THE FILM ANSWERS BACK

THE VALLEY OF THE GIANTS
(A Warner Brothers' Technicolor Production)

THE FILM ANSWERS BACK

AN HISTORICAL APPRECIATION
OF THE CINEMA

BY

E. W. & M. M. ROBSON

LONDON
JOHN LANE THE BODLEY HEAD

First published 1939
Reprinted 1947

Printed in Great Britain by
BUTLER AND TANNER LTD., FROME, SOMERSET
for JOHN LANE THE BODLEY HEAD LTD.
8 Bury Place, London, W.C.1

CONTENTS

LIST OF ILLUSTRATIONS

7

9

ACKNOWLEDGMENT

For permission to reproduce the illustrations contained in this book, grateful thanks are due to—

> Mr. C. L. O. Cattermoul.
> Denning Films, Ltd.
> First National Film Distributors, Ltd.
> Mr. Fried, Film Sales, Ltd.
> Metro-Goldwyn-Mayer Pictures, Ltd.
> Paramount Film Service, Ltd.
> Progressive Film Institute, Ltd.
> Radio Pictures, Ltd.
> United Artists Corporation, Ltd.
> J. G. & R. B. Wainwright, Ltd.
> Mr. C. J. Wakeling, The Forum Cinema,
>   Charing Cross, W.C.2.
> Warner Brothers Pictures, Ltd.

Cliftonville,   E. W. & M. M. ROBSON.
July, 1939.

PART ONE

THE CINEMA:
EUROPE AND AMERICA

For these indeede doo make to imitate; and imitate both to delight and teach; and delight to move men to take that goodnes in hande, which without delight they would flye as from a stranger; and teach, to make them know that goodnes whereunto they are mooved; which being the noblest scope to which ever any learning was directed.

SIR PHILIP SIDNEY, 1554–86.

There's a lot of new angles—things move faster—ten years faster. Everything's streamline—you know what I mean? We get to the point quicker, get me?

From *The Last Gangster*
(M.-G.-M. 1938).

I

EPPUR SI MUOVE! And yet it moves! In the face of the might of authority, in spite of the notion of a fixed earth which had held the minds of men for thousands of years, Galileo spoke of the world as it revolves.

But not only the earth but everything upon it and beneath it, and out beyond into the Universe, all is in motion. Even the eternal hills are not eternal. From an electron to an atom to a solar system, from an amoeba to a plant to a lizard to a man, to groupings of men called society, all is animation, interaction, movement.

Action, movement is the core of life as it is the core of man's life among his fellows.

If whilst you are reading this book at an open window, a bee or a bird or a bluebottle were to cross your line of vision, your attention would be instantly centred upon the moving object. This involuntary action is primary and instinctive and takes momentary precedence over every other activity. If a mouse were to run across the floor, or if a sheet of paper were to be disturbed by a draught of air, your eye would be focused on that mouse or that sheet of paper in a fraction of a second. You would hardly realize how it happened, but the moving mouse or the fluttering sheet of paper would take precedence over the book you are reading. This is because watching things move has two roots in human and animal nature. It is at once a pleasure, like eating and mating, and a part of your defence mechanism. It is nature's way of prompting you to exert eternal vigilance over every change in your surroundings, because that change may involve a question of life or death. In this respect human beings are as fresh in their sensory reactions as any mammal you can mention.

Our basic instincts were formed during our pre-human development, in common with those of the animal kingdom. In point of time the acquisition of rational thought which man possesses is a gift which was developed but yesterday. It is our extremely fine sensory equipment which is fundamental.

It amounts to this: without the basic primary instincts and their satisfaction, no higher form of mental activity could have developed. During the struggle to subdue the forces of nature, man has developed the capacity for conscious thought—the ability to generalize, synthesize, classify and memorize his experience. This new quality of thought brought about a change in the structure and functioning of the brain. The increased size in the frontal part and the way it functioned in new linkages with the older parts of the brain had to be paid for. One step back to get two steps forward. The human child can no longer use the power of locomotion from the moment of birth like the foal, the calf and the monkey. Infancy has increasingly extended and has become ever more helpless as early man evolves into man as we know him to-day.

The basic instincts of man are concerned with:

> Food.
> Mating.
> Self-defence.
> Investigation.
> The social urge.

Every one of these instincts in being satisfied is accompanied by pleasure.

Now let us see how this relates to the movies.

Not only do we find pleasure in satisfying the 'investigatory reflex,' in Pavlov's phrase, by watching things move when we go to the pictures, not only do we find pleasure and comfort in the company of our fellows, but the pictures satisfy and please because they are concerned with every kind of variation in the operation of our basic instincts. This may sound very well in theory, but does it work out in practice? Does it add up?

We find it does add up. It adds up to about twenty-two million patrons who attend the cinema in Britain alone every week; not every year or month, but *every week*. Patrons to the number of nearly half the population of the country satisfy a basic need in the pleasure of seeing a picturization of the emotional and instinctive lives of all kinds of people like themselves. In the U.S.A. the proportion of weekly cinema-goers is even higher; they number over eighty millions, close on 70 per cent of the population.

The instinctive needs that people satisfy in going to the pictures are satisfied in this particular manner because the film is a cultural medium which corresponds to the special structure of modern industrial society. But this basic need has always existed and has always been satisfied in one form or another. In man's earliest social existence, the actions he had to perform in real life, in hunting the buffalo for instance, were reproduced in what we may call man's early cultural life, in the buffalo dance, or the bear dance, or a dance named after any animal he intended to capture for food. These dances served the double purpose of being preliminary, preparatory exercises for the real business of the hunt, and they were also intended as demonstrative exhortations to the appropriate gods as to what was expected of them: the granting of a successful issue to the forthcoming expedition.

In those days the gift of speech had been so newly acquired that people dared not entrust their message to the gods in the form of words. Their prayers were enacted in mime and dance so that there should be no misunderstanding. Certain writers on early civilizations, thinking in terms of their own age, have spoken of the early fertility rites as 'obscene' and as 'orgies,' which is perfectly absurd. People in those days had none of the distortions nor the pruderies that afflicted so many of our Victorian investigators. All that men were concerned with was making sure about the fertility of the earth, and so the act of fertility was performed on the fields, again so that the god may make no mistake about what he was expected to do: to make the earth bring forth in due season. For thousands of years it was thought that unless this were done every year, calamity would befall and there would be no food. Without knowledge, without science, they could afford to take no chances.

From the earliest times to the present day, man has always had two parallel satisfactions: the practical, the actual business of getting food, getting a mate and defending himself against enemies on the one hand, and a social reflection of these activities, which it is permissible to call cultural activity, on the other. This cultural activity has taken various forms throughout the ages corresponding to the type of civilization existing at any given moment in history.

The strength of the social instincts which impel twenty-two million people to go to the pictures every week in this country alone is accounted for by the fact that of the two million years roughly of man's existence upon the earth as a distinct human type, only during the last ten thousand has he lived in class-divided society. In other words, man has lived two hundred times as long under some form of primitive communism as he has lived under the varying forms of class division. Hence the enormous strength of the social instincts which often transcend thoughts of class, especially at a time of great social stress.

Only with the greatest, with the most painful effort was it possible for men to subjugate men in slavery, in order to expand the making of socially useful things to a higher plane. This process was a very painful but a very necessary one in the evolution towards a higher degree of material satisfactions. It was rather similar to the way in which the earlier, the more primitive form of organic life evolved from the asexual method of reproduction. As soon as a higher form of life became possible and the individual became more complicated in structure, reproduction could no longer continue in the old way. And so the function was divided between two, male and female.

So violent, so difficult was that first break from the communal way of life that the man on top who had done violence to his native social instincts had to justify or rationalize his position in order to allay his pangs of conscience, his own misgivings. And those who were the subjugated were also faced with the need of explaining the predicament in which they found themselves. From being free and enjoying a community of goods they were now slaves. How was all this to be reconciled?

The stories and legends and allegories that arose to explain this dilemma always had as their central core the problem of good and evil. The Garden of Eden allegory and the legend of the Golden Age are undoubted references to that long communal phase which remained tenaciously fixed in man's memory. It is highly significant that the allegorical Tree of Knowledge is associated with social evil. That is to say it is realized quite clearly that only with the coming of the knowledge of the higher productive process did this evil arise and men lost their Garden of Eden, primitive communism, in which all things were enjoyed by all men in common for untold thousands of generations.

In classic times, in the days of Greece and Rome, the memory of the brotherhood of man was still so vivid and strong that there was a yearly festival called the Saturnalia, for the Golden Age was also known as the Reign of Saturn. During this festival all people abandoned themselves to complete joy and revelry, dancing, singing and feasting;

and it is significant that an inevitable, necessary part of this celebration was a change of roles between master and slave. The slaves were decked in the raiment of their masters and were accorded every honour, while the masters, wearing the rags of slaves, performed all the menial labour. This is undoubtedly a form of alleviation of conscience for the wrong that had been done to man's social spirit.

This Saturnalia is still celebrated in a more attenuated form as carnival in France and Italy and in all other countries in some form or another. In the mediaeval Church a variation of the Saturnalia was the Feast of the Fools and the Feast of the Asses. Every form of bitter ribaldry was levelled at the dignitaries and dicta of the Church. Everything was permitted on this one complete day of freedom and equality.

From the earliest times and in every cultural sphere in drama, comedy, poetry, in every form of expression, this apparently divided personality, man, this Jekyll and Hyde enigma, has always been under examination.

In the Old Testament, it is the story of the Garden of Eden and the Fall of Man. In the New Testament you get it specifically in the story of Jesus ascending the pinnacle and being tempted by Satan. The problem of the social good set against the social evil, the problem of the individual who sacrifices the social good to gain riches for himself, is treated in every form of cultural expression through every age. From the fifteenth century onwards you get it in the form of the Faust legend. Faust is a word which signifies 'good,' and he, being tempted by the Devil, barters his soul for riches, for the ability to pursue his own egotistical ends. This story is found in many languages and in many lands; and a Faust drama written for the puppet theatres still goes the rounds to this day, especially in Eastern Europe.

From Euripides to Milton, Shakespeare and Molière, right to the subject-matter of the most advanced cultural

18

LOVE FINDS ANDY HARDY
with Judy Garland and Mickey Rooney

(*M.-G.-M.*)

medium to-day—the film—the problem has always perturbed the minds of men. Thus, the film is in direct line with every preceding cultural expression. But it is more. It is a synthesis, a unity of all that has gone before, in song, music, dancing, picture composition, drama, comedy, rhetoric, costume and architecture. The film is performing the function of culture. It is the animated picture-book study of life for the people, and an instinctive satisfaction at one and the same time. The film, like every preceding cultural medium, is concerned in explaining life and in advancing the social process through the circulation of new and vital ideas.

II

JUST as there are people who think of a film or its story purely as something that comes out of a studio, just as they are unable to recognize that the whole background of contemporary society produces a film with all its plot, its ideas and expressions, so does the habit persist of attributing the origins of the cinema to the exclusive brain-waves of certain individuals here and there, upon this or that date.

The cinema owes everything to society as a whole, not only as an economic activity, but as its source of inspiration. It owes its existence to the efforts of myriads of humans upon whose accumulated store of knowledge and experience the cinema has been built. The inventors who were most directly concerned with the specific invention of the cine-camera and projector and celluloid film, had obviously to start with things and manufactured materials. They had to have the knowledge of physics, optics and chemistry; sciences which were there to hand but only because of the painful struggles, the trials and errors, the dreams and achievements and failures of men throughout scores of centuries. The cinema is thus not only a facet of the social process of to-day: it is the unbroken continuation of the social process that has been going on since man began to think.

The real genesis of the cinema is similar to that of a great many other discoveries of social importance. Inventive ideas on the problem of making moving pictures cropped up almost simultaneously and apparently independently in different countries.

If you read an American account of the subject you will gather the impression that most of the credit is due to Edison and other American inventors. In works written from the European side, more stress is naturally laid upon the achievements of Paul and Friese-Greene of England, of the Lumières, the Pathé brothers and Gaumont of France, and of Max Skladnovsky of Germany. The truth is that it is impossible to attribute exact priority to any one person or group of persons. There is nothing clear-cut and definite about the dates that are being offered to us as the sequences of the cinema's early developments. It seems obvious from the facts, and also from the known history of so many other inventions, that there were numberless other men working on identical lines of research, but whose names, for one reason or another, had no chance of coming into the limelight. This hypothesis is strengthened by the fact that in a general way the invention was little thought of except as a kind of scientific plaything. Indeed, Edison thought so little of his Kinetoscope that he had no idea of applying for patents until too late.

In England, Friese-Greene could get no encouragement from financial circles, nor from scientific bodies, and he was accorded only lukewarm interest by the Photographic Society. But when he opened a shop at 92, Piccadilly, London, and projected on the window a moving picture of a dancing gyrating skeleton, the result was sensational beyond even Friese-Greene's expectations. It drew such crowds as had never been seen before, and the police in clearing the street had to intervene to stop the show. It was not the first time that the general public saw farther ahead, and divined what it wanted far better than the man who sat higher up, in comparative isolation from the people. And it was not going to be the last time for such a thing to happen. In political and cultural life it is happening every day.

As long ago as the twelfth century, an Arab astronomer,

Al Hassen, wrote a treatize on optics; but for hundreds of years before and subsequently scientists and philosophers had occupied themselves with the mysteries of light and with attempts at the reproduction of movement. Towards the end of the fifteenth century, Leonardo da Vinci made the problem one of his studies. This preoccupation with light led to the invention of all manner of rather crude instruments for producing strange optical effects. They were called magic lanterns, a name which came into use about 1640.

It is easy to realize the significance of such a word as 'magic' at such a time. One can imagine the awe in which these new instruments were held when mankind stood at the crossroads between the recent superstitious past of the Middle Ages and the science of the approaching industrial era.

In 1824, Roget (who is famous for his *Thesaurus*) explained his thesis to the Royal Society on 'the persistence of Vision with regard to Moving Objects.' From this date onwards, long before the invention and commercial exploitation of photography, a veritable flood of toylike inventions appear which consist in the main of simple grotesque painted figures arranged in series like coloured cartoons, which, when twirled around, in or upon a cylinder, give the illusion of the figures coming into motion. To give an idea of how widely ingenuity was exercised to achieve this very simple and very limited end, it is worth recalling some of the names that were attached to what we would now regard as toys, but which held great scientific interest to our great grandfathers.

There was the Traumatrope about 1827, the Phenakistoscope about 1830, and the Zoetrope or the Wheel of Life. In 1838 there came the Daedleum, invented by Dr. Horner, an American. This was an improvement upon the rotating Phenakistoscope, but it was not until twelve years later that Dr. Horner took the trouble to patent it.

In 1829 two Frenchmen, Niepce and Daguerre, solved the problem of photography, a problem which had eluded scientists and alchemists for centuries; but it was not until 1841 that photography was made a commercial possibility by Fox-Talbot, an Englishman.

There followed in the 1860's and onwards a whole battalion of 'scopes' and 'tropes' and 'graphs.' The grotesque, figured, coloured drawings of the 1830's gave place to still photographs in motion sequence, until we arrive at Edison's Kinetoscope. For the first time, Edison used sprocket-propelled film. With the elevation of the Kinetoscope to the public peep-show status, it begins to assume the appearance of the cinematograph in early embryonic form. The Kinetoscope and the Kinetograph came in about 1890. Their invention was made possible by the appearance of celluloid film, manufactured by George Eastman. But for many years prior to this date there had been the Zoetrope, this time with photographs in series instead of cartoons, the Zoopraxiscope, the Tachyscope, and the Mutoscope.

During these years, electrical sound transmissions were made possible by the invention of the telephone by Alexander Graham Bell, and Blake succeeded in photographing sound vibrations, which, many years later, led to the possibility of recording sound on film, that is, sound and picture on the same base as practised to-day.

In 1885, a photographic camera led to Friese-Greene's successful experiments with a camera that would take photographs in rapid succession. All previous attempts at motion photography had been made with batteries of single shot cameras, each set to go off at short intervals.

It was not until 1895 that the first Kinetescope public peep-show arrived in full force, to open up on Broadway, New York, at an arcade. To this day, the second cousin to the Kinetoscope machine, the Mutoscope, is still drawing its modest harvest of pennies at seaside promenades and fair grounds everywhere. Above each machine there is usually an alluring picture of a buxom maiden in the naughty half-undress of the early 1900's, with varying titles such as *The Ladies' Turkish Bath*, or *Nights of Passion*, or *The Chemise Girl*, *The Sultan's Favourite*, *What Happened in Her Bedroom*, *Why Men Leave Home*, titles which drew the pennies like a magnet from the imaginative male adolescent until about twenty years ago, but which no longer exercise the same attraction. For one thing the young, especially of the working class, have a much healthier outlook on sex than in those days of repressions and taboos, and for another they see more, whenever the Hollywood lovelies parade and dance upon the cinema screen. Which is all to the good.

In the early days of the peep-show Kinetoscope it was hardly necessary to harp too much on sex in order to attract the public that swarmed into the penny arcades opened up by showmen all over the world. The sheer novelty of movement was enough. Short subjects showing moving trains, waterfalls, boxing, wrestling, horse-racing, were vastly attractive.

It is interesting to recall, in the light of what has happened in the comparatively few years that have elapsed, that when it was suggested to Edison that he should have the pictures enlarged upon a screen, he refused to listen for some time. He thought that if this were done too many people would see the pictures all at once, and that the demand would thus soon be exhausted and the business come to an end!

But by this time the March of Progress had become a regular trot at the double. In England, around 1890 the moving picture projected upon a screen was being made into a feasible proposition by the work of Paul, a Hatton Garden scientific instrument maker, and Friese-Greene, a professional photographer. In France the Lumière brothers had developed their Cinematographe. And so it seems that

Edison found himself caught up again in the stream of his own part creation. In April 1896 the first performance with Edison's newest projector, the Vitascope, was given at Koster and Bial's Music Hall on Herald Square, New York.

It figured as item No. 8 on the programme and was described in the following terms:

THOMAS A. EDISON'S LATEST MARVEL
presenting selections from the following:

SEA-WAVES, A BOXING BOUT, VENICE SHOWING GON-DOLAS, UMBRELLA DANCE, BURLESQUE BOXING, KAISER WILHELM REVIEWING HIS TROOPS, BUTTERFLY DANCE, CUBA LIBRE.

Very wisely, item No. 9 was the ten-minute interval which gave the astonished audience time to regain their breath whilst listening to 'Dr. Leo Sommer's Blue Hungarian Band in the Grand Promenade.'

A year before the Herald Square show took place almost simultaneous but at first rather diffident shows were offered to the public; by the Lumières in a café basement in Paris and by Latham at 156, Broadway, New York. It is interesting to note that both Paul and the Lumière brothers have freely acknowledged that they used the Kinetescope as the basis for the Cinematographe, as the Lumières called their projector, and the Animatagraph, as Paul called his.

In France and in England the performances naturally aroused a great deal of interest and curiosity, but there were very few who thought of the invention as having any kind of future. People had got used to the ever-recurring appearances and disappearances of all sorts of queer inventions. Hard-boiled men in the show business were familiar with the different fads and fancies like roller skating, ice skating, diabolo and so on, that took hold of large sections of the people like a series of epidemics and then quietly disappeared. The general dubiousness was shared by the Lumières themselves. Méliès, whose remarkably advanced early trick films survive as the most authentic and exciting primitives extant, was advised by the Lumières to have nothing to do with the Cinematographe. It might become a scientific curiosity, but there was no commercial future for it; it was a passing fancy and he would lose all his money. Méliès, of course, persisted and obtained his equipment from another source.

The year 1896, it seems, was the year in which the infant cinema was to make its first appearance as a serious form of entertainment, for good or ill. Whether there was to be a future for it remained to be seen. Late that year, Mr. Paul gave a series of shows at the Alhambra Music Hall, Leicester Square, London, where now stands the super-Odeon. All over England similar shows in populous centres were beginning to be given in obscure halls and shops obtained on short-term hire.

No history of the cinema could possibly trace the sporadic beginnings in all manner of places during this year. As yet there was hardly a glimmer of an attempt to convey a theme in any of the pictures shown. An idea of the nature of the films and their lengths will be gathered from the following extract from the *New York Herald* in its Sunday edition of May 3rd, 1896, in describing the Koster and Bial's show:

As stated, the films now used in the exhibition of the Vita-scope, are each fifty feet in length, but they are to be improved shortly by films from 150 to 500 feet in length.[1] *Pictures for these films are now being taken, and among them are Niagara Falls, a steamer going down the Lachine Rapids, and an ocean greyhound leaving her pier with her*

[1] The three-hour single film of 1937, *The Great Ziegfeld*, was over 20,000 feet in length.

26

decks crowded with passengers waving adieus to their friends on shore.

An earlier edition of the *New York Herald* dated April 24th, 1896, headed an enthusiastic article about the first Vitascope performance of the night before:

WONDERFUL IS THE VITASCOPE

Such was the verdict of the audience which saw Edison's invention.

It went on:

The feature of the programme last evening at Koster and Bial's Music Hall was the first public exhibition ever given of Edison's Vitascope. This invention has already been described in the Herald. It has been called an enlarged Kinetoscope because it works somewhat on the principle of that machine, but in the case of the latter one must look into it to see reproductions of pictures about three inches in size, whereas in the case of the Vitascope these same pictures are thrown through a lens and appear on a screen magnified six hundred diameters. Moreover the Vitascope reproduces all the colours of a picture.

The Vitascope was the eighth number on the programme last night, and it was nearly ten o'clock when it was reached. The house was packed and as picture after picture was thrown on the screen the applause was tremendous.

REALISTIC PICTURES

The first picture shown was that of two dancers. It seemed as though they were actually on the stage, so natural was the dance, with its many and graceful motions. Next came a picture of a tumbling surf on the Jersey shore. The waves were high and boisterous as they dashed one after the other in their rush for the sandy beach over which they ebbed and

27

flowed. The white crests of the waves and the huge volume of water were true to life. Only the roar of the surf was needed to make the illusion perfect. A boxing bout between a long thin man and a short stout man was the next picture. The boxers were photographed in their bout by the Kine-toscope Company, some time ago. Every move and step and blow of the boxers was faithfully reproduced on the screen last night.

In every country in the world, the first appearance of the screen show was greeted by the Press with the same wonder and unstinted eulogy, but ten years of itinerant wandering from hall to hall and from store to store had to elapse before the business attained to the dignity of a habitat of its own, the specially built 'Electric Palace.' From then on, the 'picture palace' became part of the language of the people; but the coming of the talkies and the appearance of luxurious Regals, Odeons, Granadas, all over the country have caused the name to be nearly forgotten.

At this distance in time, the early cinema seems to have been a very uncertain-footed, tottering child indeed. Reared in the atmosphere of the nickel-odeon in America and the penny gaff of the English scene, it is little wonder that it still bears the stigma of its ignominious origins in the minds of so many superior people. The cinema has never been quite forgiven for becoming so quickly available to the masses for a matter of coppers. If only it had been kept remote and exclusive, if only it had been endowed with the halo of the Conservatoire, all would have been well.

Instead the horrid thing was taken up by gruff-voiced showmen people who stood bawling outside their gaffs or shop entrances, inviting all and sundry to 'Step this way' and 'See the world before your very eyes!' for all the world as though they were at their erstwhile business of showing 'The Fattest Woman in the World' at some noisy fairground.

From about 1900 onwards, a new showman class whom certain critics refer to slightingly as 'fur-dealers and clothes-spongers' were drawn to the business.

There were big profits to be made and they were going to be in on them. In a competitive social system who could blame them? Among the leaders of the industry to-day, in all parts of the world, but especially in England and America, are many who at one time were fur merchants and clothing merchants, diamond salesmen, butchers and bakers. This fact appears to be a source of grief to many refined students of the cinema, and yet the reasons for it are intelligible enough.

At the moment when the cinematograph appeared it was precisely these people who were best fitted to accelerate its progress. They were, of course, not aware of this. They were concerned solely with profits for themselves.

They were no more aware that they were advancing a social process than were the merchant princes of the fifteenth century aware that they were laying the foundations of nineteenth and twentieth century industrialism. Given the particular social background, the peculiarly speculative nature of the cinematograph as a means of livelihood and its 'lowly' origins, it was inevitable that a type of person with certain aptitudes, trained to understand the ways of thought of the common people, and starting with initial monetary advantages, would gravitate towards leadership in the industry.

London, for instance, abounds with ex-butcher and ex-baker proprietors or lessees of groups of cinemas. If we regard the butchers and bakers as Group One, and the fur merchants and diamond dealers as Group Two, we need only a superficial knowledge of the nature of these businesses to understand why it is that Group One has stuck rigidly to the comparatively safe side of the business, cinema ownership and the sure return of the pay-box, while on the other hand Group Two has soared to the heights of banking finance, the gamble of film production control and huge chains of theatres.

The period from 1905 to 1920 favoured the master baker or the butcher with a shop in any populous working-class district. If you were a baker with a good reputation in your district you would learn to know how much to bake from day to day with as little left over as possible. The end of the day would show you a profit *in cash*. You employed manual labour and you had no need to invest in machinery. The business was steady and regular, you knew each customer almost as a friend, and you acquired a good working knowledge of human psychology. But, most important of all, the profits you made did not need to be re-invested in a large stock. In the case of a draper, a grocer, a chemist or an ironmonger a good deal of the profits have to be kept tied up. This matter of accumulated liquid cash is the essential factor, because it enabled the butcher or the baker to find the money when the opportunity offered to acquire his small picture palace.

There was, of course, no other thought except that of leaving one business for another. It was a matter of business pure and simple.

From selling sides of beef or loaves of bread, you sold thrills and relaxation in your picture palace, and the money came in just as before, cash on or before delivery. This is how the thing happened and it could not have been other-wise. It savours of extreme petty jealousy or intellectual blindness to throw up one's hands and say: 'Oh! how awful.' The point is, these people, without knowing it, were performing an extremely useful function. They were paving the way for a social development of immense significance. The millions who are to-day capable of assimilating and enjoying such films as the *Good Earth*, *Dead End* and *The Life of Emile Zola* can only do so because the standards of appreciation and the intellectual capacity of the world's inhabitants have grown with the growth of the cinema.

Appetite increases, and becomes ever more selective and critical, and better and still better films have had to be made in recent years to keep pace with the rising understanding of the people if the profits on huge investments are to be maintained. And it is precisely those early entrepreneurs who did this immense thing with the accumulated pennies that the people have subscribed during these forty years.

If any one doubts the tremendous gulf that separates the public standards of to-day from those of forty years or even ten years ago, let him compare only one aspect of a film like *The Life of Emile Zola*, the nature and extent of the vocabulary employed, with the vocabulary at the command of the mass of the people in the hey-day of the melodrama and the music-hall. It is easy to see that such a film as *Zola*, had it been available in the early days of the cinema, would have been far beyond the comprehension of the people. It would have needed to be cruder and simpler to meet with any success.

No film can succeed if it arrives before its time, before the public mind is ready for it. It was inevitable that the first story films should be crude and primitive in execution and content. But it was also inevitable that those early efforts should start a process of mental training amongst the people, cumulative, irresistible and profound.

As the banalities and the ballyhoo and the simple crudities were recognized for what they were, pay-box receipts would begin to fall off, and the film makers were thus driven to the next upward step in film production. Every year that passed showed that the public were beginning to acquire some kind of measure, a standard of quality hardly consciously expressed, but still a standard.

This can be seen to some extent in the rise and fall of the stars who have occupied the centre of the screen from time to time. There also arose a keener desire for the kind

31

of mental food more suited to the growing adult mind than to twelve-year-old children.

Those among the film producers who had their ears closest to the ground, and could keep abreast of the demand, survived. Others who thought they could treat their public with contempt by imagining it would for ever be content with 'blood and thunder' discovered their mistake when it was too late, when they found themselves against the wall. There is very little quarter given or taken in the film business. The café tables of Wardour Street are haunted by thin grey-haired men who could tell you exciting tales of the pioneering days, but who could hardly be expected to give you a coherent reason for their own eclipse.

It was in America, where living standards and mechanical aids to comfort come into general use at least fifteen years before they do anywhere else, that the enterprising clothes-sponger, the owner of a suit-cleaning shop, got his chance long before trustification set in.

The Americans take quickly to ideas of improvement and 'service,' and the habit of getting old suits and dresses to look fresh and new grew like wildfire. Here again the transition from the shop where you steamed heated clothes to the place where you offered thrills was easy and logical. You had no stocks to worry about, and after the usual out-goings such as rent, light and heat had been met the profits were your own *in cash*.

Most of the fur merchants came in at a stage when the picture palace was becoming the cinema and a form of centralized control was getting into shape. It is no accident that both in England and America men who had considerable training in the fur business control huge properties in the cinema field.

No other business in the world, except perhaps diamonds, demands such finesse, such razor-edge keenness, so all-round an understanding of the funny ways of human beings as do furs. To be in the fur game working in family groups, and in a fairly big way, is to acquire the skill of a tight-rope walker, the knack of instantaneous decision, a nose for staking your money at the right moment, not too soon and not too late, a keen understanding of your fellows, the most skilful adaptability, and an insight into the psychology and practice of banking.

It is but a step from this hectic existence to the equally nerve-tingling game of the cinema. The suave, nonchalant, delicate touch of an Adolphe Menjou is of great assistance. The acquisition of one group of cinemas after another is but a continuance of the business of gaining the confidence of bankers. The basis is acquired for floating public companies, and then with the money from the investing public it is possible to travel from strength to strength, to branch out in all directions, build studios, start film production with the Quota Act to help you, show the films at your own cinemas and arrange reciprocal exploitation of films in the overseas markets.

Film producers or cinema proprietors, either as individuals or grouped in trusts, are neither good nor bad, neither benevolent nor greedy, neither cruel nor kind. It is childish to elevate them as gods or denounce them as demons. You cannot blame people for being born into a world not of their own making. You cannot blame or praise people for being born into a competitive world at a moment in time when the development of the cinema like an 'ill wind' became a veritable tornado which left some floating in comfortable boats, others on shaky rafts half in and half out of the water, others clinging to spars, and others, countless others, to disappear below the waves without a trace.

III

FROM the first, the meteorology of the cinema has been stormy, and the wind would change with very great suddenness for many. The first people who came into the business were naturally those who were as interested in the sheer excitement of technical achievement as in any monetary reward. Friese-Greene, who had quite a tidy sum to start with, spent his life and his fortune in various experiments and was able to give great impetus to the cinema's development, but he died in poverty. Méliès, who made many very wonderful trick pictures and contributed much that was remarkable in cinematography, also died in poverty.

In 1895, the Lumière brothers gave their first show to a private society in France, but the first show in public to an audience paying at the door was given the same year in a café basement in Paris. The sceptical proprietor demanded his rent daily in advance. Bird in the hand! He was not going to be caught with any nonsense about sharing terms. During the whole of the first day about thirty people attended. Three weeks later the takings were 2,000 francs a day!

Then came the shows at the Polytechnic in Regent Street, London, whilst Paul was giving his shows at the Alhambra. These shows made money, but it was only as grains of seed compared to the harvest that was to be reaped by those who came after.

The next phase was that of the penny gaff, mostly run by showmen of the old school, who, by the nature of their business, were always on the lookout for any novelty likely to attract the pennies of the people. The moving picture was as marvellous at least as any of the other entertainments offered in fair-ground booths.

A type of motion picture entertainment that suited the showmen still better was the introduction in 1903 of what became known as Hale's Tours. This was invented by an ex-fireman named Hale who saw the possibilities of uniting the cinematograph with the scenic railway.

It was a sideshow which was built to look like a railway carriage. At the door you were greeted by the ticket collector in conductor's uniform who took your fare. When the barker had done his job and all the seats in the carriage were occupied for the tour, a bell rang, there was a blast on the whistle and the carriage began apparently to move. Before you a panorama of scenery began flashing past (by means of a concealed cinematograph projecting from behind the screen instead of facing it), whilst the carriage rocked and the noise of wheels filled out the illusion of a speeding train.

So immensely popular did these tours become that the Hale Company of America netted 500,000 dollars in two years, a colossal sum for those days.

The spread of Hale's Tours from coast to coast in America and throughout Europe started a new development. An immense stride forward was made when for the first time the film began to carry a definite story. This was Edward S. Porter's *The Great Train Robbery*, a film that contained the germ for the next stage at a time when showmen were beginning to worry as to how long the craze for the sheer novelty of movement in the scenics would last.

The appearance of this film in America started a goldrush fever which has had no equal since. It became immediately apparent that there was infinitely more gold in this than ever came out of Alaska or California. It brought in a vast heterogeneous collection of people from all walks of life who were to become the new showman class.

People like real-estate salesmen, owners of legitimate stage shows, newspaper reporters, owners of road show melodramas, market hucksters, travelling salesmen, as well as the diamond merchants and furriers, clothing merchants and cleaners, butchers and bakers already mentioned; people who had always been in close contact with the fluctuations of public taste and who had acquired skill in catering for it with profit to themselves. These were the people who now helped to create a greatly widened audience for the moving picture among the polygot masses that crowded the great industrial centres of a rapidly expanding American industry. Whether you were a labourer from Russia, Italy, Hungary, Poland or Germany, whether you spoke Slovak or Magyar or Chinese, whether you could read or no, you could always meet in the store picture show in common understanding with your fellows. You might not understand each other's languages, but you could all understand the common universal language of the moving picture on the screen. And you could enjoy this simple form of culture for the price of a packet of fags.

All the claims during that gold rush have now been staked. To-day, without substantial capital, newcomers have about as much chance of entering the cinema business as a camel has of passing through the eye of a needle. Some of the men who entered the business at this phase now dominate the industry in the United States. Zukor, Selznick, Lasky, Goldwyn, Loew; and Laemmle until a year or two ago. Even these, however, no longer rule in their own right but through their intricate connections with powerful banking interests.

Consider the hunger for this form of entertainment at its inception. Here is an instance of what happened at one of the first store picture shows that were opened in America.

In Pittsburgh, the steel city, in 1905, two partners, Harris and Davis, real-estate men, found they had an empty store on their hands and an old projector.

When a copy of *The Great Train Robbery* came into their possession they decided to furnish the store with a couple of hundred chairs, rig up the projector and open with this first story film, which was in one reel, lasting about twelve minutes. The first day's takings were 22 dollars; the second day's 76 dollars. At the end of two weeks the picture was running continuously from eight in the morning till midnight and showing a profit of 1,000 dollars a week. This lasted for several weeks, all with the same picture, until almost the entire population of Pittsburgh had been to see this miracle. The news spread throughout the American continent, and store shows sprang up in New York, Chicago, San Francisco, Cincinatti and other big centres, and in the smaller towns and villages. Anyone who had a few dollars to invest for a projector and chairs, and could put down the first week's rent for any kind of shop or store, could start as a showman and almost literally start coining money.

The manufacture of projectors was kept at frantic pressure, and it was not long before small companies sprang into existence to supply the suddenly awakened clamour for films, films, films—any kind, no matter what the style or content, so long as they were films. In America such names as Kalem, Vitagraph, Lubin, Selig, Essanay, Keystone, Biograph and IMP were becoming familiar, in England Hepworth, Samuelson, Jury, British and Colonial, in France Gaumont, Pathé and Méliès.

In America, the land of the vast open spaces, where men still lived with the memories of the Wild West, an internecine patents war developed between the Edison Company, who claimed the patents rights, and all the other U.S. film companies mentioned above.

There were fights, tricks, stratagems, strong-arm men and shootings a-plenty. There were midnight flights to distant places with illicit equipment, and much dodging of court process servers. If the industry did not quite resemble a jungle at this period, it somehow did have the appearance of a crowd of Keystone characters, cops and robbers, travelling at top speed in a cabriolet whilst arms and legs were flying about, eyes were blackened, and noses bled in the struggle for control and the cash.

And it was not funny either.

It was not only a private fight but, in the words of the Irishman, it was one that anybody could join if he wished. All that was needed was a little money to start with, a heart that could stand a lot of palpitation, a coat, a waistcoat and a shirt to strip off if need be as the fight got warmer.

The eminent American historian of the motion picture industry, Terry Ramsaye, in his book *A Million and One Nights*, describes the period in the following words:

> *Every studio was a guarded stronghold in* 1907. *Pictures were made behind locked and guarded doors . . . all the makers were in fear of being discovered in their infringements and because they had methods of production, inventions and formulae of their own to keep secret. The business of the motion picture was in a state of feudal war. But the coming of the story picture, the photoplay and the consequent rise of the screen theatre made the profits of the business so alluring that laws, patents and ethical customs were futile. Peace had to come before progress, and peace had to be a compromise finally settled in December* 1908 *with the formation of the Motion Picture Patents Company which included Kalem, Vitagraph, Lubin, Selig, Essanay, Méliès and Pathé.*

Biograph held out for a considerable time, claiming patent rights equally valid with those of Edison, but they came in following a settlement.

In pooling their patents in this way under the Edison flag, the companies hoped to place the rest of the industry under tribute. It was expected that exhibitors would submit to a licence fee of two dollars a week, and that smaller users of cameras would be made to pay a fee for every foot shot. It was thought also that production could be restricted to the one- and two-reel subjects which were then in vogue and which were highly profitable. It worked, but only haltingly and not for very long. That the attempted monopoly was bound to fail at that stage is evident when one remembers that a one-reel film lasts as long as, or a little longer on the screen than the average Disney cartoon. It is impossible to imagine a present-day audience tolerating a battery of short dramas, comedies and interest films each lasting from ten to fifteen minutes throughout a three-hour programme.

If those who formed the Motion Picture Patents Company thought pictures could be made to stay put like canned peas, monopolized at the one- and two-reel stage, they had evidently never heard of King Canute.

The war started afresh with the emergence of the Independent Motion Picture Company under Laemmle. To Carl Laemmle is given the credit of forcing the first big breach in the monopoly. But it was the public which really decided the outcome of the war in favour of the independents. Very unreasonably from the monopolists' point of view, the public mind could not be held in a strait-jacket. The public insisted upon preferring the type of film that was taking them a stage farther than some of the monopolists were prepared to go. Nevertheless, while the going was good the profits of the associated companies were almost fantastic, even before the business had reached the dignity of the picture palace.

Here is the story of the Kalem Company which is typical of many others. Early in 1907 three friends got together and agreed to start up on their own. They were

Kleine, Long and Marion. The last two had had some experience working with Biograph, and Kleine had a small business of a film exchange. Long put in an interest he had in a loft where the studio was to be, Marion put in 600 dollars, and Kleine stood surety for the purchase of a camera from Charles Urban in London. Profits were immediate, and in twelve months had reached 5,000 dollars a week, continuing to rise throughout their association with the Motion Picture Patents Company. In about 1911 they decided the time had come to quit, and did so, with 1,500,000 dollars to their credit. What with sky-rocketing star salaries and rising quality standards, the game was getting expensive and risky. During this short term of years they had made their money supplying a market which was desperately hungry for films. Quality, story or stars had hardly begun to mean anything, and the films they made on factory lines were sold outright direct to exhibitors at about 5d. per foot in English money, say about £20 per reel. This was before the practice of renting or hiring out films had gone very far.

The profits these companies made is but an index of the tremendous demand there was from the world-wide public. The speed with which these profits were accumulated is explained in this way: The prime total cost of a film is always embodied in the negative. The picture that goes on the screen is the positive print which is taken from the negative, and the number of prints that can be taken from a single negative is almost limitless.

The raw unexposed stock may have cost the film producers about one penny per foot. A film would be shot and ready in a week, and after selling four or five prints, the cost of the negative would have been recovered. Thereafter, each print would show about £16 gross profit out of every £20, and as many as two hundred prints of one film might be called for.

In this period, nearly all the profits went to the film-producing companies and to their customers, the exhibitors. Technicians and players hardly counted. The films were crude and unsophisticated. Unknown, unemployed actors were picked up and thrust into their parts for a matter of a few dollars a day. Camera work meant the ability to stand beside a tripod, which was always trained upon the scene in one stationary position, and to crank a handle street-organ fashion. Camera, lighting, script workers and actors were expected to lend a hand shifting furniture, lifting planks, knocking up sets and painting scenery.

All sorts of chances led to actors appearing on the set. One actor might get a job because a story required someone to appear in morning dress and he happened to be the one and only lucky possessor of such an outfit, another would be engaged because he could shoot a running rabbit whilst riding on horseback. All kinds of people were roped in, relations, friends, wives, or even any stranger off the street if he fitted a particular part.

After the film was shot and developed, it was taken to the editing room, where there would be hanging from spools in a row, like spools of ribbon in a draper's shop, rolls of stock film with stock sub-titling that would easily fit into stock situations in film after film.

In addition to the stock of 'End of Part One' and 'Beginning of Part Two' there would be found rolls of sub-titles such as 'Ten Years Elapse,' 'One Hour Later,' 'Two Hours Elapse,' 'Revenge,' 'The Next Day' ('Came the Dawn!' came very much later in film evolution), 'Forgiven,' 'Happy Ever After,' 'Wedding Bells,' 'The End.'

There was another company contemporary with Kalem which ran successfully for years. It was formed from similar small beginnings by G. Spoor and G. M. Anderson whose initials made Essanay (S. and A.). They, too, retired, a few years after Kalem, well satisfied, it is known, with millions of dollars.

Many readers in the forties may remember kindly-eyed, hatchet-faced, stocky 'Broncho Bill,' who put the bad men on the spot and got the girl and the gold in the end. Well, that was Broncho Billy G. M. Anderson.

There was one memorable year in this company's career in which fifty films were made. Fifty! One a week, and Anderson appeared in nearly every one of them!

There were many who retired on their gains. Others, like Rothapfel, who was one of the first to set a standard of comfort high above that of the earlier cinemas, and who built the sumptuous Roxy in New York years later, died in obscurity. Those who remained and are now in the lead have travelled through each phase of picture development amidst titanic battles for position, power and supremacy. At each phase the weapons have altered but the scale of the battle has increased. It is still on. And it is a battle which has given rise to one constant triumph: for it is the people, the audiences of the world, who have forced the pace and determined the ground. The people had, and still have, the final say. The people are not quite the sheep that the coteries might like to think they are, as the following chapters will show.

IV

ALL things in the Universe, whether planet or a grain of seed planted on its surface, whether men and women or the drama or anything else, conform to certain habits of movement common to all. These habits or characteristics have been observed by men who, for the sake of convenience in terminology, call them universal laws.

A part of the inner nature of things is the law of the spiral progression from quality to quantity and from quantity to quality. Then upwards to a higher plane from quality to quantity again, and so on continuously. People are apt to be frightened by such theoretical formulations, but nowhere is this law of progression more clearly or easily demonstrated than in the story of the cinema. A grasp of this law may make a great many things understandable which at first may have seemed obscure.

Let us start at any point in the cinema's history, say the period 1890–95. As we have already seen, this period is characterized by the intensive research that was going on both in America and in Europe to advance the motion picture peep-show to a point where it might be seen by more than one person at a time, that is, projected upon an enlarged screen. This period, therefore, presents an appearance of a huge quantitative dead level, a wilderness of dwarf Kinetoscopes, Mutoscopes and hosts of other 'scopes.'

Thus we start with quantity on a very low qualitative plane. Here and there, however, are tiny little shoots struggling to force themselves up above the dead level.

Out of and proceeding from quantity, there emerges the new quality, the picture-on-the-screen machine, the cinematograph. The moment this machine makes its appearance, no matter how limited its quantity (there may have been only three at one time in all the world), progression starts again immediately, and the new machine begins to multiply and is spread to the four corners of the earth.

Now we have quantity again, but on a higher plane, and for some little time there appears to be no forward upward drive to the next stage. This is quite understandable because the urge is for expansion, multiplication. The urge for quality is temporarily overwhelmed by the insistent primary need of satisfying millions of people who are content to thrill at pictorial movement and very little else.

But the apparently insatiable wonder and curiosity of the people does eventually reach a point of saturation. Things are now ripe for sprouting a new quality, and again isolated shoots begin to be visible. Until finally the new quality emerges. It is STORY.

The Great Train Robbery in 1903 was the first of this new growth to appear in America. But as early as 1901, Méliès was making truly wonderful pictures about ten minutes in length which deserve to rank as classics amongst early primitives of the screen. An example is the famous *Trip to the Moon*. Méliès was the proprietor of the Théâtre Houdin, a home of magic in Paris, and in a most skilful way he managed to capture the atmosphere of his theatre in every picture he made. His training as an illusionist enabled him to think up all manner of ingenious tricks with the camera, long before its potentialities were discovered by anyone else.

Again, nearly the whole world had to have its surfeit of scenics, trick films, short crude story films, cowboy dramas, mawkish domestic problems, chase comedies before the ground was prepared for the next qualitative stage, a period which started about 1909 and coincides with the emergence of the long feature film, the photo-play and the rise of the stars.

So throughout the history of the cinema, progress has taken place in stages from quantity to higher quality. The higher quality first appears in small doses, and then becomes widespread; then a new still higher quality appears. This process is still continuing. It cannot stop, as will be made clear in the course of this book.

It must not be thought that the upward climb was always steady and uniformly even. Sometimes it may have seemed exceedingly slow, at other times it would make up for it with a terrific whiz forward which left one gasping. Many of the intelligentsia both in Europe and America have for years laboured under the extraordinary delusion that the cinema has been an instrument in the hands of certain unprincipled people, individuals who attained great wealth and power merely by banging the drum of publicity ballyhoo, and thus persuading the masses (poor masses) to troop into their cinemas like a flock of sheep.

This is a fantastic distortion of the truth.

It arises from an inability or unwillingness to recognize that what had been the dream of philosophers for centuries, the first international, universal, effortless Esperanto had arrived. Peoples of diverse races, language and levels of culture, children of three years and upwards, old and young of both sexes could thrill to its pictorial message. It was the one touch that made the whole world kin.

Observe a crowd of kiddies at any matinée performance. 'Look out, he's behind yer!' comes the cry from every part of the house, as the villain creeps up behind the unsuspecting hero. The children are extremely absorbed and agitated. It is as if they were witnessing the scene in real life. Even dogs have been known to jump up and fly at the screen, barking, as a dog or a cow appears.

True stories are told of the early days of the cinema when grown-up audiences would shout imprecations and would hiss the villain just as they did a little while before from the pit when *Maria Marten or The Murder at the Red Barn* was being staged.

In these circumstances, any entrepreneur or showman who brought the cinematograph show to the people could not help at first but make money. He was fulfilling an insistent public demand and the money was there to be picked up. Historical evidence, however, is overwhelming to show that the entrepreneurs and the film makers did all they could to hold the film within the then existing bounds for as long as they possibly could. At every stage this tendency has operated, and at every stage it has been surely and decisively countered by the people, exercising their democratic right of the pay-box.

This pull between the desires of the producers and the developing mental and emotional needs of the people themselves increases in tension right up to the present day. It could not be otherwise.

If things could have been left to the film maker there might have been nothing but scenics perhaps to this day. But there came a time when the public said it had had enough. Money talks, and never more effectively than when it says NO. It was only with the appearance of the first acted story film that the money started rolling back into the pay-box. This was the one thing needful to keep up the patronage which had been started with the scenics.

Audiences were still uncritical. Technique was necessarily of the crudest, acting the sheerest stage mime. Films at first could only be made by sunlight, and sets were built in back gardens in the open air. The transference of stage acting technique from the stage to the screen was but the normal natural progression from the known to the unknown, in the same way as the first motor-car was a converted horse-gig or pony-trap.

The type of story that appealed most was the type of story the people had been used to. Blood-and-thunder

46

melodrama suited them because this was the cultural level at which an industrial society had left the people at the moment when the story film came upon them. Nevertheless commendable attempts were made very early to interest the public in fifteen-minute versions of the plays of Shakespeare and the poems of Dante. Even Sir Herbert Beerbohm Tree was persuaded to appear in one of them. But these pictures cut very little ice with the general public. Showmen, no matter how well intentioned, had yet to learn that nothing has ever been known to grow from the top downwards.

Always from the roots upwards.

And it was only amongst the people that the film was to find its roots. The real staple food of the people quickly became the cowboy drama, professionally known as the Western, the religious story picture, the crude chase comedy and the domestic problem picture from the old melodrama.

The chase was a style in comedy that could only be developed to its limits by the film. It usually started with a comedian upsetting a basket of fruit outside a shop, the proprietor of which would start chasing the delinquent down the street. At the corner he would bump into the butcher boy carrying a tray of meat. The boy would join the chase, and, like the stick that beat the dog that bit the cat, the film would run its fifteen-minute length with the whole community running and waving their arms about with farcical threatening gestures, the butcher, the fruiterer, the house painter, baker, ice-cream vendor, postmen, women with shopping baskets, navvies, sailors and policemen—especially policemen! The audience exulted in seeing the pomp of authority suitably humbled and in humorous situations. It seems hardly credible that countless numbers of films were made to this generic formula and avidly consumed for years. But it is so.

The Western held the public interest longest and

achieved the greatest success in every country in the world. There was something tremendously satisfying about the cowboy dramas to men and women clamped to an urban existence, smoky and governed by the clock. Here at least were wide plains, space, freedom, where any man was as good as his neighbour, where justice was rough but swift, where the very clothes of the cowboys were sensible, rational, comfortable, open at the neck, not the maddening, fussy, buttoned-up armour prescribed by the standards of Edwardian respectability. The popularity of the Westerns can only be explained by this subconscious longing for a way of life as far removed as possible from the urban existence of the people. The violence and the shooting and the thrilling chase across the plains were imaginative escapes from a narrow, convention-bound existence.

The type of the domestic problem picture would usually come to a close by showing the husband, agitated, on one side of the picture standing with his back turned upon the woman, his erstwhile erring wife who pleads for forgiveness. All to no purpose.

Ah! the little child upstairs in the bedroom has heard. She comes down the staircase in a long white nightgown, takes the hand of the woman, her mother, then the hand of her father, and with herself in the centre joins their hands in a clasp. Sub-title—FORGIVEN. Embrace. Sub-title—HAPPY EVER AFTER. Another embrace—THE END.

To us in 1939 the appearance of the room in which this idyll takes place with its fussy curtains and its pretentious, uncomfortable-looking furniture, would seem unattractive enough, but how would it strike the working people say from Flower and Dean Street, East, or those from the neighbourhood of New Cut, Lambeth, in 1905? Never mind the heartaches of the characters for a moment. Here were people who lived in a house where there was actually room enough for a table, upon which was placed a gorgeous aspidistra in decorative isolation.

48

A riot of spatial splendour.

That is not all. For sleeping, these people on the pictures had wide comfortable beds in separate rooms, and for eating yet another room, and there was a spacious kitchen and perhaps a bathroom. In the daytime they would wear clean immaculate clothes of one kind, and at night clothes of another sort. At bed-time they would wear special garments called nightgowns, not the shirt and pants you wore all day and at work and changed once a week. One had heard rumours or occasionally read in the papers that there were beings somewhere in another world who lived like that, beings of whom it was said that they had no need to cook, eat, sleep, live and die all in the same room.

But here at the pictures, you were brought almost right into their homes and could live amongst them for a while in active imagination. If you looked at them closely and went to the pictures often enough, you would realize that they were humans just like yourselves.

And so the working people would start making comparisons. Their conclusions were not consciously expressed. Nevertheless, a process like the slow fermentation of yeast had begun, which would gain terrific momentum within a decade or two. In the world of letters, science and philosophy the genesis of this new factor in the stimulation of critical faculties amongst the people was either ignored or treated with contempt.

No one seemed to dream that the popularity of the pictures had the remotest relation to fundamental human needs. It was just an insignificant excrescence. It was little more than a low popular fancy somewhere about the level of the fair-ground. So it was thought.

That it was deserving of scientific observation and evaluation, or of political guidance, would have been thought absurd. When at last, in 1925, after about thirty years, the cinema achieved the honour of being noticed by intellectuals, there were some who still spoke of it as

49   D

'dope for the masses,' an expression which still does service among the culturally immature.

From the short ten or fifteen-minute cowboy, chase, domestic or religious drama there had to emerge a new quality in the upward climb of the cinema. But not before the public had had their surfeit, and not without the usual resistance of vested interests, which is the expression of the law of inertia in the cinema's history.

The new development started with a dissatisfaction at seeing dramas and comedies presented as impersonal and general. Patrons began to take an interest in particular actors and actresses who appeared regularly on the pictures and for whom they developed what seemed almost a personal affection. At this time producers were getting their actors for the most part from the bread line of the profession. Studios in New York, for instance, were placed as far away from Broadway as conveniently possible, so that the professional disgrace which then attached to working for the movies should not affect the actors' prospects on the stage. This arrangement suited the producers admirably, because as long as the actors remained anonymous they could obtain their services for no more than chicken feed. Again, all the influence of the producers is weighted on the side of the *status quo*.

But the public wanted what the public wanted.

At this time no credit-titles giving a list of parts and studio personnel ever appeared to preface a film on the screen, as is the practice to-day. What follows is exceedingly instructive. We have Terry Ramsaye's authority as well as a great deal of other evidence for the way the star system started. The initiative came from the people. The producers could only direct it once it had started. Ramsaye describes how, after the American pictures had been circulating in Europe for some time, the producers began receiving reports from their agents and distributors in London, Paris and Berlin with some very disquieting news.

Patrons at the pay-box were beginning to ask specifically for pictures in which certain of their favourite players appeared. They usually asked for, 'You know, that chap with the nice face and curly hair who was such a fine handsome hero' or 'You know, that girl with the ringlets and the charming way with her' or 'That jolly old fat man, you know whom I mean, the one who is always seen patting children and dogs and who is so friendly and affable.'

These personalities were afterwards identifiable as Maurice Costello, Mary Pickford and John Bunny respectively.

As this specific demand became more insistent it drove the producers near to panic. Here they were, getting along quite comfortably, getting good prices for outright sale of their films at so much per foot, with actors content to work for a few dollars a day, and then this had to happen. Now they would be compelled to enter into competition with one another for the services of particular actors and actresses, and heaven knew to what heights their salary costs might rise. As if there was not enough trouble over the patents wars! There was sure to be another battle with the exhibitors over the question of increased charges. But there was nothing they could do about it except to adapt themselves to the new situation.

Coincident with this development, there came a demand for better stories and better direction. It was becoming increasingly difficult to keep the public satisfied with the short, sharp, staccato films that dashed their way to a conclusion in ten or fifteen minutes. People began to become sophisticated enough to want to see a story that required a little more time in the telling, and which told a little more about the characters and the situations they had by now got used to.

About this time, pictures were being shown for the most part on single machines. The two-machine system, which allows for continuous projection, was only just coming into vogue. The majority of places showing pictures were given to the one-machine system, which would run one reel of film of 1,000 feet and stop. END OF PART ONE. Two or three minutes elapsed in darkness, for lacing up Part Two before the show could continue.

At first, when the longer feature film made its appearance, showmen would vie with each other in describing the lengths of their offerings. The red-nosed comedian of the contemporary music-hall was able to make fine capital out of this situation by describing how he had been invited to see *A Woman's Heart* in ten parts, or *She Would Not Hold Her Tongue* five thousand feet long, or *The Drunkard's Remorse* in three reels and a stagger!

By about 1908, five years after *The Great Train Robbery*, the mere ability to set a camera upon a tripod and crank a handle was no longer the way to fortune. The cinema was entering the path of big business. Players were coming into public esteem and were becoming a big economic factor in film production. Story writers and directors had to be seriously considered, although for a very long time the public took hardly any interest in who the writers or directors were. The wish-fulfilment ideas of the people were expressed in their allegiance to the types who appeared on the screen, types that most nearly represented a slight advance on their own current ideas of manly men and womenly women.

But even at this early stage the film makers sought to cash in on the publicity value of well-circulated books which had run into several editions. Such was *Quo Vadis* from the story by Henryk Sienkiewitch. It met with very great success partly because it was in line with the current religious trend, but mainly because of its then unusual length (it was in ten reels), its lavish sets and huge crowd casts employed in the making of the film.

Many film makers in those days were in the habit of

making short films on the quick, from well-known novels, without even a by-your-leave from the authors concerned. The first film that started protracted litigation in America over author's copyright was a one-reel *Ben-Hur* made by Kalem. This was made without seeking the permission of the author, Lew Wallace, the publishers or anyone else. Kalem settled at last for 25,000 dollars in 1911, but they had made a big profit from the circulation of the film during the three preceding years. The case established author's copyright in the U.S.A. definitely as far as films were concerned. It was probably this case that finally decided Kalem to quit with their gains in that year.

Fifteen years later another *Ben-Hur* was made as a feature by the Metro Company of America. It was on the most lavish scale imaginable and had many sensational new features. It netted four million dollars, thus beating the record held by Griffith's *Birth of a Nation* in 1915 by half a million.

V

M ANY have speculated upon the reason for the
ascendancy of the American over every other film
industry in the world, but the real reason is to be sought
in American history itself, in the fresh unhampered movement of ideas which gained its impetus from the American
Constitution with its regard for the rights of man; in the
history of transport of a whole people over a vast continent; and in the terrific tempo of American industrial
advance. This accounts for the vitality of the American
film and its spread to almost every market in the
world.

There has always been a receptiveness of ideas among
the Americans. Even the poorest recent immigrant from
Europe immediately becomes affected by the American
social atmosphere. Until the great slump of 1929 America
seemed to offer everything to everybody. The idea of log-
cabin to White House was encouraged by the endless
vistas of progress which were said to be open to every
humble citizen.

American film producers had this advantage too. They
had the poorest peasants and immigrant labourers from
every country in the world in vast masses right on their
door-step as consumers. Very early they discovered what
sort of picture it was that the greatest number of people in
the world wanted to see.

While the Swedish, German, French and Italian film
contributed to the world's common stock with interesting
nationally individual characteristics of their own, the

American film was international by *its own national necessity*. When the war of 1914–18 to a large extent stopped or hampered film production in European countries, it placed America at a still greater advantage. But all the evidence shows that even had the war not broken out, America would still have been in the lead.

The Americans were living in a vital ferment of expansion which produced a quickening of personality. Terms like 'live wire' and 'go-getter' were all native expressions of the type most likely to succeed in the U.S.A. The very atmosphere was stimulating to all sorts of people in all walks of life, from the vigorous, rugged, aggressive members of the I.W.W., the Industrial Workers of the World, to the sharp-witted entrepreneur and the ruthless, determined leader of industry. It was all indicative of an extraordinary creative tempo never before seen in the world's history.

Small wonder then that America was the cradle of the most enterprising film producers, distributors and exhibitors, the most appealing stars, and the most influential and idea-inspired directors, such as D. W. Griffith.

It has been seen that the initiative for change, the demand for something better in film fare came from below, from the people. However slight an advance it may appear to us to-day, the exercise of discrimination in favour of one player rather than another is a distinct sign of progress. It was the first sign of the exercise of taste, limited, rudimentary if you like, but the definite beginnings of a process which it would be impossible for anyone to hold in check for any length of time. Discrimination was now a factor and would inevitably evolve until it came to affect every component of the film; story, direction, theme, treatment, photography, social outlook, music and the dance. All in good time.

The American producers were the first to recognize the importance of the new phenomenon, the star.

As soon as they had reconciled themselves to the new situation they entered into the fight for the possession of the people's favourites with the same gusto as heretofore. Did that mean higher salary costs? Well then, the new films would have to be hired out at four or five times the price at which they were previously sold outright. And they went all out for the stars.

While the Swedish cinema before the war developed on the lines of intense feeling, superbly poised photography, beautiful landscapes and themes full of meaning and tragic implications; while the basic French cinema was the light comedy and the Italian cinema specialized in spectacular mass presentations of early civilizations in the manner of *Quo Vadis*; and while all these tendencies stopped in their tracks and faded out through lack of international support, the American cinema was able to forge that link in the chain which would unite the cinema's past with its future. That link was the star.

The American producer realized almost in a flash just what the star really portended. The star was the focal point upon which the newly awakened critical faculty of the people centred, and the American producer knew it. He knew it by intimate personal contact with the people whom he regarded as his equals. When it comes to fundamental needs, food, security, warmth, love, all men are alike. The American producer knew this because he had studied his psychology at close quarters, in the real, in the life, as it works.

Later, he would be obliged by necessity to comb the universities and art schools, and to buy all the learning and specialized knowledge he needed, in the same way as he was compelled to buy the services of stars. He would become more sensitive to derision if he put too many anachronisms into his historical pictures. He would therefore be compelled to employ competent research workers, antiquarians, as well as others working in specialized fields.

Whatever faults we may find in the cinema's American past, there is one thing for which we may be profoundly grateful. You may examine the tens of thousands of films made these forty years past in America, and never once will you come across that peculiar and obnoxious trait which is so constantly to be found in English films—the patronizing attitude towards working-class characters. In most English films all the nice people conform to the most correct West End theatre standards, in character, accent, mannerisms and attire right down to the last crease in the last pair of flannels, but a taximan or a charwoman is made to talk and act like a mental defective.

To explain why you get this kind of thing in English films and not in American films is to go a long way towards explaining why the English film has a restricted appeal and why the American film is enjoyed all over the world. With few exceptions, the English fictional film derives from the artificial, hot-house realm of the smart set and the West End stage. Our film makers mistakenly imagine that what is part of their own system of ideas will serve as currency for the rest of the millions of the population. They do their utmost to cater for the widest market, but they omit to do the one thing essential to success, to delve deep amongst the common people for ideas and for inspiration, and also so that they may understand the needs and tastes of their 'customers.'

The story is quite otherwise in America. The close study of the tastes of the widest mass of the people has always been part of the very texture of American commercial practice. Rationalized mass-production began in America before anywhere else. The corollary to this was a necessary study of the psychology of the people in order to effect mass sales. The Carl Laemmle who helped to organize the sale of clothing in a store in the rising town of Oshkosh was in no way different from the Carl Laemmle who organized the production and sale of films, who had the public on his side when he helped to bust the trust, the feudal Motion Picture Patents Company.

We have stressed the importance of the star as a necessary focal point at a certain stage in the cinema's history. But, with almost lightning succession there followed new qualitative developments. The first was theme. The intelligent synthesis of theme and star in turn called for an advance in technique. The director became as important as the star, although in the nature of things he would not come within the range of public awareness as often or as insistently as the star.

Next in importance came the cameraman and lighting experts who would employ light, shade, angle and composition in their new dynamic medium, with the same painstaking care exercised by their predecessor, the worker with paint-brush and canvas.

The further merging and inter-relation of qualitative factors had its effect in bringing the theme up to a higher level. And so the upward spiral continued, always at the demand of the audiences, the people who regulated the tap whence the money flowed.

VI

IN the year 1907 there came to New York a young man who was about to achieve the position of one of the world's leading figures in the cinema's technical and cultural advance. The young man was David Wark Griffith. The moment was conducive to the exercise of intelligence, far-sightedness, imaginative sympathy, technical skill and a well-developed knack of team work. It was given to Griffith to lay the basis for the theoretical examination of cinema technique; and it was to Griffith that many directors, including the Soviet directors, would years later generously acknowledge their indebtedness.

It is very significant that Griffith's antecedents were similar to those of Mary Pickford, Charlie Chaplin and countless others like Anita Loos, for instance, who was amongst the first to introduce a more intelligent sub-title technique in the 'Came the Dawn' manner. Griffith, like Miss Pickford and Miss Loos, had worked in a travelling show. The tradition of the real people's theatre, of the strolling players, of the Commedia Dell'Arte lives strongly in the hearty melodrama which is the staple offering of these companies.

The travelling show appealed to rural audiences, whilst the music-hall, whence Chaplin graduated via Fred Karno's company, was more the urban expression of the people's theatre; a little more sophisticated perhaps, tinged with urban cynicisms, but still of the people.

Griffith had the advantage also of having been a newspaper reporter and a book agent. (There are many ex-

59

reporters turned directors, amongst them René Clair.) Griffith left Louisville with ideas, a script in his pocket, and an impressive physique. Arriving in New York he sought out E. S. Porter, who had made *The Great Train Robbery* some four years earlier, and offered him the script. Porter would not buy his script but he was ready to hire his physique. He offered Griffith a part as a sturdy mountaineer in a film called *The Eagle's Nest*. The offer was accepted and Griffith earned his first ten dollars in New York in front of a camera. It was not long before he became a director for Biograph.

In the period of comparative peace that followed the formation of the Motion Pictures Trust of which Biograph was a member, Griffith got his chance to try out certain ideas that had been simmering in his mind.

Biograph was beginning to acquire a reputation on the market, with visible results at the pay-box and repercussions upon competitors, thanks to Griffith. This is how Terry Ramsaye describes his work:

Griffith began to work out a syntax of screen narration, and started to use close-ups for accents and fade-outs for punctuation, with cut-backs and manipulations of sequence and new intensity of suspense.

The importance of Griffith's innovations was realized in a practical way by the American cinema, which continued to use his technique without realizing it in specific terms as a science, because knowledge of psychology had not been developed to the point of accurate scientific measurement of cause and effect. It was only fifteen years later when the Soviet directors Kuleshov, Eisenstein and Pudovkin had studied Griffith's films in conjunction with the results of Pavlov's laboratory experiments on conditioned reflexes, that it was possible to demonstrate for the first time how mind-conditioning was effected through the silent film.

The application of this synthesis led, for instance, to the discovery that the extremely short flashes of short scenes cut into the story of a picture galvanized the attention of the audience like a shock. The whole story could be heightened to such an intensity of meaning as can only be realized when one has seen films like Eisenstein's *Battleship Potemkin* and *General Line* and Pudovkin's *Storm over Asia*.

Another characteristic of Griffith was his incurable curiosity in human affairs and social evolution, a pointer to which is his third or fourth film, *Man's Genesis*, a drama of our hairy, cave-man ancestors, complete with animal skin and club. An epoch in one reel!

Griffith by no means had it all his own way in the making of his experiments at Biograph's. One of the most curious demonstrations of man's resistance to the impact of new ideas is to be found in the treatment that some of Griffith's innovations of technique received at the hands of both his business chiefs and the public.

Until Griffith came upon the scene, all films were shot just as if an exact photograph were being taken of an entire theatre stage. Characters made their exits and entrances, indulged in exaggerated mannerisms just as the current stage convention demanded. When a person entered a scene, you always saw the whole of him from top to toe. For the sake of emphasis of meaning Griffith began to show characters in threequarter-length, half-length and close-up. The Biograph bosses and the audiences both started objecting. The producers complained because they were paying full salaries and were only getting their actors photographed in part, which was sheer waste of good salary and good paid-for anatomy; and the audiences objected because they thought they were being cheated. 'We want to see his feet' became the cry.

But after a while the obvious superiority of Griffith's films reconciled the public to the swindle!

One morning a young girl of seventeen presented herself

at the reception desk of the Biograph Company on the off-chance of getting a job, and asked to see Mr. Griffith. Mr. Griffith was impressed by her appearance and the list of plays she had performed in on the 'kerosene circuit'—the one-night stands at country fairs. He engaged her on the spot, and the whisper went round the studio that Griffith had found a winner.

He undoubtedly had, for the young girl was Gladys Smith, who was soon to be known to the world's inhabitants as Mary Pickford.

She was a success in every picture from the start, but her talents were by no means limited to acting. Both Miss Pickford and Griffith had gone through the hard school of the strolling player and were able to hit it off very well in the pooling of ideas in making pictures which had the effect of elevating Mary to an unprecedented height of stardom.

Griffith was never a man to adopt a high-handed attitude towards his co-workers, and he generally enlisted the help of the entire studio personnel in the solution of day-to-day problems. At every odd moment, whilst resting, at the studio café table over shilling lunches or travelling to and from the studio, the only topic was film.

From the beginning the Americans have always treated the film seriously. It is not only a means of getting a living. It is a collective means of expression full of exciting possibilities. It is a job to do with competence and gusto. That was the spirit that made itself evident in the Biograph studio from the earliest days.

The first of Mary Pickford's pictures was *The School Teacher*, made while she was still anonymous. The flood of insistent enquiry that followed made it impossible for Biograph to continue the policy adopted with their first woman star, Florence Lawrence, whose identity was conveniently cloaked under the designation 'The Biograph Girl'; and within a year Mary Pickford had achieved greater fame than had any one person in history, up to that time.

Another worker at the Biograph studio was Mack Sennet who, too, worked like a Trojan, and watched every new technical step that Griffith took. Terry Ramsaye remarks humorously that nearly every scenario that Sennet submitted had a policeman in it, and not one was ever accepted by Griffith. This disappointment, says Ramsaye, must have worked itself out as a repressed policeman urge in the now famous classic Keystone cops which Sennet first established when he left Biograph for Keystone. Undoubtedly, Sennet has made his contribution in the field of comedy. He learned a lot from Griffith but it is quite obvious that the two men were worlds apart in temperament and in outlook on life, and it is this difference in outlook which was to determine the nature of the creative work that each was to undertake.

Mary Pickford, however, could work with Griffith. The eventfulness of her road-show career afforded her an enormous store of material which she was able to convert into scenario form. Griffith took nearly all her stories, and turned them into amazing film successes. Some of the titles are worth re-calling: *Caught in the Act*, *Getting Even*, *The Girl of Yesterday*, *Fate's Desire*, *The Awakening* and later *The Human Sparrow*, *Daddy Longlegs* and many others. The value of Mary's services to Biograph shot up with meteoric suddenness, and in a year or two her salary had risen from 35 dollars for her first week's work to 10,000 dollars a week. But even this ratio of increase in terms of money can give no inkling of the popularity her films were achieving. The lion's share was still going to the producers, distributors and exhibitors between them. The huge increase in profits arose from the circumstance already explained, that once a film is complete as a negative any number of positives can be printed therefrom. The players engaged in a production would get paid the one salary whatever it may be, but to all intents and purposes the stars might have been appearing at three or four hundred different theatres every day, several times a day, all in the same week in the U.S.A. alone. If the markets of the world are counted it might mean four or five times that number of theatres playing the same star simultaneously.

In those early days a tremendous amount of piracy went on which it was impossible to control. Especially was this the case with the Pickford and Chaplin films, which made piracy a worth-while risk to those who were prepared to take a chance. To-day the practice has ceased completely because of tighter world control.

The method of the pirates was simple. Just as a positive print is taken from a negative, so, with a good clean unscratched positive, it is possible to have a negative printed from this positive. In the trade this is called a dupe negative. The resulting positives from the dupe negative will be quite good, with only a small loss of definition in the picture. A clandestine arrangement with the transport man, an exhibitor and a not so particular film printing firm, and you have the pirated copies ready for export. This is where all the pirated copies come from that dot the more obscure corners of the earth and draw untold millions of dollars which will never find their way to the original players, or to the makers of the film.

It was not until 1910 that piracy was practised on a wide scale. A year before, an established star like Marion Leonard, one-time actress in melodrama, had been getting the record salary of 75 dollars a week from Biograph. Screen programmes still retained a strong seasoning of primitive scenics. Comedies and dramas were reel length, and sometimes only half-reel length, with a stage technique which by contrast made Griffith's early work appear quite revolutionary. There was not the same incentive to piracy at this stage.

It was Miss Pickford's rise to the 10,000 dollar a week

standard that made pirating really pay, and it was Chaplin's films in 1915 that turned this illicit traffic into a real gold mine.

The first picture that was to presage the multiple-reel film was *The Fall of Troy*, imported into America from Italy. Then came *Dante's Inferno* from the same source. A little later Adolph Zukor imported Sarah Bernhardt's *Queen Elizabeth* and *The Lady of the Camellias*. This gave him the idea of offering 'famous players in famous films,' and so was started Famous Players Lasky, later to be reorganized under the name of Paramount.

Another ambitious production from Italy was *Homer's Odyssey*, which was toured by showmen all over America. In the Middle West everyone wanted to know whether Mr. Homer was touring with the company to make a personal appearance! With the people at their then cultural level it was inevitable that these pictures of classic times should bring disappointing results to the showmen. Audiences preferred the Wild West, with its action and its Indians, and the charm of Mary Pickford, to the stories of Greek civilizations, all knowledge of which had been obscured for them by the necessities of the day-in, day-out struggle for existence. Broncho Billy was more of a poet to them than Dante, and Mary Pickford was much nearer to their hearts' desire than was Sarah Bernhardt.

The infiltration of these films, however, upon the American scene had the effect of influencing Griffith to try his hand at multi-reel films, the first of which was his *Judith of Bethulah*. It was this picture which proved to be one of his ideological stepping-stones towards *The Birth of a Nation* and *Intolerance*, the two major classics for which Griffith will always be remembered.

VII

AGAINST this background of fast changing technical standards, against the shifting organizational base of the film industry, and the impact of European films upon American ideas, the figure of Mary Pickford began to assume the brilliance of the first star of the first magnitude. How is it possible to explain the almost legendary popularity of Mary Pickford?

She was nice and she was sweet, say many to explain the phenomenon; but so were such of her predecessors as Marion Leonard, Mary Fuller and Florence Turner, who have since faded from memory. Others who came after, such as Mae Busch and Theda Bara, have been forgotten, but the fame of Mary Pickford still persists.

The reason can only be found by relating the star to the social and cultural background of the time. We have seen that the people will persist in admiring that type or that tendency which is taking them a step, but only a step, forward at a time. Only the American civilization, a civilization materially in advance of the rest of the world, could have produced Mary Pickford.

We must try to realize the impact of Miss Pickford's appearance and acting upon the consciousness of the world's population as it existed around 1909. The current male idea of a woman's place in the scheme of things was extremely well mirrored in the films before Miss Pickford wrought a change. Let us take a sample.

The manly hero appears in the nick of time just as the heroine is about to be subjected to a fate worse than death.

66

'So—we meet at last!' A terrific fight ensues between hero and villain. It takes up a considerable length of the film. But what is the heroine doing while this schemozzle is going on? Does she ever have the sense to pick up the revolver which has been dropped and for which the two men are struggling? Does she even kick it out of the villain's reach?

Not a bit of it.

There she stands, frightened and aghast, on the verge of fainting, shrinking in a corner and swaying from side to side, clasping her hands to her brow: the perfect woman in a world where men vie with each other for their women as if they were passive chattels.

In those days this was the current male idea of a woman's role in life, imported from Europe into America; it was the masculine notion of how a woman should behave in the emergency just described. She must be sweet and weak and helpless, so that when the handsome hero has conquered he can puff out his chest and claim his bride, who will lower her eyes and blush.

But a change was beginning to take place in the real world. Increasingly women were entering into commercial and industrial life. The idea of the helpless creature was gradually disappearing from men's minds. The Suffragette movement in England was a reflection of the resentment that women felt at being looked upon as inferiors or as frail beings for whom men would always play the gallant. And the Women's Movement was followed with interest by the rest of the world's women as well as men.

The time was ripe for a change, and Miss Pickford arrived at the psychological moment and gave the world what it was waiting for. The world's women loved her as someone who had charm as well as spirit; someone who was not afraid to assert herself as well as win the man of her choice. The world's men loved her because she was lovely to look at for one thing, and because she afforded a fascinating glimpse of the woman of the very near future, although she wore the nostalgic ringlets of the past. Here was a girl with all the attributes, and a companion who could stand up to trouble when it came; someone who could give a man a hand in an emergency instead of shivering like a jelly in her corner as her predecessors had done in the films that had gone before.

It will perhaps help us to realize the depth and extent of the influence of the film upon social consciousness, and the phenomenal speed at which the social outlook has been altered, if we compare woman before Mary Pickford with the woman in 1938 in a picture called *Stand-In*. In this film, Leslie Howard is an accountant who is sent to Hollywood from New York to learn a few things about studios. He makes the acquaintance of Joan Blondell, who is surprised to see him one day come home with a black eye, the result of an argument. Joan questions him sympathetically and then says: 'Look, this is what I do when anyone tries changing gear with my knee,' and before Leslie Howard realizes what is happening he finds himself lifted in a ju-jutsu grip and sent sprawling dazed across the floor. Just a friendly sympathetic wrinkle from one human being to another, without, for the moment, the slightest self-consciousness about their differences in sex.

Between the woman of 1908 and 1938, there is not thirty years' difference but three thousand years. And the change has been advanced as well as recorded, step by step, first by Mary Pickford, then by the luscious, sinuous vamp of the Theda Bara and Lya de Putti type, who disappeared to give way to the Elinor Glynn 'It' girl, Clara Bow, who was in turn supplanted by the Gloria Swanson type. Then came the Garbo and the Dietrich and the full-hipped Mae West who, in turn, have led to the much more individual and realist women of the American screen to-day.

THE EVOLUTION OF THE SCREEN WOMAN

(a) Before Mary Pickford—a Vitagraph one-reeler.
(b) Mary Pickford (1922).   (c) Gloria Swanson (1923).
(d) Claudette Colbert and Clark Gable in the 1934 IT HAPPENED ONE NIGHT.

All these represented distinct and necessary stages in the evolution of women as they exist in social life to-day, an evolution in which the cinema itself has played an immensely important part.

In 1910 Miss Pickford was getting 175 dollars a week, which was about 100 dollars more than the most favoured screen actress had ever got before. Between 1910 and 1915 she was lured away from Biograph by Carl Laemmle's anti-trust Independent Motion Picture Company, which gleefully announced in trade advertisements 'Little Mary is an IMP now!' A little later she went back to work with Griffith at Biograph, then again back with Laemmle to Cuba, to escape an angry mother and a panic-stricken flying squad from the Biograph studio.

In 1915 she signed a contract giving her 1,400,000 dollars for two years' work with Zukor's Famous Players. In the space of six years she had in truth become the world's sweetheart.

There are many who write about the cinema as if it were controlled by sinister money ogres. They start off with a fixed conception of personified finance capital performing all its underhand manipulations to confound the innocents. That Miss Pickford was able to command over a million dollars for her work for two years in 1915 was but an index to the desire of millions of people all over the world to indulge in a new experience.

The public was buying something. They were buying a glimpse into their own future evolution and the sight pleased them tremendously. They were experiencing the same pitiful yearning deep in their hearts which inspires millions to-day to watch Shirley Temple. It was no accident that whilst a certain star might be third in popularity in U.S.A., and, say, tenth in England, and whilst another might be second in U.S.A. and fifth in England according to pay-box figures, Shirley Temple for years was 'box-office' in the same position in England, in America or anywhere else in the world for that matter, right at the very top of the list.

Shirley Temple is what all parents would like their children to be, beautiful, clever, sound in body and brain, adventurous, but not precocious, and full of good spirits. Just as there are many sound psychological reasons to explain Shirley Temple's popularity, so there were good reasons for the popularity of Mary Pickford in her day; and one of them is that, consciously or unconsciously, Mary Pickford was contributing her share in the acceleration of the social process towards a healthier relationship between the sexes.

Another aspect of cultural progress between 1998 and to-day is indicated by the way people behaved in crowds then and now. At the entrance to any pit and gallery of any music-hall or theatre, you shoved and you pushed and you cursed to get through the crowd at the narrow entrance where you handed in your fourpence in exchange for the metal check which entitled you to enjoy the show sitting on a hard seat. The more civilized queue of to-day was hardly known. Beer and oranges and peanuts were consumed all over the house, and now and again an argument about a seat would start a fight which would bring the chucker-out to the scene. At music-halls and at picture-halls (the converted furniture stores mostly), slides would appear on the screen at intervals reading: 'Do not expectorate on the floor'; 'Will ladies please remove their hats'; 'If drunk, your patronage is not wished for'; 'No whistling please during songs.' As recently as twelve years ago, a famous dance-hall at Margate displayed the following notice over its portals: 'Gentlemen are requested not to dance wearing their hats and overcoats.' Which is rather like the notice put up at a Moscow hostel for visiting peasants immediately after the Revolution: 'Citizens are asked not to get into bed with their boots on.'

We have, indeed, travelled a long, long way in these

few years. Is not, for instance, the more sensible clothing we wear directly traceable to the influence of a civilization newer and younger than our own? And by what means could this civilization affect our judgments, our tastes in clothes or cars, in hygiene and clean living and our more rational attitude towards sex, other than by its films? By what means, other than by means of the film, could our womenfolk in their millions admire and emulate a type of woman who is a step ahead of themselves on the road to complete equality with men? Everyone can see the change that has occurred in the way women are regarded by men in those countries where going to the cinema has become a regular custom.

But the influence of the film is exerted in innumerable other directions. There is the effect of the documentary, the interest film of travel and science, the newsreel, the advertisement film, *The March of Time*, the public relations film and the direct political propaganda film. Each has its own method of appeal, but of all, the fictional is the most important, because the social commentary it contains (however slight or distorted at times) is the most easily assimilable and palatable.

It was in the year 1913 that a great figure was to come to the screen who, with Mary Pickford, was able to shoot forward the cinema's progress at a terrific speed. This was Charles Chaplin. Chaplin was not only a comedian of the highest rank, but a real man of the people, and one whom history will accord a position amongst the truly great, for a man's greatness is to be measured not by the armies he can raise and the death, destruction, misery and devastation he can spread, but in the solid contribution to the store of human values which he has effected. To this day, Charlie Chaplin's films are among the most popular in the 16 mm. and 9·5 mm. circulating film libraries. They are still enjoyed by young and old, and will probably be cherished when the very name of Hitler has been forgotten. Hitler adopted Chaplin's moustache, but his feet do the goose-step instead of the Chaplin straddle. Chaplin's moustache spells sympathy and joy, whilst that of Hitler . . . They are the outward embellishments of inner contents as opposed as any two things can be.

The present generation can have little conception of the effect of Chaplin upon an audience which had never seen his pictures before. In the early months of 1914, you would be sitting on a form in a converted store, watching the end of a picture. The drama over, you would wait for a minute or two, then on to the screen would flash an introductory title which is a signal for a concerted scream of delight from the children—KEYSTONE! Everybody knows Keystone. They all look forward to seeing the fun and the grotesque characters, plenty of action, plenty of custard pies. There is a gurgle of delighted anticipation from the adults.

The main title over, he comes—someone quite new—waddling down the street, twirling his cane—Charlie Chaplin. From that moment, for the rest of the fifteen-minute run of the film, the whole audience is convulsed with such laughter as it is beyond the power of a pen to describe. Raising the roof may seem a metaphor, but here you see the walls, wall brackets, chairs and forms literally rocking with the whole packed mass of people in helpless, uncontrollable mirth. A happy release from the emotional tension of everyday life.

Now, and for many years, the world will set up a clamour for Charlie Chaplin. From his first picture to his latest word in *Modern Times*, it can be seen that a strong social commentary runs through all of them. Charlie is everywhere the butt of circumstance. The brutes and bullies may humiliate him, he gives as good as he gets, hoisting them with their own petard.

His highly stylized movements and masterly pantomime served to throw a sharp beam of light upon human experi-

72

ence. His manly stance, his amorous passes, his mistakes, his self-deceptions, his chivalry towards women, his fastidiousness amidst squalor; the acrobatics, the tricks and tumbles, the morning after the night before, the disillusionments were all of the very stuff of life, presented with extraordinary sympathy, comedy and unprecedented ability.

VIII

TO appreciate Chaplin correctly, it is very necessary to take a look at the social background in which he spent his early years. To anyone living in poverty and possessed of feeling and a highly sensitive imagination, an area like Kennington in South London would offer plenty of scope for the observation of the frailties and foibles of men.

In the early 1900's, long before the fast tubes to Edgware and Morden and Ealing and Harrow, and long before the one-hour Pullman to Brighton, Kennington was one of the nice residential districts of the middle class. To this day, the wide, spacious thoroughfares and the pretentious façades of whole streets speak eloquently of the days when the world for the prosperous seemed solidly built for ever. A faint air of the topper and the crinoline of a past age still seems to hang about the place.

In Chaplin's time, parts of Kennington were being gradually converted into crowded working-class tenements. The imposing façades were beginning to serve the purpose of hiding the poverty which was hitherto more prevalent in the East End and in dockside London. There are many such districts in a periphery of two or three miles from the City or West End of London, now populated by the artisan working class mostly, but still retaining the outward shell of pre-war middle-class gentility; places like the area around Hampstead Road near Mornington Crescent, North Kensington, Dalston and Stoke Newington and the south side of

74

Victoria Park, all within reasonable horse-bus distance of the City and West End, centres of business and pleasure.

The physical appearance of Charlie on the screen is the very symbol and essence of the district in which Charles Chaplin spent his impressionable youth. *Toujours le gentleman* might well be the motto below the baggy-trousered figure. No matter to what straits of poverty the average little Kennington resident may come, he will always conform to the civilized habits of the real gentleman. If he bumps into a lamp-post not looking, he raises his bowler to it in apology; when he floors his opponent, the bully, with one swipe (it hurts him to do it, but he must!) he raises his bowler again as he steps on to the prostrate body to further adventure.

There is no doubt that struggling respectability at grips with poverty was the dominant feature which fixed the character of Charlie in young Chaplin's mind. He must also have had ample opportunity to observe the middle class drunk, whom he caricatured for years. One can easily imagine that drunkenness was quite a common way out for many for whom the problems of life were really too much, and the frequent sight of an inebriate in evening dress must have made a very vivid impression on Chaplin.

As if in preparation for his future career on the silent screen, he went through a considerable apprenticeship as the monocled dude in Fred Karno's Company touring in *Mumming Birds*. In this music-hall sketch, most of the characters had plenty to say and to sing, but Chaplin's antics were always silent. *Mumming Birds* was presented as a stage upon a stage, and the theme was a burlesque of the current English music-hall. The Mumming Bird boxes were placed one on each side of the stage. In the left-hand box, a party of Karno visitors came to applaud or to make facetious remarks as each burlesque music-

75

hall turn appeared. In the right-hand box was the dude, with eye-glass complete, and almost *non compos mentis.* That was Chaplin.

It required a great deal of inventiveness to run through the whole half-hour performance and act as a kind of inebriated silent chorus. He would sway about, throw things at the annoying people in the opposite box, and when a fat-cheeked smiling soubrette appeared with her exaggerated padded hips, his intense excitement would cause him to sway right over the side of the box, bumping his head on to the stage.

There was a hearty, meaty tang about the music-hall of those days, something that reflected the hard life of the London working class, expressed in Cockney satire and a form of humour of extraordinary vigour. Every Monday, a new six-day programme was put on at the halls. People would say to each other '. . . good company up the Cambridge this week.' It was never a programme, always a company; and you always went *up* the Cambridge or the London, or *up* the Paragon or the Forresters. You never went *to* or stayed *at* any of these places, not even if you could afford a shilling for a stall on the ground floor.

Contemporary with the popular Fred Karno's Company, there was George Carney's Company, with Carney as a policeman who had always something sarcastic to say about policemen. Then there was Lew Lake's Company; Lew Lake and Bob Morris in the *Bloomsbury Burglars*, which ran for years under the advertised wise-crack: 'Watch 'eer, Jerry! Go it, Nobbler!' This sketch finished with an exciting battle and chase over the roof-tops, with a score of coppers being scattered all over the place. How the audiences loved it! And how the promoters of these sketches knew it!

There were, of course, the big single stars, whose names alone in thick, bold letters at the head of a playbill would ensure a full house at every performance. Such were people like Chirgwin, the White-Eyed Kaffir: *My fiddle is my sweetheart*; Marie Lloyd, the Cockney predecessor of Mae West: *A little of what you fancy does yer good*; lugubrious Sam Mayo: *'Ladies, don't be frightened, I'm an Indian, I come from Timbuctoo, three four, five, six'*; Harry Lauder, years before he became Sir, with his wiggle and his waggle and his crooked walking-stick; and the Jewish comedian with his bowler pulled well over his ears, who was accepted with genuine good humour by Jew and Gentile alike.

There was a strong streak of sentimental chauvinism in the music-hall before the war. The unfolding of the flag brought wild applause. The idea taught at school that one Englishman was worth six of any other nationality prevailed, until it was knocked on the head so completely since the war that there is hardly a sign of its revival.

Despite occasional displays of jingoism, a bold expression of a national culture other than English would receive unexpectedly warm appreciation from the audience. They liked to see people stand up for themselves. They listened with great respect to the songs of yearning of the Negro, about the *Swannee Ribber*. There was genuine warmth for John Lawson's tableaux, in which he was seen outside a synagogue with the light streaming through its stained-glass windows, singing *Only a Jew*. And sentimental songs about Ireland had a great vogue.

Treatment of sex as a subject would range from the realism of Marie Lloyd through varying nuances to the sentimental idealism of something like the following:

> *If those lips could only speak,*
> *If those eyes could only see,*
> *If those beautiful golden tresses*
> *were there in reality.*

77

> *Could I only take your hand*
> *As I did when you took my name:*
> *But it's only a beautiful picture*
> *In a beautiful golden frame.*

Perfect specimen of a hybrid, resulting from Kipling's *If* and Marie Corelli.

The average current standard of comedy is rather well epitomized in this:

> *Is the old house still in the same old place*
> *With the same old picture on the wall?*
> *Does father wear the same old trousers*
> *Mother the same old shawl?*
> *Do you still keep a lodger in the top back room,*
> *Still without a carpet on the floor?*
> *Does the old tom-cat still spoon upon the mat*
> *With the ginger-whiskered cat next door?*

An examination of the significance of Chaplin to the cinema can have no validity whatever, unless his emergence is related to the extraordinary fertile soil thus lightly sketched. Anything else would be like trying to explain a plant from the stem upwards, ignoring the roots.

Chaplin was not only a first-class comedian and mimic. There have been others who were good at the mechanics of their profession. Chaplin deserves his position amongst the great, precisely because he has his roots deep down amongst the ordinary folk of the earth. His imaginative sympathy for the common man, the result of his early life's experiences, is expressed in everything he does. At the height of his activity he was flattered by an innumerable number of screen competitors, who went so far as to imitate his every item of attire, from bowler hat to leaky boots, even to his moustache, his waddle and his amazingly funny way of rounding a street corner when in a hurry. The more they came, the greater was the

THE CIRCUS

MODERN TIMES

THE GOLD RUSH

MODERN TIMES

(All United Artists)

The pathos, comedy and unbounded chivalry of Charles Chaplin

demand for the genuine article. The others just petered out.

Chaplin's greatness is attributable to the fact that his experiences and his observation of human beings have left indelible impressions on his mind. Behind the scenes of the music-hall he had opportunity enough of meeting men and women of every nationality under the sun, people given to every form of human kindness, weakness and idiosyncrasy. To observe, to absorb with intense imagination and to express with an unbounded pity for human kind. That is the road to greatness.

In the late summer of 1913, Fred Karno's Company was at the Hammerstein's Theatre in New York, performing in *A Night at a London Club*, which, from its title, was probably a variation of *Mumming Birds*. Chaplin was in the cast. One night, after seeing the show, a Mr. Adam Kessel of the New York Motion Picture Company, the makers of Keystone films, went round to the back to put a proposition to Chaplin. According to Terry Ramsaye, Chaplin's first reaction was: 'What the blooming hell, no!' However this may be, in the end he and Mr. Kessel came to terms.

Chaplin's first film was *The Kid's Auto Races*, and a number of films were turned out at the usual rate of one per week. The period of the multi-reel film was now setting in. Higher standards of comfort in the halls were beginning to be established, consequently the time was ripe for the new development, the longer film with a theme. It was known in the world of the studios that Griffith had left Biograph and was making huge preparations for a very long, spectacular picture, based on the American Civil War.

Mack Sennet, who was director of operations at Keystone, decided to make a long comedy. To the outside world of exhibitors the idea seemed perfectly crazy. It was all right to put on a picture like *Quo Vadis*, which was a serious subject, with spectacular Romans and with Christians being thrown to the lions in the arena, but who was going to stand six reels of belly laughs?

Nevertheless, *Tilly's Punctured Romance* with Charlie Chaplin and Marie Dressler in the first six-reel comedy ever made was an enormous success.

Keystone were selling their pictures at 10 cents per foot. Chaplin's salary was going up and up. Keystone thought they would raise their price to 11 cents per foot. The showmen started complaining, not because the films were not worth it, but because they sensed it was the thin end of the wedge for yet bigger demands. There was still only the haziest appreciation of star value to a film. Greater pains were now being taken over the making of films. The six reels of *Tilly's Punctured Romance* took fourteen weeks, instead of the usual standard tempo of one reel per week.

While Keystone hesitated, Essanay put in a bid for Chaplin's services at 1,250 dollars a week, almost a tenfold increase upon his first week's salary in pictures. Off he went to make an Essanay two-reeler, *Charlie's First Job*. Then he made his second Essanay success, in which he helped cross-eyed Ben Turpin to make a name for himself. This was *A Night Out*, a title which suggests that Chaplin was turning his *Mumming Birds* experience to good account. Then came the very famous *The Champion*.

By autumn 1915, almost exactly two years after he had made his first screen appearance, Chaplin had proved himself to be the most important factor in pictures, not only as a star, but as one who was setting the tempo for the cinema's future development at an unprecedented speed.

Griffith, Miss Pickford and Chaplin were all responsible

for the quickening pace of advance, but whilst the technical and cultural contribution that each has made has been absorbed into the fabric of present-day film technique, Chaplin alone remains unique in type and character. There never was such deserved fame accorded to any one man in history. In a world passing through the agony and torment of war, he, at least, helped to take the pompous and the vainglorious down a good number of pegs in the public mind.

The de-bunking of his chief enemies, the fuss-pot little martinet, or the brute taking advantage of an officer's uniform, was as near as he could go to propagate the anti-authoritarian and, therefore, anti-war idea. The 'great I am' who could inflict any amount of suffering upon the less fortunate was exposed by Chaplin as a fraud. Let no one be surprised, therefore, that Chaplin's films, all of them, are under a thrice-fold ban in Germany to-day. Trust Hitler. He knows something.

In a famous long picture, *Shoulder Arms*, made in 1917, soon after America's entry into the war, Chaplin is a recruit in the American Army. In due course, he gets 'over there' and is in the trenches. In one short, masterly sequence, he exposes all the pre-war music-hall jingoism which sang songs like *Yes, let me like a soldier fall*. True, Chaplin passed life over in a joke, but there were plenty of little medicinal doses inside the sugar.

When Keystone lost Chaplin to Essanay, a phase of the picture business set in which has had no parallel in pictures before or since. All the Keystone prints of Charlie in existence started working overtime until they were in ribbons. Every possible Chaplin that was ever made was pressed into service and served up by showmen time and time again, and nobody seemed to get tired of them. Films, copies of which had been sold to foreign countries, came back to America as bootleg duplicated copies, and were distributed by film exchange firms at great profit. Exhibitors found themselves paying four times as much as the original hire fee for an old Chaplin, a thing that has never happened to any other type or make of film at any time.

It is on record that one cinema in New York, the Chrystal Hall on 14th Street, played nothing but Chaplins solidly for ten years, from 1913, when they first appeared until 1923, except for one week when one of his best imitators was shown as an experiment. The takings in that week fell with a bump, but the patrons returned the following week for Chaplin.

What Chaplin did has a two-fold significance. He has proved, more clearly and unmistakably than perhaps any other type can do, the falsity of the myth of the sinister money barons weaving their plots to degrade the public taste for the sake of lucre. Chaplin's popularity came when the cinema was on the border between ebullient youth and maturing adolescence; and he, more than any other· one person, consolidated the cinema-going habit amongst the widest possible masses of the world's population.

The money barons may, if you like, scheme and plot and intrigue against each other, which they did. They could juggle for position in the world market, grab each other's stars, use every subterfuge to gain advantage over an opponent, and they could spend an enormous part of their gains upon ballyhoo. Ballyhoo will be effective for a time, but only for a time. For if the films with which the publicity is concerned fail to live up to what the people expect, if they fail to correspond to their mental and emotional needs at a given historical moment, that publicity will be money down the drain.

The tail has never been known to wag the dog, and every phase of the cinema's history shows it. Public taste is something that grows and expands continuously. A film never can succeed with the public unless it deepens their sympathies, widens their consciousness, enlarges their experience and confirms their efforts in the day-to-day struggle.

There can be no possible room for doubt that during those horrible years of war, the symbol of the little humble average man, who could demolish the great big blusterer as if it were all in the day's work, found a tremendous echo in the hearts and minds of the people who were growing weary of supporting their own great ones of the earth.

Those who have succeeded on the business side of the film industry are, in the main, those who were aware of this aspect of public mental growth. They knew how to keep films at a certain intellectual level for just so long; then at the slightest fall in the barometer—one step ahead of the general level of appreciation, and again the public would offer its support. It would be tilting at windmills to try to jump too many steps ahead. The cinema magnates were wiser and knew far better than the secluded and sheltered intellectuals who for years had moaned that intellectual life was going to the dogs, all because of those terribly low pictures.

It has taken thousands of years for a literary form to develop from the narrative to the novel. It has taken nearly five hundred years of print to endow the book with the respect and the dignity and the appreciation which has all the weight of age-old tradition; yet it was expected that the film should achieve the same level of maturity before it could walk.

They expected miracles, and miracles do not happen, unless you regard from peep-show Mutoscope to *The Life of Emile Zola*, and the intellectual growth of the people of which it is indicative, as a miracle that took forty years instead of four hundred years.

During the Essanay period, which lasted until January

1916, Chaplin continued making two-reelers like *Champion Charlie*, *Charlie the Perfect Lady*, *Charlie at the Bank*, *Charlie at the Show*, and *Shanghaied*. He began to take much greater pains in the making of these films. It speaks volumes for his sense of responsibility that he would at times shoot as many as 15,000 feet to obtain 1,200 or 1,500 feet for his final completed picture.

In February 1916, Chaplin signed up with the Mutual Film Corporation, who were a distributing and film exchange firm, hitherto dependent on Essanay, Keystone and other companies for their supplies. For months the hotels and cafés in the neighbourhood of Los Angeles were alive with spies and touts working for competing film producers anxious to get Chaplin on their pay-roll.

Essanay tried to scotch these attempts by offering Chaplin 500,000 dollars as his guaranteed share of the profits on a profit-sharing contract for one year.

But it was Mutual's Mr. Freuler who made the best impression on Chaplin. The contract between them gave Chaplin an immediate cash payment of 150,000 on signing, and 10,000 dollars to be paid every week. Total for one year, 670,000 dollars.

This contract, barely twenty-seven months after his first picture was made, is but a slight index of what Chaplin signified in public esteem. It has been estimated that about 25,000,000 dollars must have passed the pay-boxes of the world up to about 1921 for the short films made with Chaplin by Keystone, Essanay and Mutual. And the big features were yet to come under the banner of United Artists.

Whilst with Mutual, Chaplin made *Easy Street*, *The Floor-Walker*, *One a.m.*, *The Cure*, *The Fireman*, *The Rink*, *The Pawnshop*. In England, a certain firm who had lost in the fight for the United Kingdom rights of Chaplin's films, tried to injure its rival by spreading the story that Chaplin was a shirker, which, ordinarily, might have been very damaging in the early part of the war. There was a slight uproar in the trade Press, but the general public took no notice. Public support in the British Empire for Chaplin became stronger than ever as the pay-box returns showed.

This episode gains greater point when it is contrasted with the Arbuckle case. Roscoe (Fatty) Arbuckle was arrested and accused of murdering a woman named Rappe, who had co-starred with him in his pictures. In one night one of the most popular comedians on the pictures was withdrawn from every screen in the world. Public hostility became so great that no exhibitor was willing to take the risk of having his hall wrecked for showing him. Arbuckle vanished as if he had never been. All the king's horses and all the king's men and all the publicity gods on Olympus could never put Arbuckle back again.

In a word, the public can be as stubbornly oblivious to what the publicity managers try to put over, as it can be assertive in its condemnation of anti-social behaviour. There is no doubt about it; a strong social instinct plays its part in the formation of public likes and dislikes. The public knew and felt that Charlie was of greater value to society than a battalion, and they loved him.

IX

THE date of Chaplin's entry into pictures, about November 1913, almost coincides with another event of parallel importance for the cinema's history. D. W. Griffith left Biograph for Mutual, the company that Chaplin was to join three years later.

A clause in the agreement between Mutual and Griffith entitled Griffith to make two films a year independently, a provision of which he took full advantage. He had been very successful in severing the cord that had kept the film tied to stage technique. The stage demanded that an actor should use emphatic gestures, so that meaning may be conveyed to the person sitting at the back of the pit or gallery. When Griffith began to bring the camera close up to the actor, it was seen at once that the much enlarged appearance on the screen would exaggerate the lifting of an eyebrow almost to the point of burlesque.

Griffith profited by this discovery by insisting on restraint in expression, whether in close-up or in long shot, with noticeably improved results in screen acting. It is curious that to this day there are any number of people in British films who seem quite unaware that the camera can do, and does, all the exaggerating necessary.

It is this sweet oblivion which makes much of our native screen acting, especially in the second feature category, unmistakably stagy.

In the face of great opposition from the producers, Griffith familiarized the public with the cut-back. This was a method of referring to a previous event in the picture by cutting into it, and showing that event actually taking place. Hitherto, what had happened in a story's past was always referred to in wordy sub-titling.

Griffith had sufficient faith in the intelligence of his audiences to believe that they would know what he was driving at when he told a story in that way.

By judicious cutting, and the assembly of the various shots according to plan, he was also able to increase the suspense. Thus equipped, he started on *The Birth of a Nation*, a film upon an unprecedented scale. It was to be in twelve reels, and would be specially distributed and shown at legitimate theatres, instead of at the store shows.

The Birth of a Nation is a milestone in film history. Griffith starred himself as the director. He was the one isolated instance for many years to come of a director upon whom the limelight of publicity was centred. But it was deserved and justified after so many years of intelligent, creative work in comparative obscurity.

The Birth of a Nation went out into the world and created a great impression. The theme was an objective treatment of the result of Negro enfranchisement in the South. It covered the Civil War between North and South, which was fought out in the film almost regardless of cost, and it placed into bold relief the Ku Klux Klan vendettas. With *The Birth of a Nation* came the birth of a realization that the film was capable of taking its place in the esteem of serious-minded people, just as much as the novel, the painting, the epic or the theatre.

The Birth of a Nation is a landmark because it represented the next qualitative step in the progress of the cinema. It is important because, for the first time in film history, it brought the film up to the plane of ideas; vital, creative, social ideas. It is this feature which gives *The Birth of a Nation* the character of a distinct break with what went before. It is this feature which created such turmoil in

87

America when the film was first shown. People took up sides with great vehemence. Some said it was anti-Negro, others said it was pro-Negro. There was so much bitterness and controversy aroused, that Griffith had to enter the field as a white-hot pamphleteer to argue that the film must be accorded the same right of expression as the novel or the newspaper.

From the scenics to the religious films, to Westerns, to melodramas, to the simple story film of the first Mary Pickford type, to the *The Fall of Troy* and *Quo Vadis*, the film had not yet attempted to get to grips with contemporary reality. In his previous work, such as *Man's Genesis*, and *Judith of Bethulah*, Griffith had been moving towards the expression of social ideas through the film. Until he joined Mutual, he had never had a completely free hand. It was only now that he was able to give full expression to those ideas. This development brought three important results to the cinema.

1. *The film had staked its claim for the expression of ideas on current social problems for the first time.*

2. *'The Birth of a Nation' set a new standard in quality, not only in cinematic technique, but in conscientious search after truth in background, costumes and action, with consequently, an immeasurable increase in the scale of monetary expenditure on films.*

3. *It set a precedent for Chaplin when he joined Mutual three years later. It gave Chaplin the latitude to make pictures for that firm over which a great deal more care, time and money was expended than upon any comedies hitherto made. It gave Chaplin a practical insight into the technical problems involved, which later fitted him to make feature length masterpieces under his own personal direction.*

The Birth of a Nation made a large sum of money for Griffith and his backers: no less than 3,500,000 dollars, a figure that no single picture had ever been within miles of approaching. At the same time, it seemed to revive all the heated passion of the Civil War, of which it was a picturization. That the film was misunderstood, even by many white friends of the Negroes, must have been particularly galling to a man like Griffith.

Evidently people wanted the film to conform to what they thought was a film's proper function, to romanticize, to idealize, to set up a mirror that would show life in a misty haze, so that sharp antagonisms are obliterated. It is not surprising that that outlook existed so widely in those days, because the self-same naïveté persists to this day.

The opposition that Griffith encountered during his campaign for the freedom of the film, impelled him to reply with the second of his independent films, *Intolerance*. It showed even better than *Birth of a Nation* the wide culture of the man. He was determined to give the public a new kind of mirror in which they could see themselves reflected. It was a mirror in which they could look down the ages and see their own kind going through the same ritual of intolerance and oppression in which they were indulging with such ferocity in the twentieth century.

This exceptionally long film was divided into four episodes, the fall of corrupt Babylon before the onslaught of the legions of Cyrus, the Christ legend of Judea, the pitiless massacre of the Huguenots on St. Bartholomew's Eve, in France, and a fourth episode telling just as heartless a story, set in contemporary industrial America. This last episode was probably influenced in style and treatment by Upton Sinclair's *The Jungle*, which had had a big circulation for some years.

Linking each episode with the other was the profoundly

moving symbolic representation of the mother rocking her child and a line from Walt Whitman:

> '*Endlessly rocks the cradle*
> *Uniter of here and hereafter.*'

Griffith showed remarkable feeling in choosing the mother and child to symbolize how intimately we are connected, how much at one we are with all that has gone before. For no other single conception has left so profound, so deeply reverent, so persistent and ineffaceable an impression on the minds of men through every conceivable age and culture as the conception of the mother and child, or the Madonna and Child. That this reverent feeling arises spontaneously from the very nature of human beings, and as an expression of gratitude to the giver of life, comfort, protection and love, the mother, can be appreciated by all who understand even a little of human psychology.

Intolerance was remarkably rich in ideas, but it was rather ahead of its time, and it was not a financial success. In the Soviet Union, a few years later, the film circulated for over ten years and was well appreciated. It was closely studied for its technical lessons by Eisenstein, Pudovkin and other Russian directors.

Upon *Intolerance* was spent a sum of money approaching the two million dollar mark. The crowds alone, it was reputed, cost twelve thousand dollars a day for long periods. The famous banqueting hall scene, during which the writing on the wall appears at the Feast of Belshazzar, cost nearly a quarter of a million dollars. The picture took nearly two hours to perform, although the actual material which was taken took seventy-five hours to view.

With *Intolerance* on the scene, it was now impossible for the cinema to turn back. The days of the cheaply-made reel-per-week film were finished. Henceforth the

INTOLERANCE, directed by D. W. Griffith

public could no longer be fobbed off. For films to show a return, more money would have to be spent on production. The store-shows will now disappear, and in quick succession there will come the Picture Palace, the Cinema, and then the Super-Cinema.

The big, spectacular, silent films will have specially selected musical scores arranged for orchestra to accompany the screening. The barker will disappear, along with the chucker-out, and in their place will appear the resplendent Ruritanian General, and the dainty, trousered Lady of the Electric Torch. Huge spectacle films will come like the *Four Horsemen of the Apocalypse*, *Ben-Hur*, *The Ten Commandments*, *The Covered Waggon* and *Way Down East*, and all will acknowledge *Intolerance* as their forerunner.

X

IN 1911 the New York *Ladies' World* was running a
series of stories called 'What happened to Mary.' They
made an arrangement with the Edison Studios to make a
series of one-reelers to illustrate the stories appearing in
the journal. The effect on circulation was phenomenal.

This was a new form of publicity which was not long
to remain without competitors. In 1912, the *Chicago
Tribune* followed by running a serial called *The Adventures
of Kathlyn*, and the paper arranged with a film company to
make a film serial of the story, instead of, as in the case of
What Happened to Mary, a series of separate stories.

The Adventures of Kathlyn let loose a spate of similar
films and Press serials which turned out to be very good
for the circulation both for paper and pay-box.

There was *Dolly of the Dailies*, starring Mary Fuller, and
Lucille Love, which was sponsored by the *Chicago Herald*,
run as a serial and filmed by IMP. The Hearst group
followed in 1914 with the *Perils of Pauline*, and there were
serials like *The Clutching Hand* and *The Exploits of Elaine*
with Pearl White in the leading role.

All these serial films were alike in that all the characters
in each of them were continually on the go, shooting and
escaping from one adventure to another. At the end of
each episode, the hero or heroine would be left suspended
from a shrub on a cliff with a sheer drop of hundreds of
feet below, or tied hand and foot to the railway line with
an express train approaching in the distance, or in some
similar predicament.

It will be observed from the titles of these serials that they were concerned mostly with Mary, Kathlyn, Dolly and Elaine. One of these characters usually occupied the centre of the story, and the things they did, the feats of acrobatics they performed to outwit the villains, the hairbreadth escapes they got away with were simply marvellous. In fact, they were a little too marvellous, for these 'sheroes,' as they came to be called by the people, were still addicted to wearing skirts to the ground, bodices, and long hair tied up in hair-pins, a most unconvincing outfit in which to go out and conquer the world.

These women, however, brought to the forefront of social consciousness a realization that women could be active, assertive and individual. We have therefore to be grateful to them for contributing, in no matter how slight a degree, to the emancipation of the sex.

The undue emphasis on women as the central characters of these thrillers was an attempt to go further along the path that had been laid by Mary Pickford. It was, in fact, an attempt to cash in on the Mary Pickford cult. And yet Miss Pickford outlasted them all in public favour simply because she was a much nearer approximation to the public idea of a desirable girl type. The others showed that women could be as capable as men, but they were just a little ahead of their time, and the men could not believe in them as they believed in Mary Pickford.

But if anything can prove conclusively and finally the far-reaching effects that the cinema can have on social trends, it is the films that exposed the vice rackets in the U.S.A. During the Chicago Vice Commission's investigations, the revelations that came through shocked the public imagination. The White Slave traffic was shown to be colossal in extent, both nationally and internationally. Newspapers and magazines were full of stories about the traffic in women. Plays like *The House of Bondage*, *The Lure* and *Damaged Goods* were written and performed and

93

publicized in book form. The best remembered play is *Damaged Goods* by the French writer, Brieux, which is still doing service as a play and as a film for societies formed to educate the public on the subject of venereal disease.

Two enterprising young men who were in the employ of Laemmle's IMP, determined to make a picture on the subject. They could get no support from the boss, so they got three other friends to put up a thousand dollars each. With five thousand dollars between them, they set about making the film in their spare time and without the boss's knowledge at the studio, a proceeding which would be fantastic under present-day studio conditions.

They called their film *Traffic in Souls*. Ten reels of the film were condensed to six, and then it was shown to the governor, who after a little hesitation bought it for 20,000 dollars.

The film opened on Broadway, New York, at a legitimate theatre and played to 15,000 dollars in the first week. Laemmle then contracted with the Shubert theatre circuit for 35,000 dollars as a minimum guarantee of a third of all proceeds at the pay-box. The picture was shown in twenty-eight theatres simultaneously in New York and suburbs and grossed 450,000 dollars.

That meant 150,000 dollars as Laemmle's share, and there was still the rest of the States and the whole of the world to draw from. It was advertised as showing 'traps cunningly laid for young girls by vice trusts . . . based on the Rockefeller White Slave Report and on the investigations of the vice trusts by District Attorney Whitman.'

The public interest in *Traffic in Souls* was something that rival film makers could not afford to neglect, and so they each made their own version.

The best known is *Damaged Goods*, which was made in 1915 and brought the makers about 600,000 dollars in profit. This public agitation on the kindred social and physical diseases of White Slavery and venereal disease had this result; of effecting an almost clean sweep of the vice traffic, as much because the customers fell away as through official action. Fresh air and light upon a dark subject helps to clear disease from the body politic as well as from the physical body.

XI

IN England during the war years it became apparent that the incidence of venereal disease was reaching formidable proportions. It became a military as well as a social problem. So the discussion came right out in the open for the first time in England's history. The question had to be faced, and films of the character of *Damaged Goods* found their social purpose. At the end of the war, the agitation could not possibly stop at that. Public interest stormily centred around the pioneers of birth control like Margaret Sanger in America and Marie Stopes in England.

In spite of the opposition and persecution endured by these pioneers and their friends, the public was avid for information upon a problem that affected the lives of every family. The films that reflected this phase of public interest were *Where are my Children?* a drama which was full of clinical detail, *Hypocrites* and *Motherhood*. A certain New York exhibitor thought he would improve the appeal of *Motherhood* by re-titling it to *The Doctor and Your Wife*.

Public curiosity on birth control having been satisfied, the psychoanalytical phase set in. Young people were beginning to question the precepts of their elders who, it seemed, had created a code of ethics in which the slaughter and maiming of millions of people was accepted as part of the day's work.

The young began developing their own ideas and to assert themselves with a swing of the pendulum that took them miles away and beyond the ideas of behaviour cherished by their parents.

They were quick to take advantage of the changing situation, and their case found advocacy and exposition in such films as *We Moderns* and *Flaming Youth*. To realize what this meant at the time, it should be remembered that the older people were still living in a mental fog persisting from the days when women were said to possess nether limbs instead of legs, when they expected 'happy events' but never babies, and when people did not undress for bed but indulged in a process known as 'disrobing.'

The Freudian theories on psychoanalysis and sex problems were by now sweeping across Europe to England and over the Atlantic to U.S.A. The frank discussions on sex relationships dispersed the sex-and-sin ideas that found their greatest expression in the sinuous, selfish, sinful and sensuous vamp type in which Theda Bara shone.

It seems hardly credible that there were responsible people in positions of social leadership who decried the films because it was thought the vamp craze was a sign that men were becoming increasingly immoral, and that therefore humanity was surely doomed to perdition. It became the fashion for certain intellectual circles to belittle the film in general and vamp films in particular.

It is, however, as unreasoning to assume that people will follow the anti-social behaviour of certain film characters who, it must be remembered, are always presented as anti-social characters, as it is to adopt a superior attitude to the film tastes of the people.

But if, after the war, certain sections of the intelligentsia sought to discredit the film, let it not be thought that the authorities were so blind as to neglect its value as an emotional stimulus during the war of 1914–18. Over fifty war films were issued by private enterprise in Britain with the blessing of official circles between August and December 1914.

Some of the titles give a fair picture of the social consciousness of the time; here they are:

Britain's Bid for Supremacy
Facing Eternity
Looters of Liége
Your Country Needs You
Boys of the Bulldog Breed
By the Kaiser's Orders
Answering the Call
England Expects
Ready, Aye Ready
The War Against the Huns
The Aerial Invasion

Apart from official encouragement, the first reaction of the public at the outbreak of war was one of curiosity, and the demand for films about the war was very great.

The Bioscope, the paper of the trade, in its edition of August 27th, 1914, states that:

Manufacturers and agents are feverishly putting to the fore any and all pictures with the faintest smell of powder or the rumble of guns.

Who can deny that there has been a change in the social consciousness since the days when the 'smell of powder or the rumble of guns' was considered good business? The advent of the talkie film and the widespread use of the radio coming about the same time, has brought about this change.

In these days it is quite impossible to work up animosities between peoples on national grounds. The statesmen and the Hitlers and the Mussolinis may beat the drums and hold back the process of international understanding for a while, but again, reckoned in historical time, it is only for a while.

Once it used to be said that the pen was mightier than the sword. To-day the talkie film and the wireless are mightier than the bombing plane and the big howitzer.

The historical process is already showing, even though things in Europe may look black for the moment, that the new weapons of international understanding will eventually put the weapons of destruction out of commission.

During the war there was a great deal of propaganda of all kinds, but not the least was the silent film. In addition to the films made by private enterprise there were films specially made for the War Office for general exhibition. One such was *Germany in Word and Deed*. This was followed by a recruiting film sponsored by the Admiralty to serve general propaganda and to praise 'the sentinels of the deep.'

It was not long, however, before the people became thoroughly tired not only of war films but of the war itself, as the food cards came in, as the lists of daily food-ship sinkings were published, as each family learnt of a shocking bereavement, as the darkness of death was painted over the street lamps and Zeppelins began dropping their loads upon the people.

In London and the provinces the people needed to go to theatres, music-halls and picture palaces or the tension would have driven them to distraction. American films, with Chaplin topping the list, were achieving immense popularity. The most successful theatre entertainments in London were those which were as remote from the very idea of war as possible.

Towards the end of 1917 the blockade of Germany was beginning to tell upon the armies of the Central Powers and upon the peoples. Adulterated bread was being distributed to spin out the wheat supplies, food of every kind was becoming short and the people were getting hungry and restive. But Krupps had a plentiful supply of steel and other metals, and so it was decided that it was good policy to make cinema projectors with the metal in hand.

In a short time, there were no fewer than five hundred portable cinema units working for the German army on the western front and over three hundred units on the eastern front, all showing films of various kinds intended to keep up the morale of the German armies. But the effort was not successful. As we have seen in another connection, you can make people believe ballyhoo up to a point and only for a while. You can make them believe that clay bread and *ersatz* food is good for them, you can make them believe even that black is white, that guns are preferable to butter and a whole number of other things. But there comes a breaking point. Herr Hitler and Signor Mussolini would do well to take note.

XII

THE film was used as a weapon during the war, not only upon the populations of the war countries and upon the soldiers, but as a means of swaying public opinion in neutral countries.

The Jackboot military mind which had charge of the war on the German side, proved itself particularly inefficient and blundering when it came to ideological warfare, a war of wits which was as much out of the range of Junker understanding as it had been part of the very marrow of English governmental practice for generations. One of the first principles of psychology, which is well understood in Whitehall, is that suggestion may be more effective than compulsion. Government circulars to local bodies wherever possible indicate or suggest, they hardly ever order or command.

By way of contrast with the consummate skill in governing and in propaganda displayed in this country, it may be well to instance the lumbering style of the German military caste, especially as it affected their propaganda in neutral countries. It was not before August 1915, one year after the war's outbreak, that a company was formed in America to import films into that country from Germany and Austria, giving the Central Powers' version of the war; but they were very crudely made, and their circulation was negligible. When America went into the war on the side of the Allies, the principals of the firm, which was called The American Correspondent

Film Company, were sentenced to prison for various offences against the State.

The French and British versions were in the field very much earlier in America. They gave their story in the manner of the chatty topical, which was in advance of the existing news-reel, and they were especially prepared for neutral American consumption and less raw than those used at home, where rawness was more effective.

It was in Switzerland, however, that the spies and agents of both sides could see each other's screen efforts at winning the war. A particularly vivid example of an effective film for German home consumption was *The Cruise of the Moewe*, the true story of a U-boat.

But would it be believed that a film intended to hearten the flagging spirits of the German people by showing them how the ruthless sinking of merchant ships was supposed to be winning them the war, was the film that was put out as propaganda in a neutral country! Yet this true record of how food ships were being *spurlos versunken*—sunk without trace—was exhibited as the Junker effort to endear themselves to the Swiss!

The effect, of course, was immediate and painfully unexpected to the monocled Brass Hats of Berlin. The film had to be hastily re-packed and returned to Berlin—the English were seldom guilty of such stupidity.

XIII

IN France, as in England and in Germany, films were made during the earlier part of the war that reflected the state of war in that country. Pictures with such titles as, *The Avenging Poilu*, *The Angelus of Victory*, *Christmas in War-time*, *The Heart of a Frenchwoman*, all indicate the same trends that prevailed in England during the first six months of the war.

In 1917, with Russia in the throes of revolution, America came in on the side of the Allies. Immediately, as in England and France and in Germany at the beginning of 1914, films came forth very like the typical *Ready, Aye Ready* of England. These were: *America's Answer*, *Pershing's Crusaders* (Pershing was America's General-issimo), *Under Four Flags* and *The Official War Review*. Then there were the war films sponsored by the Army and Navy and a film which was made specially for the U.S. Treasury, and which helped in the sale of Victory Loan Bonds, *The Price of Peace*.

It was whilst MacAdoo, the Treasury Secretary, was soliciting the American film industry's co-operation, that he put the suggestion to America's chief stars that they should have their own distributing organization. The suggestion was followed by the formation of United Artists, with Mary Pickford, Charles Chaplin, Douglas Fairbanks, and D. W. Griffith, as the chief stockholders.

The time was ripe in any case for the big stars to unite their forces to protect their interests against some of the leaders in the film business, who seemed to be getting too much of the lion's share of the proceeds. There have been constant fluctuations and manœuvring for position, and perpetual struggles in the film industry, but in this respect it only resembles every large industrial group, whether it is oil, steel, cotton or chemicals.

The industrialists of the film have had to display that toughness in their business dealings which is necessary for survival in any industrial enterprise conducted on a world scale. But there is this at least to be said for the film magnate, the nature of the film industry itself seems to develop a puckish, intensely alive quality in his psychology which is very much absent from many of the leaders of other industries. To illustrate this, we may quote again from Terry Ramsaye:

One morning, Selznick awoke, to discover that the news headlines screamed of revolution in Russia and the overthrow of the Tsar. Selznick wrapped a brocaded silken dressing-gown about him, rang for Ishi and demanded tea from the samovar. A secretary came panting, a pencil poised, to take dictation. It was a cablegram, sent paid, which, translated from the Russian, read about thus:

NICHOLAS ROMANOFF,

PETROGRAD, RUSSIA.

WHEN I WAS POOR BOY IN KIEV SOME OF YOUR POLICE-MEN WERE NOT KIND TO ME AND MY PEOPLE STOP NOW HEAR WITH REGRET YOU ARE OUT OF A JOB OVER THERE STOP FEEL NO ILL-WILL WHAT YOUR POLICEMEN DID SO IF YOU WILL COME NEW YORK CAN GIVE YOU FINE POSITION ACTING IN PICTURES STOP SALARY NO OBJECT STOP REPLY MY EXPENSE STOP REGARDS YOU AND FAMILY.

SELZNICK,

NEW YORK.

Now say what you will about the big-wigs of Hollywood, call them all the names you can think of, you have still to hand it to them for being able to hold their positions by this perpetual youthful ebullience which is so characteristic. There is something intensely human, kindly and generous about that cable, all the more so because it is politically so childlike in its naïveté. But there is also a vivid imagination sweeping over wide horizons. Let a man possess the gift of imagination and a sense of humour and you can forgive him almost anything.

Well, the war ended for us in November 1918, but its after-effects persisted in Central and Eastern Europe. If there be any who imagine that it is the rational side of men that determines their actions, that men learn from the past to plan a better world for the future, let them read the following passage from Huntly Carter's book, *The New Spirit in the Cinema*, published in 1930, in which he describes his journey through Eastern Europe immediately after the war:

> *I passed through civilization shattered and stinking. I recall those everlasting breaks in the journey, changes, connections, the truly horrible carriages not fit for skunks to travel in, the fragments of stations where platforms were completely covered with excrement flowing from stopped up or smashed-up lavatories and overspreading the line for long distances, the cattle trucks filled with cholera and typhus-stricken refugees who died by the score each day, and whose bodies were thrown out at every halt, the mad baggage examinations at frequent intervals at wayside halts and in the pouring rain. I remember the fanatical examiners who threatened to shoot me the moment they found anything of a Russian character among my belongings, and the sickening hours of waiting whilst the whole train load of human beings was being vaccinated. . . . Sick of being cramped up in odd*

corners of compartments filled with vomiting and dying folk, I told the stationmaster that I would walk and get some fresh air. He warned me of the danger. There were two frontiers to be crossed guarded by savages. The stationmaster was right. I was lucky enough to miss the first consignment of savages, but I ran full tilt into the second lot.

The boundary ran across the middle of a little street of cottages, thus cutting the street in half. . . . The woman who lived in the east side and brought home the laundry to the west side was compelled to have her passport visaed every time she made the crossing.

In his attempt to cross the absurdly arranged frontier he is arrested and incarcerated in a small guardroom. After two days of this, he mentions the word *kino* to his two armed guards, and all three march off to the village cinema, which he describes thus:

We passed from semi-darkness without to semi-darkness within, from sickly yellow lights to dim blood-red ones. At one end was a worn-out silver screen, at the other a projector balanced upon a pile of bricks. Between were old benches and chairs tied together for security upon which we herded. A murmur rose from the audience, eyes brightened, depression fled. The picture came, I forget its title. It was one of a series of the marvellous exploits of a man whose valour, courage, daring and chivalry roused the audience to an intense pitch of excitement. All the time I seemed to be surrounded by armed men whose bayonets pressed against me; might go through me should the picture cause the soldiers to start with emotion. But nothing happened except the effect upon the audience. . . . And my rough guards. As we splashed homewards, I noticed that they went not behind me but before me. Something had humanized them, had made them no longer guards but guides.

106

The bestiality, the utter senselessness, the complete chaos that was Europe produced its effect through every form of expression, through the novel, the painting, the theatre and particularly the film, for it must be remembered that the social consciousness does not *correspond* with social reality. It *reflects* the social reality.

Recall the mood of Central Europe at the end of the war. Gaunt and nerve-shattered people, millions of them, were thinking:

> . . . *our professors tell us that clay bread is good for us, but our children have died from eating it. Why has the flower of our youth been destroyed? Why have we had to kill and maim, and to be killed and maimed in turn? Why have our leaders failed us? What have we done to deserve such suffering and torture?*

In this mood, workers took up arms and established their short-lived administrations in Hamburg, Saxony and Bavaria, Austria and Hungary. But these attempts to establish a new social order that would banish wars were overthrown, stifled and suppressed.

So the questions were being repeated with ever greater frustration. Why? Why? Why?

And to a distracted Europe came the answer in all the forms of an expressionism which was at the same time a revolt, an escape from the mad outside world, from objective reality to introspection, to speculation, to an enfeebled rationalization of that which it was impossible for so many to face. In painting, in literature, in the theatre, in the film, the spirit was everywhere the same, a spirit of morbidity, of terror of the unknown and the apparently inexplicable. It gave impetus to introspective speculations on the 'soul' and the ego when Freud and Jung were only beginning to be understood.

Expressionism, Futurism, Cubism, Dadaism were sweeping through the upper and middle layers of society everywhere. One of Europe's favourite playwrights was Pirandello, whose *Six Characters in Search of an Author*, for instance, come upon the stage in turn and argue their respective 'inner being,' before they are born in the mind of an author!

In England, the whimsical J. M. Barrie, who had written *Peter Pan* before the war for the children, wrote such well-attended plays as *Mary Rose* and *Dear Brutus*. Strange fairies and enchanted islands and magic trees. Escape from reality.

And the youth of Europe, those who had barely escaped from the shambles, danced and jazzed with relief, to the sound of the saxophone in palais de danses which bobbed up like mushrooms in city, town and village from the Vistula to the Tweed. But whilst youth jigged to the Charleston and pirouetted to the tango, the thick, all-pervading, inescapable atmosphere of Central Europe was one of unutterable gloom, the very bottomless pit of despair. Hunger, misery, hopelessness. Death through epidemic. Every family bereaved. Canons of civilized behaviour shattered to pieces. The very earth seemed to have slipped its moorings.

It is against this background that *The Cabinet of Dr. Caligari* appeared in the year 1919. Not only is this one of the distinct milestones in film technique: it will remain as one of the most revealing documents by which future generations will judge the Europe of 1919–20.

All the major films of that period display the same unmitigated gloom, the same signs of a civilization whose rational basis has disappeared. But *The Cabinet of Dr. Caligari*, pursuing the ancient German cult of the *macabre*, is also the supreme expression of headlong flight from a world become too horrible to contemplate; flight to an escape world of introversion, of speculation, amid the apparently inscrutable workings of the human mind; flight to the prostrate worship of the ego, to subjectivism.

The film opens in a world of twisted streets and fantastic crooked houses where beings live their twisted lives apparently unconscious of the menaces that surround them.

Dr. Caligari is a showman at a fair-ground. After enticing a sufficient audience into his booth, he opens the doors of an upright cabinet to reveal the somnambulist, Cesare, dressed in long, black tights, immobile and lifeless as a statue. Caligari proceeds to demonstrate his powers. He commands Cesare to awake and walk before the audience. He then ingratiatingly tells the audience that Cesare knows the past and foretells the future, and will foretell the future of anyone present. A young man steps forward and asks his future, and Cesare slowly turns his stare at him and says: 'You will die before midnight.' The young man recoils with horror at this inexplicable sentence of death when he is on the threshold of life and innocent of any crime.

Observe here the resemblance between this death motif and the one that runs through another of Pirandello's plays, *The Man with the Flower in his Mouth*. The flower is epithelioma, a sudden and inexplicable cancerous growth in an otherwise healthy body. A man innocent of any crime against his fellow men is thus under sentence of death. There follow endless mind-wracking soliloquies and questionings in an attempt to explain this horrible fate.

There can be only one explanation of such pre-occupation with the thought of unmerited, pitiless death. It was the wanton destruction of young lives during four years which blazed the insistent question mark across the European sky: WHY?

The story of Dr. Caligari runs its course.

The young man is found murdered, nobody knows by whom. A casual passer-by is at first arrested on suspicion and is hauled to the police-station where, in a room full of remarkable symbolism, sits the universal bureaucrat himself, upon an extraordinarily high stool to indicate his very high position, and writing with a quill pen in a huge tome like the Domesday Book.

The suspect is not the guilty one.

It is Cesare, the somnabulist, who, with the expressionless hollow-eyed mask of death, emerges from Caligari's cabinet to wreak his unreasoning, unmotivated destruction.

Cesare walks his stiff measured tread, through streets of unearthly light and distorted shape, yet at the same time remains asleep in the cabinet. The inhabitants spot Cesare and give chase, but Cesare eludes them. They rush back to Caligari's booth and insist upon seeing the cabinet opened. Lo, Cesare, deathlike and immobile, is there all the time.

Later Caligari is seen by a friend of the murdered man to pass through the gates of a mansion. This friend follows him into an inner office, where to his amazement the Caligari of the fair-ground, with the sly expression and fantastic clothing, dissolves into an apparently normal-looking individual who stands at an ordinary office desk, a doctor, and none other than Dr. Caligari, the head and principal of the establishment, which is a hospital for the mentally deranged. The young man creates a disturbance and accuses Caligari of being a murderer, whereupon attendants come into the room, put the young man into a strait-jacket and throw him into a padded cell.

Out in the courtyard sits an empress with pallid face and flowing hair, surrounded by her council of ministers, all seriously engaged in discussing affairs of state. Another woman sitting with staring eyes and playing on an imaginary piano is the greatest musician on earth. The whole place is full of flesh-creeping human characters, deranged, mutilated beings. It turns out in the end that Caligari himself is a lunatic who has been put under restraint, and that the whole story has been told through the imagination of a lunatic.

Werner Krauss as Dr. Caligari, and Conrad Veidt as Cesare

THE CABINET OF DR. CALIGARI, directed by Robert Wiene

Is there a more perfect allegory of Europe 1919? Could symbolism reflect more closely the bitter outside reality? In a hundred or a thousand years from now, which is likely to be regarded as the truer reflection of the social reality which was Mittel-Europa in 1919, *The Cabinet of Dr. Caligari* or, say, the numerous volumes of statesmen's memoirs?

The most interesting thing about *Dr. Caligari* and the German films that followed, right up to about 1925, is that they hardly show any evidence of having been consciously or deliberately planned as symbolizations of Europe's tragedy. This is easily intelligible when one bears in mind that the *social consciousness does not correspond to the social reality, it only reflects it.*

This is abundantly evident during the period under review in Germany between 1919 and 1925. A flood of questioning, re-valuation and re-statement was let loose in every field, in science, literature, the stage, painting, sculpture, architecture, the cinema and in many other directions.

Visitors to Germany in 1925 were amazed, for instance, to see the freedom of the Press extended even to groups who had elevated perversion to a cult. Their publications were issued regularly, complete with photographs, and openly displayed at every respectable book-stall. Many of the Nazi Party leaders, future members of the Government, such as Captain Roehm, were followers of this cult.

As for *Nackt-kultur*, this was a well-established form of sun worship in Germany at least eight years before the nudists sought to found their first timid colonies in England. All sorts of cults and beliefs and strange practices arose, including that of a return to the worship of the elements, personified by gods with Teutonic names, such as Wotan and Thor.

This crowd of devotees was led by General Ludendorff, Hindenburg's right-hand man during the war, which shows you the kind of mental case in whose charge the lives of millions were entrusted.

Such was the Germany that succeeded the war, the hunger blockade, the lowering of national pride through the Allied occupation of German territory and the monetary inflation that wiped out middle-class possessions. The whole of this immense nation-wide mental ferment is clearly mirrored in the films of the period commencing with *The Cabinet of Dr. Caligari*.

The titles alone are extraordinarily revealing: *The Joyless Street, Dr. Mabuse, The Spy, Secrets of the Soul, Warning Shadows, Pandora's Box, Crisis, Waxworks, The Golem, The Student of Prague, Diary of a Lost Girl, The Woman in the Moon, The Living Corpse.*

It is curious to note that although at this time the intelligentsia of England were beginning to recognize the film as a medium for ideas, when these films from Germany and those from Russia and France were trickling into this country, the cinema was still looked upon with disdain.

And yet, the silent film was the most effective vehicle for the exchange of ideas and *feeling* between nation and nation that had ever appeared, if only it had been better understood.

You may take a play, say by Molière, and translate it into another language. No matter how conscientious and painstaking the translation, it is bound to lose some of its spirit and meaning in the process, and when it is acted upon a foreign stage it will be impossible to avoid details of décor and characterization that would have seemed preposterous to the playwright. Peculiar national characteristics, mannerisms and habits of thought make certain incongruities almost inevitable.

The same applies to the translation of a novel. Nor can you inscribe in a musical score just that *feel*, that hardly definable rhythm, with which the Budapest orchestras render their native compositions. It would be as difficult for a foreign orchestra to play in that precise manner as it would be for an educated Englishman to speak French with the native gestures and facial expressions, unless he had lived in France for a very long time.

But a film, provided it is run at the standard rate of sixteen frames (separate pictures) to the second, will make upon any audience in any country just that visual impression that it was the intention of the film director to convey.

In a film like *The Cabinet of Dr. Caligari* you will see not only the extraordinarily fantastic backgrounds just as the designers painted them, not only the lighting and the fine camera work of the craftsmen as it was photographed twenty years ago, not only the highly imaginative make-up and costume and remarkable acting of Conrad Veidt as Cesare and Werner Krauss as Caligari, but the very tragedy of a continent, fixed upon a roll of celluloid and yet visible in motion for future generations to ponder over.

XIV

WE have seen how the social reality of a given historical moment is reflected in a particular country. You may therefore ask how is it that the Russian films of the same period, or of just a little later, say between 1923 and 1929, are so different from those that came from Germany.

You will be correct in saying that outwardly, in physical conditions, the two countries had been passing through like experiences. Both countries had been led by autocrats when the war started. Each country had known defeat, hunger, devastation, civil war, chaos, bereavement in every family. Russia, moreover, had had to contend with fourteen armies whose efforts to overthrow the Bolshevik Government had only been defeated after a series of appallingly destructive wars.

Russia's agony lasted from 1914 to 1917 and from 1917 to 1923 before warfare ceased. Nearly nine years of torture, five years longer than Germany had undergone, with what little industrial economy there had been almost completely destroyed; and yet the social consciousness that is reflected in the major films following this period is precisely the opposite in spirit and in content of that which prevailed in Germany.

In direct contrast to the morbidity, despair, introspection and crippling subjectivism of the Germany of *Dr. Caligari*, *The Joyless Street* and *The Secrets of the Soul*, there came from Russia films the very titles of which were a challenge to the world as well as a new form of cultural expression:

such films as *Battleship Potemkin, Ten Days that Shook the World, The Strike, The End of St. Petersburg* (a title that clearly suggests the beginning of Leningrad), *The Old and the New (The General Line)* and *Storm over Asia.*

Here were no introspective speculations, no fear complexes, or preoccupation with metaphysical souls. Here there was no gloom and despair and groping in the darkness, but hope and buoyancy, a determination to travel from weakness to strength, to face the real world fearlessly, with all its dangers and difficulties, and to proceed resolutely and scientifically to the building of a new world. Let the dead past bury its dead!

The Germans in their frustration, betrayed by their leaders, tried to explain the world. The Russians determined to change the world. That is why, in contrast to the German, you get in the best Russian silent film that clear determinism, objectivity and absence of self-pity.

In the main, it may be safe to suggest that the Germans made the greatest contributions in the realm of lighting, architecture, and extremely fine camera work. The French brought to the cinema the long-standing tradition of the painter's studio, a fine appreciation of pictorial composition and a native sense of social satire. But the Russian cinema had the most profound influence of them all.

It may be said that, where the French were concerned with aesthetics and the Germans with aesthetics plus metaphysics, the Russians were devoted to social dynamics.

That the Russian cinema was instrumental in influencing the social consciousness of America, for instance, can be noted in a single classic example. Everyone remembers how the Chinese were depicted in American films until comparatively recently. They were usually assigned the most villainous roles, treacherous, evil-looking characters, fit for nothing but the hangman's noose. Such characters have vanished from the American film as if they had never been. Two Russian films have helped to create a complete *volte face* in the American studio. Chinese characters are now more accurately depicted as dignified humans, cultured, and belonging to a civilization of great antiquity. The two films which have helped to effect this change are *Storm Over Asia*, directed by Pudovkin, and *The Blue Express*, directed by Kosintsev and Trauberg.

In *Storm Over Asia* we are shown for the first time in film history a nation of nomad peasants and fur-trappers, people of a Mongol type, living in a region where the none too peaceful penetration of the white man is making itself felt. These peasants are simple, kindly folk, exceedingly like the ordinary people of any other race or colour in feeling and temperament.

In *The Blue Express* the suffering of the Chinese people is shown with extraordinary sympathy and feeling. The cumulative effect of these films over a number of years culminated in the great American classic *The Good Earth*, produced by the late Irving Thalberg.

The Russian influence upon this film is clear and unmistakable; not only in the sympathetic way in which the characters are treated and the great care taken in conveying the Chinese national characteristics and manners of speech, but in detail and photography you can observe innumerable shots that might have been taken bodily, some out of Victor Turin's *Turksib*, from Eisenstein's *General Line*, from Dovshenko's *Earth*, as well as from Pudovkin's *Storm Over Asia*.

The influence of *The Good Earth*, coming at this moment, in creating sympathy for the Chinese people in their present extremity, may be well imagined.

There is, however, a debit as well as a credit side to the influence of the Russian silent film. Where the Americans took what was best from the Russian cinema, the Germans during the Weimar Republic adopted those features which were over-intellectualized and ill-considered. Pudovkin's early work contained much that was socially progressive, but his tendency to follow the literary method by dwelling too often and too long upon the pernicious aspects of the old regime, as in his film translation of Gorky's *Mother*, was taken up and extended by Pabst, Dudow and others in Germany. Pudovkin was not the only offender. In Dovshenko's *Earth* a member of the village commune is murdered by a kulak. In an American film the strongly prevailing sense of social preservation would demand that the murderer be brought to justice. If an anti-social act is shown on the dynamic screen *in action*, it must be balanced in the minds of the audience by social retribution *in action*. In *Earth*, however, you are not shown the community on the hunt to prevent the killer from committing further murders. No, you are shown the father of the murdered man, weeping at the funeral which ends the picture in an oration, *in words*, on sub-titling, about the glories of the future.

But the point that Dovshenko has forgotten is that in the realm of objective reality, the murderer has got away with it.

Mental abstractions and aspirations cannot be photographed, the murder of a man *does* photograph not only on the film but upon the minds of the audience. The anti-social liberalism of Dovshenko's ending could only occur to an intellectual out of touch with basic social realities. The strong instincts that men possess for the preservation of society are undermined when such an example as this ending is set before them as a picture of the real world.

These derogatory features of the Russian silent film not only influenced the pre-Nazi film directors seeking to find a social solution for the plight of Germany, but they remained endemic in the Soviet film itself. These faults became proportionately magnified with the coming of sound.

XV

WE have said, in another connection, that evolution does not operate like a guillotine. All kinds of old and new elements may co-exist at one and the same time, and react upon one another. This occurs in the world of material things. It occurs in all forms of life, organic and inorganic. And it occurs in the realm of social and cultural life and thought.

In comparing the film titles of the predominant trend of the Russian cinema with the film titles of the post-war German cinema, we saw that the German film was turned inward towards an unhealthy subjectivism, while the Russian film was mainly turned outward towards a clear examination of the objective world. The Germans sought an individual, a personal solution to the world problem, whereas the Russians looked upon the world as a place where great social and economic forces were in constant movement and where the individual is of importance primarily as a social unit, taking his place in the social scheme of things.

Whilst this new way of looking at life was gaining ascendancy in the Russian cinema, the old way of thought still persisted in Russia for many years; the old habits of the old civilization, the habit of introverted obsessions and subjectivism, of trying to explain the objective world from the personal emotional states of isolated individuals, the same habit of introspection which produced Pirandello in Italy, the precise cult which expressed itself in England through an amazing number of individualist war descriptions and autobiographies, this cult was still to be met with in Russia.

Mainly, it took the form of Trotskyism, but it was also to be met with in the cultural sphere, in the poet Essenin for instance, who married Isadora Duncan, and whose crazy, egotistical, anarchical outlook led him to all kinds of anti-social behaviour and finally to suicide. In the film world, the subjective tendency survived in the work of Otzep, Touriansky and Protozanov, whose films were hardly known outside Russia, and who eventually left the U.S.S.R. to settle in Germany and in France, where their work achieved a little more recognition.

The leader of the school of objective realism in the Russian silent cinema was undoubtedly S. M. Eisenstein, whose *Battleship Potemkin*, in 1925, came upon the world like a thunderbolt. It would be well to examine the reasons for the emergence of this school, which has had so great an effect upon the development of the cinema in other countries.

The Russians started with two advantages. Firstly, since they were last in the field in mechanical production, they were able to examine this new form of expression with minds free from the obsessions current in Europe, and they were greatly assisted by Griffith's excellent ideas from America. The whole theory of cinema was examined afresh in the light of the latest scientific discoveries in technique and human psychology, and without the handicaps with which long years of literary and stage tradition had encumbered ideas on cinema in other countries.

Secondly, the Russians were the first in Europe to realize consciously that with the cinema had appeared the emotional expression of an age in which production was carried on co-operatively by masses of people. They realized that just as the machine and co-operative methods had to displace the individual craftsman for the making of things, so that more people could have more of those things, so the machine and co-operative method must supersede the individual writer or craftsman, who simply remains content to work in comparative isolation and to mirror the life of a narrow set.

They realized that corresponding to this shift from the individual to the mass, the film had no longer any use for the petty themes with which so many had pre-occupied themselves for many years.

The cinema, by its nature, is compelled to employ hundreds of craftsmen working in co-operation, to produce one film which will express the emotions of millions of people to whom a book or a picture may be beyond immediate reach through lack of means, or through lack of leisure and opportunity.

In Russia, events had newly taken place which were of the very stuff of epic drama, events that brought about one of the most fundamental changes in human history, and which still presaged great struggles in the near future, before the change could be consummated.

The events which accompanied this change were not something the Russians had merely heard or read about, they had seared themselves into the very brain and marrow of every man, woman and child in the whole of that vast continent. History had made itself felt in hunger, in wounds, in the death of loved ones and in the destruction of their homes by white and foreign invaders.

It is not to be wondered at that the films which resulted showed such white-heat intensity of feeling and passionate indignation. It is no marvel that they produced *Battleship Potemkin*, *The End of St. Petersburg*, and *Storm Over Asia*. To produce such films there must be correct cinema theory, but above all, there must be intense sympathy and complete kinship with the people, the vast masses. There must be the capacity to rid oneself of the obsession with the narrow theme about the individual and about the petty family squabble. And you can never make films such as these by order from above, from authority. That is inconceivable and quite impossible.

It is known, for instance, that Dr. Goebbels, of the 'Ministerium for Propaganda and Public Enlightenment,' called a conference of German Nazi film chiefs and exhorted them to make a film that would elevate the Nazi idea: 'give me a National-Socialist *Potemkin*.'

He might as well have asked for the moon! Instead of *Potemkin*, the Nazi German film industry achieved *Der Ammenkoenig*, which has been shown in England. The title means King of the Wet-nurses, although it was circulated here as *King of the Nurses*, to make it sound more respectable.

The central character in this film is a great hulk of a leering blacksmith, who goes around impregnating a village full of girls. It is a kind of imaginary village, in which the main business is the making of babies, just as certain villages in the Alps are specifically noted, some for their woodcraft, others for their lace. The village is shown as full of laughing, joyous, unmarried mothers, who accept their task as incubators in the spirit of Herr Hitler's Strength Through Joy movement.

The setting is eighteenth century, and therefore the message of the film glides down the gullet of many naïve worshippers at the unworthy shrine of 'art for art's sake' who miss the point and purport of the story. The most horrible thing about this film is not its frank advocacy of barnyard promiscuity, but that its purpose is to advocate the having of babies, by any means, any time, anywhere. The emphasis is on the babies, lots of babies, children, plenty of them—you get the idea?

Such a staggering glimpse into the Nazi mind as *Der Ammenkoenig* passed without the faintest realization of its real significance when it was first shown in England. When one remembers that not one foot of film is permitted to be shot in a German studio without the stamp and certificate of Dr. Goebbels' department, is it not amazing that not a single critic in this country saw the slightest connection between the film and official Nazism? Nowhere did a criticism appear which adequately interpreted *The King of the Wet-Nurses*.

No one film in history has had a more potent influence upon motion pictures than has *The Battleship Potemkin*. As a production, it takes its place by the side of some of the greatest works that the human mind has been able to conceive, by the side of the works of Euripides, Shakespeare, Beethoven, Rembrandt, all of them among the greatest gifts that social man has produced to advance the social process and the welfare of mankind.

Battleship Potemkin may be compared with such works precisely because it plumbs the deepest founts of man's social being. Boys at Eton College, with their basic social instincts still unimpaired, have raised the rafters with their cheers as they watched the sailors upon the battleship *Potemkin* throw off the yoke of their brutal officers and run the flag of freedom up to the mast. There is a sequence in the film known all over the world as the 'scene on the Odessa steps.' The sailors who have succeeded in taking charge of the battleship have been fraternizing with the townspeople in the port of Odessa. Thousands of people are standing on the wide stone steps leading for a considerable distance to the quayside, men, women and children, old and young, workers, professional and middle-class people waving handkerchiefs to the sailors of freedom in the distance, watching with delighted faces, the scores of boats leaving the quayside with provisions for the battleship.

Suddenly the soldiers of the Tsar appear from a street at the top of the steps. Drawn up in ranks, they occupy the full width of the steps. No order is given to the people to disperse, and no chance of escape is offered. The soldiers commence their inexorable march down, down the steps as they calmly and deliberately fire salvo after salvo into the people who drop writhing in agony all around. Still the soldiery march, tramp, tramp, tramp, down the steps firing every few paces as they go.

A mother in charge of a perambulator, frantic with anxiety to save her child, receives a bullet and falls. The perambulator bumps down the steps in rhythm with the unthinking, murderous jackboots of the Tsar's soldiers, who pass on, leaving behind them agony and death. The picture reaches the greatest heights of emotional intensity ever touched by a film in the silent medium.

Around the years 1925–27, quite a number of Soviet films began to trickle into Germany and the rest of Europe. In England, in those days, they were only given at isolated showings to Film Societies. *Battleship Potemkin* acted like a stick of dynamite in every film studio in the world, and brought profound changes in film technique. The ideas that Griffith had embodied in his films *The Birth of a Nation* and *Intolerance* had been reduced to a scientific principle with the advent of *The Battleship Potemkin*.

As an instance of the widespread effect the film has had all over the world, it need only be mentioned that John Grierson, the founder of the documentary school in England, has fully and generously acknowledged his indebtedness to the inspiration of *Potemkin* for much of his film technique, especially in his first silent film, *Drifters*.

In Berlin, the picture received its première at a large West End cinema and ran continuously for months to packed houses. It was in Berlin, too, that a special musical score was written for it which enhanced the emotional effect of the film.

Hitherto, most musical accompaniments to the pictures were compilations from the classics, chosen to fit the mood of each sequence as it appeared on the screen. The lessons of the emotional appeal of a sympathetic combination of sound and image had repercussions in many early experiments, and the fruits of these may now be seen and heard in film after film from the U.S. studios.

Another Soviet Director whose name is often coupled with that of Eisenstein, is V. I. Pudovkin. His first big film to come westwards and eventually reach England, was *The End of St. Petersburg*. This was the first major Soviet film to receive the certificate from the British Board of Film Censors, which enabled it to be distributed commercially. It was handled by the old Atlas Film Company and was shown very widely up and down the country, until the talkies came in.

Nothing from any other country in the post-war years has had the effect upon world culture that these films of Eisenstein and Pudovkin have had.

While these films were being made, the old school still survived. As in everything, traces of the old have a habit of surviving side by side with a more vigorous new. Touriansky left Russia for Germany to make *Volga-Volga*, a story which centred round, as was to be expected, the *private* life of Stenka Razin, the Russian Robin Hood of the eighteenth century; and Feodor Otzep left for Germany, to make *The Brothers Karamazov*, with Anna Sten and Fritz Koertner, a story also dealing with love troubles in the Russia immediately before the war. The vast social upheaval of the Revolution had left these directors unmoved and untouched.

A very interesting point emerges from an examination and a comparison of the two groups of films represented by the works of Eisenstein and Pudovkin. Here is the list:

Directed by Eisenstein:	Directed by Pudovkin:
Battleship Potemkin	*End of St. Petersburg*
Old and the New	*Mother*
(*The General Line*)	*Storm Over Asia*
October (Shorter version,	(*Heir to Jenghiz Khan*)
Ten Days that Shook the	*The Deserter*
World)	

We have said that Otzep and Touriansky represent the old subjectivist school in the Russian cinema, which, for a time, became submerged and almost completely disappeared because of the triumph of objective realism.

Eisenstein's work represents that spear-point in the field of realism which discredited the old ideas and old methods, and scattered the forces of subjectivism from the Russian scene. Eisenstein's silent productions are largely free from any trace of introspection. The same, however, cannot altogether be said of the work of Pudovkin. Pudovkin once acted in a post-war German film, *The Living Corpse*, from the story by Leo Tolstoy, in which he played the wronged husband. The nature of the role would suggest a tendency towards subjectivism. But later, a study of Pavlov's reflexology and psychology drew Pudovkin into making a documentary film of the subject called *The Mechanics of the Brain*. This film is still widely circulated in the U.S.A., and a copy of it is doing service for the University of London.

The making of this film would obviously incline Pudovkin in the direction of the clearest objective study of reality.

When, therefore, we come to his major films, we observe a very curious intermingling of these two tendencies in his own person, in the way his personality is expressed in his films.

Take the first, *The End of St. Petersburg*.

Although this picture gives an objective portrayal of

Russia before the war and during the Revolution, of the reaction during the Kerensky period, and finally of the storming of the Winter Palace in St. Petersburg, and the triumph of the Bolsheviks, it nevertheless revolves around one central figure, a peasant whose career is traced throughout the period of social turmoil. The picture is, in fact, the story of the Revolution with this peasant in bold relief, although it must be stated that it is far more concerned with social movements than with the inner workings of the peasant's mind. At the time this film was made the German film directors were giving themselves up to the introspections of their film characters, with the result we know.

By contrast with *The End of St. Petersburg*, we see in Eisenstein's *Ten Days that Shook the World*, or *October*, as it was called in the longer version, an entirely different treatment of the same event—the Revolution.

From beginning to end, no single individual stands out from the rest. There is a commissar who takes a vigorous part towards the end, but the whole impression is of people working together as a single social unit, and not as individuals with a personal axe to grind. Lenin appears as an individual playing his appropriate part, but only as one amongst the many, the millions. There is never the slightest suspicion of hero-worship.

The films that followed Pudovkin's *End of St. Petersburg*, in every instance, portray a central character around whom the background of the picture is built. The titles alone show the pre-occupation with the fortunes of individuals. *Mother*, based on the story by Maxim Gorky, deals with two characters, a mother and son. In this picture, Pudovkin himself takes a small part as a Tsarist officer who leads a search party into the home of the revolutionary, and who deceives the mother by promising a pardon for her son if she will reveal where some illegal literature is concealed.

The original Russian title to *Storm Over Asia* was *The Heir to Jenghiz Khan*, again the individual. Here, again, the Mongolian trapper, Baer, is the central character. The picture, however, presents the Mongol people with a remarkable reality and sympathy. This aspect has had an effect upon the U.S. cinema, especially in films like *The Good Earth*. Still, there is that slight trace of subjectivism in Baer, who is made to occupy the centre of the screen in almost every other shot.

The title of Pudovkin's fourth major film, *Deserter*, speaks for itself. Not only is the deserter the central character, but one might say he is nearly the whole film. Here there is almost a complete decline into subjectivism, into that close pre-occupation with the fluctuations of the mind of a divided personality, the Deserter who suffers pangs of conscience, the same kind of pre-occupation that affected the German directors years before in the period of *Dr. Caligari* and *Secrets of the Soul*. In this film you get enormous close-ups that stay put on the screen for what seems minutes on end, as if in an attempt to photograph what was going on in the character's brain-box.

The picture suggests that there must be something lacking in Pudovkin's social philosophy which prevents him from taking a firm grasp of objective reality.

Let us contrast with Pudovkin's films those made by Eisenstein. If there was a hero in *Battleship Potemkin*, it was the people of the Russia of 1905, represented symbolically by the sailors upon the battleship itself. One of the leaders of the revolt, who is but one of many, calls out: 'Brothers, whom are you shooting?' and with this cry creates a ripple of wavering along the line of pointed rifles. As the ripple develops, it bursts into revolt. The rifles that pointed a second ago at their own comrades are turned in the direction of the officers who gave the order to shoot. The leader who gave out the cry of revolt is killed in the fighting that ensues. The sailors take control of the battleship, and then take the leader's body to the quayside of Odessa, where the people of Odessa pay homage as he lies in state on the quay. But even in this sequence, there is not the slightest impression that it is an individual to whom homage is being given. He simply represents the deathlessness of all who die for freedom.

Again, in the *Old and the New*, or *The General Line*, as it was called in England, the objective title indicates the content. It might be contended that Martha, the peasant woman, who is the leader in the formation of a village collective farm, is the heroine. That is not so, for Eisenstein has simply used the individual character as a means of bringing the lesson of collectivization home to the thousands of peasants who in those days were strong, hard-bitten anti-collectivists, petty individualists, distrustful of progress.

Martha, the peasant woman in the *Old and the New*, cannot be regarded as a subjective character in comparison with any of Pudovkin's characters, for in Pudovkin's pictures you find that it is always events that shape the character, the central figure, who is always the victim of circumstances. This happens in *St. Petersburg*, in *Mother*, in *Storm Over Asia* and especially in *Deserter*. It is only almost at the very end of *Storm Over Asia* that Baer, hitherto the victim, takes things into his own hands and symbolically sweeps the Imperialists out of the country in a storm.

By contrast, where Eisenstein is obliged to use an individual to illustrate his theme, as in *Old and the New*, that character almost at once starts battering at events, shaping them to his or her own desire, the social desire. From being the anvil, as in Pudovkin's film, the central character in Eisenstein's production becomes the hammer; a very profound difference. Two concepts as wide apart as the poles.

Right at the start of *Old and the New*, you get this vigorous determinism that inspired Eisenstein's early work. He first states the problem by showing how the peasants' age-old habit of petty ownership and division of property only serves to cripple their resources and keep them poor. Martha is in the fields working with the most primitive equipment, struggling with an old wooden plough and a half-famished ox to break up the earth.

She had already tried the other method of applying for assistance from the local kulak, the rich peasant, who tells her 'nothing doing.' Sweating and struggling in the field, in a spirit of determination, she rams the wooden plough into the ground.

Enough.

An end to this foolishness. An end to this waste of human effort on an outworn individual basis. A new way must be found, and the scene merges to the first open-air meeting in the village, inaugurated by the local district agricultural commissioner to discuss the formation of the village co-op. All the old peasants turn away in disgust and mistrust of the 'Bolshevik tricks,' but Martha, determined Martha, and a few others form the first nucleus of the village co-operative farm. From then on, Martha steers the fortunes of the village, teaching them by example to achieve through co-operative effort a better and more civilized life. Thought. Determination. Action. The hammer not the anvil. Such was the method and social outlook of S. M. Eisenstein at the height of his creative powers.

There have been very few other silent Soviet films shown in this country. *Bed and Sofa*, directed by Room, was a recapitulation of the old triangle problem. It showed one effect of the housing shortage in Moscow of 1926, which, in that year, contained three times as many inhabitants as it had done before it became the centre of government. Although the story revolved around a man and his friend, the film was clearly a mirror of the current questioning and re-evaluation on sex problems which was going on in Russia at the time. A similar ferment of discussion on sex was going on about the same time in Western Europe and in America, as we have already pointed out.

A picture of very great importance for the future of the documentary film all over the world, was *Turk-Sib*, directed by Victor Turin. It came as a surprise to many people to realize that it was possible to construct an exciting hour-length drama from a subject apparently so prosaic as the building of a railway, in this case the building of the first single track that linked the cotton of Turkestan with the timber of Siberia.

John Grierson's talkie, *Night Mail*, is a worthy descendant of the pioneer *Turk-Sib*.

The Man with the Movie Camera, directed and cut by Dziga-Vertov, was a documentary, which received considerable notice in this country because of the director's much discussed theory of the Kino-eye. The film, having no narrative interest running through it, as in *Turk-Sib*, and no personal appeal, was not very widely shown.

Men of the Woods was a three-reel documentary of infinitely greater interest. It pictured the life of a small Mongolian tribe who lived under Soviet influence beyond the Arctic circle. It showed the men engaged in trapping and fishing, the tribal customs in marriage, the custom of isolating a woman in a separately built hut before childbirth; but it also showed the gradual displacement of these age-old and backward customs by more civilized ways of behaviour. It showed at first how the tribe gathered in a circle to watch the local shaman or medicineman in full panoply performing his wild evolutions, but towards the end of the film, you saw the same circle of men gathered to discuss the election of one of their number as a delegate to the local Soviet or district council, in far-away Vladivostock.

The outer form, the tribal circle was the same, but the inner content had changed.

These were amongst the most important of the silent Russian films that were shown publicly in England.

XVI

ALTHOUGH the U.S.S.R. was, until 1936, very poorly equipped with sound-recording apparatus, she made a contribution to technical advance as early as 1931, when the first Russian talkie, *The Road to Life*, directed by Nicolai Ekk, was shown in this country and in America. It demonstrated the idea of orchestrating sound with action, as opposed to the contemporary American use of sound, dialogue and song exactly synchronized with action of the lips, and very little more.

The sound in *The Road to Life* is imaginatively architectural and is used to heighten the dramatic meaning of the action taking place on the screen. As in real life, there are silences in it more potent than words or song. And there are sounds that insistently seem to deepen one's consciousness of the vital processes that nourish the growth of human life itself. That is what the film, in truth, is about—The Road to Life—for millions of orphans, hitherto outcast youngsters, who had been a menace to themselves and to others, a legacy of war, civil war and intervention.

The Road to Life, which was made about 1930, serves as a reflection of one of the most tragic phenomena in the world's history. In the year 1923, in the U.S.S.R. nine years had elapsed since the world war had begun, years of the greatest social upheaval the world had ever seen on any continent.

Literally millions of homeless orphans, boys and girls, deprived of parental or adult guidance by war and civil war, were roaming the streets and countryside in hordes, like little savages, sleeping in hedges, barns, caves, cellars, railway trucks, completely lawless, stealing, destroying and even slaying. Their social instincts were expressed in only one way, by running round in gangs like little marauding animals, a menace to the existence of society.

Although *The Road to Life* tells the story of one such group of children, it is a picturization of the method employed to reclaim the millions of these unfortunates; to turn them into orderly decent citizens.

Mustapha, a young leader of a gang, an engaging little criminal of about fourteen, is rounded up with his followers. The following morning, the problem of Mustapha and his gang is discussed at the headquarters of the committee of social workers. After a good many pros and cons, one of the committee (acted by Batalov) prevails upon them to permit him to try an experiment which, until then, had never been made. From this point, we see the experiment being unfolded in action.

Batalov visits the boys at their place of detention and persuades them to follow him voluntarily to a distant centre in the country, where they will be given every facility for running the place as a commune under their own control and responsibility. At first, the boys suspect a trick, but at last, under the nodding wink of Mustapha, they decide to go.

As soon as they find themselves outside the gates of the detention home, they stand surprised and irresolute, and ask Batalov: 'but where are the guards?'

Batalov, amused, replies: 'we have no need of guards, have you not all volunteered to come on your own?' They pass through Moscow's streets, across squares and tramway junctions. Not one attempts to escape. So strong is the faith of Batalov in the strength of the social instincts that after they are seated in the train, he gives

Mustapha, the erstwhile leader of thieves, money with which to buy food for the group on the journey.

Sure enough, Batalov was right. Mustapha comes dashing back to the train, just as it moves off, loaded with good things, amid the hearty, joyous acclaim of the boys. As he unloads the eatables for distribution, Mustapha pulls a surprise. With a broad wink, he makes a dive into his capacious coat, slowly draws out a long, thick sausage and says with mock innocence: 'I didn't steal this, I just borrowed it.'

Loud laughter from the little ex-thieves, but a look of reproach from Batalov: 'This must never happen again!' At each inevitable, subsequent misdemeanour, Batalov, like a good psychologist, repeats: 'This must never happen again,' 'This has happened for the last time!' knowing full well that a suggestion in the mind tends to carry itself out in practice.

The sausage incident is only one among many that occur during the progress of the picture, to show the realist understanding of life's problems. There is no such thing as a sudden and miraculous change of heart in human beings.

At the commune, the boys are taught all kinds of crafts. After a while they work on their own initiative. One morning, after several days of satisfying creative work, the hungry boys sit down to dinner at a long table, and lo and behold! the spoons have disappeared, and no one knows anything about them. The boys are obliged to eat their porridge with their snouts. When they are finished, the only one with a clean face is the house-dog, whom nature has provided with a means of eating porridge without a spoon.

Mustapha, his face covered with wrath and porridge, gets up to make his after-dinner speech with great vehemence: 'The spoons have got to be brought back, no stealing here!' The following morning, sure enough,

THE ROAD TO LIFE, directed by Nikolai Ekk, the pioneer Soviet film about problem children

DEAD END, the Samuel Goldwyn production, with Humphrey Bogart and the Dead End Kids *(United Artists)*

the spoons have found their way back in the cabinet where they belong!

In far-away Moscow, there still lives a fellow who is a kind of field-marshal, or grown-up leader of groups of young thieves living in the underworld, a relic of Moscow's pre-revolutionary days. He is beginning to find business very difficult now that so many stray children are being assisted to establish their own communes by the Soviet Government.

This chief decides that something must be done about it, so he collects a number of women from his gang and travels down with them to a spot not far from Mustapha's commune, and in a hut starts a kind of drinking saloon and cabaret in order to entice the boys back again to their old thieving life.

A few of the boys fall into the trap of 'vodka and girls' during their spare hours, and come rolling back to the commune in the early hours of the morning, drunk. But the majority remain solid and sensible and stick to the life of the commune.

One night, Mustapha, who by now has shed every sign of his old thieves' mentality, and is a determined, responsible young leader of the commune, organizes a raid upon the hut by means of a ruse, and helps to break up the drinking saloon for good. The chief criminal escapes, and lives to take his revenge. He waylays Mustapha and kills him.

Mustapha has died in order to safeguard the integrity of the commune. He dies by the hand of an assassin, by the hand of a decayed past. And his death only strengthens the proud resolve of the boys to justify his faith in them, by working doubly hard to achieve the welfare of the whole of the community.

The Road to Life is a reflection and a symbol of what was actually taking place at that time in the whole of the U.S.S.R. All her people, the 170 millions, bore within themselves the legacy of earlier days. Every single person in the whole of that vast territory was faced with the task of re-making himself, and of helping to build up industrial technique at one and the same time.

Until 1926, the Russians were occupied in reconstructing the ruins left by the wars and civil wars which had only finally ended, three years before. From 1926 onwards, the process of electrification and vast scale industrialization, the making of the first *Piatiletka*, or Five Year Plan, had the same effect upon the world as *Potemkin* itself.

There was galvanism in the very word *Planning*. It began to creep in everywhere, even into the speeches of Conservative statesmen.

The Russians were building for the children who are the future. The consideration and care accorded to the boys in *The Road to Life* was paralleled by the consideration they were receiving everywhere in real life. Milk supplies were often entirely reserved for children and expectant mothers and invalids.

The system of education was changed right from the beginning of the Soviet regime, and had passed through various phases of development by 1926. The children themselves were guided into responsibility just as in *The Road to Life*.

In this young State, only in its teens, everything was growing before one's eyes: factories, collective farms, housing estates, rest homes, railways, roads, schools, public buildings, parks and libraries; everybody was learning to read in his own national language one of the two hundred languages spoken in the Soviet Union; and for the first time, the unification of language was taking place.

When the cultural heritage of the world is being devoured by millions of people, when an enormous percentage of them are reading books for the first time, then it is spring in the U.S.S.R. It is the hey-day of youth.

These salient aspects of the social consciousness cannot help but be reflected in their talkie films, only a few of which have been seen in this country. There is something striking about the titles themselves: *The Road to Life, The Youth of Maxim, We from Kronstadt, A Greater Promise, A Generation of Conquerors, Moscow Laughs, Young Pushkin, Peter the Great, Son of Mongolia, Youth, Three Songs of Lenin, The New Gulliver.*

There still remains, however, the union of opposites that we noticed at the beginning of the Soviet silent films. The titles convey joy and a forward drive, but many of the films unfortunately tend towards subjectivism. Historically there is a powerful onward wave, and then the wave recedes. The Pudovkin who makes *Storm Over Asia* follows it with *The Deserter*. The Eisenstein who makes *Battleship Potemkin* makes *Alexander Nevsky*.

Other Soviet film directors follow the prevailing trend, the stress upon the individual, and with that stress—subjectivism, as in *Peter the Great, Professor Mamlock, Lone White Sail* (accent on the 'Lone') and *Lenin in October.*

The real Peter the Great left Russia for the Thames shipyard at Deptford and with his own hands learnt to saw and to plane and to construct ships. This historical episode which would have delighted a Soviet audience is never shown in the film except as a recitation *in words*, on a chart, about topsails and mainsails. But the barbarities, the incitements for looting and women, the rising tide of a disastrous flood in Petersburg and other subconscious indulgences of the directors are given the most vivid expression.

Here is another aspect. Let us suppose that an American director in Hollywood is making a film about the American Revolution. Let us suppose that in the course of the action a thousand rugged armed colonists come upon a company of about thirty well-drilled professional English soldiers. The colonists descend upon them and surround them. Instead of disarming the soldiers and taking them prisoner, the colonists and the English soldiers face each other for a few moments, then the colonists give vent to one huge 'boo' *and the soldiers, still in possession of their weapons,* are chased away. How long would an American director last who could put this incident in a picture? Yet this is precisely the incident that occurs in *Lenin in October* when the armed counter-revolutionary Cadets are chased out of the Putilov factory, *still with their arms in their possession,* a few hours before the timed Revolution!

The derogatory aspects of such mistakes will do little to harm the healthy social instincts in an advancing society. But it is amazing that a people with a capacity for self-defence that the Russians possess should allow free scope to individual film directors who seem to have lost touch not only with basic reality but with common-sense everyday psychology.

So far from cramping its directors, the Soviet Union is allowing them unheard of freedom, a latitude that in America would soon meet with a well-deserved check at the Box-Office.

Contrast the Russian *Professor Mamlock* with the American *The Confessions of a Nazi Spy.* The Russians, with the best intentions, harbour upon the problem of the individual, upon barbarities, upon the contemplation of suicide. *The Confessions of a Nazi Spy,* on the other hand, is treated as a social problem that has to be cleaned up, and *is* cleaned up with determination and clarity of purpose. There is objectivity, firmness and a strong sense of social preservation that touches on the horrors of Nazism only long enough to ginger the American people into further protective action.

The Soviet Union has the most magnificently equipped palace of psychological study in the world—the Pavlov Institute in Leningrad. A closer study of film production on scientific lines is called for. Culture must lead. Culture must direct the attention of the people not entirely upon what was or upon what is, but upon what should be.

XVII

HOW are we to account for the comparative inadequacy of the English cinema, when the industry was developing so rapidly on the Continent and in America?

The culture of a country can only be understood in the light of the social scene and its past history. The cultural soil of England differs greatly from that of Europe and of the U.S.A. The difference springs from certain physical advantages which were counter-balanced by corresponding disadvantages.

With William the Conqueror, hundreds of years before any such thing happened on the Continent, England achieved a stable monarchy, a unified regime, in the widest sense of the term, which was to rule a unified nation. England as a nation owes the physical virility of her people to the same causes as does America of the nineteenth and early twentieth century. The virility of the American people is in a great measure due to the extraordinary admixture of races and cultures. Similarly, the country that the Conqueror acquired was one whose population had been fertilized by successive waves of Roman legions, Celts, Picts, Jutes, Angles, Saxons, the successive Danish settlements and the invasion of peoples from other Scandinavian countries; and finally by the Normans themselves.

England was thus first in the field as a national unity. This, and her immunity from invading armies, enabled her to be the first in the world to plant effectively the seeds of an industrial society. She was assisted in her fight with the

Papacy by being furthest away from Rome geographically and least accessible. When the scramble for colonies took place, she had a people who lived by knowing how to sail and trade, and she had a merchant and fishing fleet from the beginning. Moreover, she was bound to win against her competitors in the long run because Portugal and Spain, and later Holland and France, were never free from the necessity of having to defend their frontiers at home.

The culture which reflected the social reality of England after the war of 1914–18 must therefore be regarded not as something which existed at that particular moment, but as something which was the outcome of all that had gone on since the Norman Conquest.

Since that event, England had enjoyed, above all other countries, unity, priority in social economic development, the greatest stability, the longest historical continuity.

This social reality, this compact pyramid which has the Norman Conquest as its base, is most vividly reflected in the social consciousness.

In view of the long, slow, uninterrupted, ever-deepening rooting-in of England's social life, is it any accident that of all countries England should have given the 'inevitability of gradualness' the widest currency and the largest following as a political concept? Is it not clear that Ramsay MacDonald, who gave expression to this notion, was in no way an historical accident?

The English slowness and unwillingness to change, their proud rigidity, is well known to our European neighbours, who often comment on the behaviour of the middle-class Englishman abroad, who refuses to learn any foreign language (Gad, Sir! let the blighters learn English!) and irately demands his eggs and bacon for breakfast though the heavens fall.

The sum total of a country's social past, and the reality of its present, is expressed in that country's culture. But culture covers every activity. Culture is how we behave to each other, how we express ourselves in speech, how we work, how we create the environment in which we eat and rest, how we love and how we dress.

As we have seen, England's geographical detachment from the Continent was of the utmost advantage to her for material progress, but it had the corresponding disadvantage that it developed a greater disparity between social ideas and reality, a greater time-lag between what has happened and the *conscious social realization* of what has happened, than on the Continent.

This is of great importance to us in our enquiry as to why the English cinema is what it is, why it is so unlike the cinematic expression of any other country. It will explain why it was America and not England which was the better fitted to absorb and make her own the best ideas and technique from the cinemas of France, Germany and Russia.

Since no one disputes that the cinema is the cultural medium of an industrial age it may seem strange that Russia, starting with a backward agricultural economy and with what little industry it possessed almost shattered, should have been the first country to achieve the highest form of cinematic expression, whereas England, with an advanced industrial technique, produced nothing of any permanent value. England, in fact, was the lowest in the list of film-producing countries.

How is this paradox to be explained?

It can only be explained if we bear in mind that the full intelligent use of a medium, any medium, is only effected where the social consciousness stimulates men to advance the social process. The stimulating social atmosphere of England during the reign of Elizabeth, for instance, when exciting new Eldorados were opening out before the gaze of men, explains the vigour, the nobility, the depth of human understanding that emerged in the person of Shakespeare.

With the comparative isolation of post-war England and its relative well-being (relative to the conditions of war-shattered Europe), there was not the same incentive to cultural expression in the new industrial medium that existed on the Continent.

The strong preference shown by the majority of people for American films rather than English is a reflection of the fact that they live in an industrial world which is all too real to them. The tempo of the American film corresponds more nearly to the speed-up of contemporary life. But for the people in the upper strata of society the tempo of everyday life slackens progressively the higher you go.

Thus it happens that the upper classes in England, living in a more rarefied atmosphere, find themselves more in tune with English films than with American. The English film is a closer expression of their particular world, and, therefore, as it exists to-day, it can never achieve the world circulation of the American product, or make an appeal to the majority of our own people.

Is it not highly significant that among the few English films which made any impression upon American patronage, were films that pictured earlier historical epochs and which centred upon private lives: *The Private Life of Henry the Eighth* and *Victoria the Great*? As we have seen, the emergence of films of this particular character can only be explained by the general social way of looking at things, which is the result of our own social past. Two historical epochs which have had the most far-reaching and most powerful effect upon the future development of mankind seem to find no higher expression than a picturization of the private life of a king and the private life of a queen. The really exciting and profoundly important things that happened in the reigns of these two figures are given to us as the faintest noises off.

The popularity of these films in America can be explained by analogy with the sentimentality that still

THE PRIVATE LIFE OF HENRY VIII
with Charles Laughton (an Alexander Korda production)
(*United Artists*)

VICTORIA THE GREAT
an Imperator film directed by Herbert Wilcox
(*R.K.O. Radio*)

TWO ENGLISH FILMS

survives and the songs that are still being sung in this country about Bonnie Prince Charlie. People sing about Bonnie Prince Charlie but no one ever dreams of really having the Stuarts back as a political issue. *Henry the Eighth* and *Victoria the Great* afford the Americans a similar sentimental link with the past.

Thus the theme and the tempo of the English film is in the main that of the aristocracy, but there is a third aspect to the situation; our own peculiar *conception of the film as a medium* is likewise pre-industrial.

The forms of expression before the age of high-speed mass machine production were the drama, the novel, the autobiography, the poem, etc. All these forms the aristocracy have made their own. Hence we have the phenomenon that these older forms have taken so tenacious a hold upon the English cinema. The force of the new impacts from the Continent and U.S.A. seems unable to dislodge these older traditions and habits of thought, which are out of keeping with the cinema as a medium.

For a medium to achieve its highest expression and the widest appeal, there must exist a social atmosphere of a fertilizing kind, a strong homogeneity, an intimate contact with the people. This is true of every cultural medium, but it is a thousand times more necessary for the cinema.

Let us take the social scene in England and that of America, and contrast them to illustrate our point.

In England there is a division between the upper and lower strata of society. In America, too, there is a somewhat analogous division, but by comparison with the rigidity and frigidity that separates the upper layers of society from the lower in this country, the Americans are living in blissful brotherhood.

You can see that clearly in any American film. There you will never find the abject deference which is accorded in this country to the doctor, the lawyer, the mayor, the councillor. You will never see a land-worker touching his cap to the American equivalent of the squire. The only person in the U.S.A. who seems to be treated a little more deferentially is the plainly dressed court judge in session. And even in court, the idea of contending counsel dressing up to look different from ordinary mortals is cut right out. All men are free and equal in attire and appearance and in formal behaviour to each other, if not in actual social practice.

The *News-Chronicle* of July 26th, 1938, reported an interview between lone-flyer Corrigan and the American Ambassador to the Court of St. James, Mr. Kennedy. All the newspaper representatives were there, and these are the first words that Mr. Kennedy is reported to have uttered:

Sit down, boys, you've got the damnedest habit of standing up in England.

That is how it strikes an American Ambassador.

Observe the average worker here in his attitude to a doctor. They belong to different planets almost. Observe on the other hand the social attitude to the American doctor in so many of their films: 'Hello, Doc!' 'Hello, Bill!'

Imagine the informality that exists in America translated to England. Imagine the mayor's parlour, with the mayor sitting in dignity at his desk, whilst the local reporter helps himself to a cigar, in a leisurely way rests his posterior on the edge of the table or desk, and asks the mayor for the low-down.

This is the sort of thing that might happen anywhere, in the local sheriff's office, at the office of an industrialist, or that of a governor of a state, in America.

In America, but not in England!

You cannot say good-bye to 1066 and all that in a hurry.

A community is a single organism. We speak of the

body politic. The body politic is like the body of a man, indivisible.

You cannot divide up a living man and say this part of him engages in economic life, and that part of him reads a book, goes to the pictures or the theatre, while the other part indulges in sport. The same one person does all these things in turn.

We can see how this analogy applies to the social consciousness in England at the present time, as compared with that of America. It would seem as if in England, a pronouncement from on high permeates in varying degrees our every social activity:

Theirs not to reason why, theirs but to do and die.

From America comes a proud rejection of such a philosophy, a refusal to acknowledge any imposition. Not passive acceptance, but a manly questioning from below, from the people—into fundamentals:

'*What's he got that I ain't got?*'—'*Brass buttons!*'

The spirit of George Washington expressed in the people's language of the twentieth century, in the twentieth century medium, the film.

There was a time in England, too, when men could ask in almost identical fashion:

When Adam delved and Eve span, who was then the gentleman?

But that was long centuries ago, centuries even before the discovery of America, when John Ball voiced the feelings of a peasantry who had not yet been taught to conform as in the days of good Queen Victoria's aristocratic poet Lord Tennyson.

It is this re-assertion of human values, this probing into fundamentals so characteristic of the American film, which

145   K

is one of the qualities which makes an irresistible appeal to the vast majority of England's cinema patronage to-day.

England also knew the vigour and the spirit of the passionate questioning of to-day's America, in the days of Elizabeth, when English sailors made London the centre of the world, when trade brought the men and the manners and the culture of every European capital into the great metropolis, when the creative heart of England beat strongly through the poem and the play, when Shakespeare wrote England's name across the eternal realms of literature and inspired the Cromwellian poet James Shirley to proclaim:

> Sceptre and Crown
> Must tumble down
> And in the dust be equal made
> With the poor crooked scythe and spade.

Vigour and independence as virile for its time, in the medium of that age, as that of America's creative impulse expressed in her own appropriate creative medium—the film.

The magnificent promise of the Elizabethan age was followed by disappointments which were reflected in a gradual lowering of the creative impulse after Shakespeare's death. The chills of our exclusive English atmosphere nipped the buds of English genius until there came the impetuous, dazzling promise of the French Revolution, whose rays enlivened the hearts and minds of Englishmen across the narrow channel and across the breadth of the country.

Tom Paine, great fighter for liberty and friend of George Washington, created the biggest ferment known until then in England's history with his *Rights of Man*, a work so clearly and splendidly written that it is as well worth reading to-day as it was then.

CATHERINE
THE GREAT
with
Elizabeth
Bergner
(*London Films*)

FIRE OVER
ENGLAND, with
Flora Robson
as
Queen
Elizabeth

(an Alexander
Korda
production)

NELL GWYN,
with
Anna Neagle
as Nell Gwyn
and Cedric
Hardwicke
as Charles II
(*British and
Dominion*)

THREE MORE ENGLISH FILMS

Robert Burns expressed the deep feeling of that time in poems which were spread in handwriting and from mouth to mouth, as well as in print, across the length and breadth of the country, hailing the time:

When man to man the world o'er
shall brothers be for a'that.

XVIII

THE force of a new great social movement, as during the reign of Elizabeth, and at the time of the French Revolution, leaves its impression on human thought and culture, then gradually slackens. The force of inertia, the grip of the past, acts as a brake, but amongst western countries this historical brake seems least effective in America. That is why the re-assertion of the Rights of Man, the motive force of the American Revolution, is as strong to-day as ever, as we shall see later in an examination of America's cultural expression.

In England after the Great War, the questioning, the ferment in the minds of thinking people was conveyed through *personal*, individual modes of expression. It found no outlet in the new *collective* medium, the cinema, for the historical reasons we have outlined. The aristocratic background of intellectual life, the powerful humanist traditions from the French Revolution that had stretched across the whole of the creative Victorian era, tended inexorably to an over-emphasis upon the individual, upon the 'I' as the centre of all things. The tremendous and truly worthy achievements in the creative field during the Victorian era, in science and in literature, established a prestige for the individual method of expression which, it would seem, has been almost unshakable.

At the end of the nineteenth century, the creative impulse derived from the French Revolution and from England's industrial expansion began to slacken, and the cult of healthy individuality tended towards a decline into a less healthy individualism. The clear objective gaze upon the world characteristic of a Dickens was gradually transformed by the end of the century, until it expressed itself in subjectivism, in escape, in speculative introspections through the work of writers like R. L. Stevenson and Oscar Wilde.

We have shown how closely the mood of Europe in 1919 was expressed through *The Cabinet of Dr. Caligari* and in the plays of Piranello. We have seen that these were the reflections of the social consciousness, a deep desire to find an answer, an explanation for man's apparently inexplicable behaviour; but we have seen also that this explanation was not sought for in the objective world, but in speculations turned inwards, about man's divided personality and irrationality.

It is therefore no accident that a period of decline in the real world, and, to men of sensitive feeling, the irrational jingoism which spread through England and culminated in the Boer War, should find its reflection in such works as Stevenson's *Dr. Jekyll and Mr. Hyde* and Wilde's *The Picture of Dorian Gray*.

Notice the similarity. Notice that a period of social sickness impels men who are, by the nature of their craft, inclined to undue introspection, to think and write of doctors. Dr. Jekyll represents that side of English culture which is sound and healthy, which upholds the amenities and humanities of ordinary decent everyday life; yet this same Dr. Jekyll, England, goes out to kill human beings, Zulus in Africa, and then other white men, the Boers. Dr. Jekyll and Mr. Hyde are one and the same person, the same community.

In *The Picture of Dorian Gray* Oscar Wilde describes a similar divided personality who meets his end as his picture, his reflection, is damaged.

In the post-war film *The Student of Prague*, the student, the person who has sold himself to the Sinister One, dies as his own reflection is shattered in a mirror which he himself has fired at.

The undue emphasis upon the ego and introspection, which is but the converse of an unduly stubborn refusal to face the world as it is, to do something about it, leads inevitably in all manner of directions. In some, such as Stevenson, it will lead to escape, to living upon an island far away from the world's turmoil, and to writing about treasure and other islands. In others, as in Oscar Wilde, an over-emphatic concern with his ego will lead to all kinds of unnatural sex practices, which people with sound social instincts could never indulge in.

The emergence of Oscar Wilde and R. L. Stevenson indicates a distinct point of departure from the past. Henceforth, the cult of subjectivism shows a greater and greater influence in colouring the social consciousness of England's intellectual life. For the moment you step over the limit of *individuality*, which is socially worthy, into *individualism*, which both by name and nature tends to be anti-social, the moment that barrier is crossed, the tendency develops into a wholesale slide down to the depths of self-examination which reaches its nadir in the sex preoccupations of D. H. Lawrence and James Joyce. This predominant tendency in our intellectual life, this elevation of the 'I,' cannot easily accommodate itself to an industrial medium which depends so much upon collective effort.

It is scarcely surprising, then, that in England the film has made little headway except in the continuance of this self-same literary trend, in the portrayal, for instance, of the *private life* of Henry the Eighth.

Most English films tend to conform to this basic pattern. Examples are *Catherine the Great*, *Victoria the Great* and *Fire Over England*, which told very much more about Queen Elizabeth than about England.

In *The Vessel of Wrath* the central character occupies the

centre of the screen. In this picture you get many of the aspects of subjectivism; escape to an island away from the world, drink, dissolution, plenty of women, sex symbolism and more than a trace of sadism.

Subjectivism takes all kinds of forms, and expresses itself in all manner of ways, all definitely anti-social, but varying in the severity of their effect upon society. They vary from the self-display of the film-critic who writes in terms of 'I like this' or 'I like that' to the ego-centric, autocratic attitude of a Hitler.

In England, subjectivism is expressed in milder forms and sometimes quite innocently and quite unconsciously.

It is strongly entrenched in the English film, as we shall see in our examination, but to show how all-pervading it is in our social life, let us see how it affects other forms of expression.

In social criticism a book was published some time ago called *I was a Tramp*, by John Brown, who, having thus confessed himself an individualist by nature, having no social roots, and being therefore incapable of comprehending a society based on a collective system of organization, proceeds to Russia and returns to write a book about it: *I Saw for Myself*. A double emphasis on the 'I.' It is characteristic of the author's attitude that his own photograph should serve as frontispiece.

If this were the isolated expression of an obscure tramp, it would hardly prove our case, but we have another book written by no less a person than Sir Walter Citrine* on the same subject and in almost identical style. He spoils his narrative completely by the innumerable complaints he makes about disturbances to his personal comfort. Like John Brown, Sir Walter calls his book *I Search for Truth in Russia*, and like John Brown, Sir Walter has a frontispiece portrait of Sir Walter Citrine complete with K.B.E.,

* General Secretary of the Trades Union Congress; President of the International Federation of Trade Unions.

which shows at once how the balance between the observer and the observed will be weighted throughout the book.

The 'I' in journalism is no less prominent. An article from the pen of a music critic appeared in the *News-Chronicle* on Saturday, August 6th, 1938. The first lines were:

> *One evening during August, five weeks before the Music Critic of this journal was born, Henry J. Wood raised his conducting stick and the first Promenade Concert had begun. Since that auspicious year both of those institutions have flourished and to-night in the Queen's Hall they will both function.*

In the *New Statesman and Nation* of March 26th, 1938, appeared the following:

> *I see myself, within the limits of my capacity, as a keeper of the truth, and if I ask to have my say now, it is lest the time is imminent when I shall not be heard any more.*

This is subjectivism of another kind, which shows itself as a fear complex. It uses three 'I's', two 'my's' and one 'myself' all in the one sentence!

It is hardly surprising that later in the article the writer gives expression to this form of day-dreaming:

> *In a lesser way, I regard their manner of living (the English governing class) particularly in the country as the most civilized I know: materially speaking it would be the height of my ambition to have a small estate, hunt in the winter, and spend the summer between my garden and my library. . . . I am not concerned with economics.*

Think of the nature of the social consciousness, when, in a world tumbling about our ears, one of the most respected journals in the country prints such pitiful soap-bubbles of escape and unreality. *My* Garden and *My* Library! Shades of Beverley Nichols!

Having examined various manifestations of the social consciousness, let us see how it is reflected in the most dynamic medium of all, the film. We may as well start with the Laughton-Pommer production, *The Vessel of Wrath*.*

The ambitions which were so poignantly expressed by the *New Statesman* contributor just quoted, for a small estate in the country, a library and a garden, find analogous expression and full realization as *The Vessel of Wrath* fades to its close. The only difference is, that instead of an estate in the country, it is an exceedingly prosperous pub in the country! Not really an essential difference, for the underlying idea at the back of each is the same: 'Thank heaven, *I'm* all right!'

This is a 'happy ending' with a very big difference when you know the story from the beginning.

It opens upon an island in the tropics held by the Dutch. Laughton is a dissolute beachcomber, Ginger Ted, who receives a monthly remittance from his people to stay away. Elsa Lanchester acts the part of a very prim and proper English missionary schoolmistress who teaches a mixed class of native children and adults. Her brother is the island parson-doctor and the other chief character is the Dutch Governor who is also Dutch Uncle to the drunken ragamuffin, with whom he is on exceedingly familiar terms.

Now the exquisite, unconscious and quite unintended irony of the ending is this: The dissolute drunk and the prim schoolmistress, who explains that her father had drunk himself to death, after many adventures make it up, and we next see them back in England, the respected lessees of *The Fox and Rabbit Inn*, achieving their own personal salvation by ladling out the poison that they

* Called *The Beachcomber* in America.

153

themselves couldn't stomach, and retiring to bed with a satisfied sigh, as of a good day's work well done.

They can't take it, but, boy, can they dish it out!

Throughout the film there is the oppressive atmosphere so often to be met with in English pictures, an atmosphere of inversions and repressions, sex symbolism and a display of the hind parts, threats of spanking and booze, always booze: all the concomitants of an unhealthy, unbalanced, over-emphasized stress upon the ego.

The picture is called *The Vessel of Wrath*, but it is actually about Ginger Ted. Charles Laughton is sharply focused against a background specially designed, not only to emphasize the ego of a black sheep of the family, but the prowess of one single performer—Charles Laughton.

At this point, a comparison for a moment between the English and American film is highly revealing. The American film to-day is travelling with enormous speed towards a greater emphasis upon the social scene and a correspondingly diminishing emphasis upon the individual. (The Marlene Dietrich eclipse is significant.)

Not only the individual character but the individual performer in the American film is giving place in importance to the society in which the character moves and has his being.

By contrast, the tendency in English films is in the opposite direction. The star, the chief character, is becoming more prominent than ever in the picture, and the importance of the social background recedes until, as in Anna Neagle's *Victoria the Great*, the thing is hardly recognizable as a social-historical episode at all.

The Vessel of Wrath refers to the sex frustrations of the woman missionary, but the sense of frustration is everywhere in all the main characters. The Governor is frustrated and lonely, Laughton talks nostalgically of England far away, and the woman's brother, the medical missionary, is sex-starved and neurotic.

The consequence is that the film is steeped with sexual symbolism and psychopathic repressions. The Americans left this historical stage of the treatment of sex twenty years ago, with the final ending of the Theda Bara vamp cycle. The Americans seem one short step ahead of public taste and opinion, always. We seem to drag miles behind. This is one of the reasons why cinema proprietors in this country have often preferred to pay heavy fines rather than show English films to fulfil their obligations under the Film Quota Act.

The majority of people who have been seeing American films for years have long solved their sex problems. They have adopted a healthy outlook, they know all about it, and it is no longer a problem. But it is still an obsession with the upper layers and the smart set, where the double standard of morals still operates and fosters the Jekyll and Hyde mentality not only in sex, but in their other spheres of life.

To the sex-starved spinster, Ginger Ted says: 'I'll spank you till you can't sit down,' and there are two further references to spanking. In another instance he asks her to 'have a banana.' The audience laugh, and you can think what you like.

At a certain point in the story, they are stranded late at night on a nearby island. The spinster protests violently: 'What, one woman alone with three men on an island, all night?'

Ginger Ted wades into the water, lifts her forcibly from the boat and carries her to the shore. Immediately he ostentatiously takes off his trousers and flaps them on to a rock to dry. The spinster shivers with apprehension and suppressed excitement at the sight. He calls out to her to take her skirt off to dry. More apprehension and still more excitement.

You are given to understand that all this is being done in the greatest innocence, because some time later the spinster's brother comes dashing into Ginger Ted's lodging and says with high neurotic excitement:

Forgive me for having judged you so harshly. You had my sister at your mercy, and you spared her!

Ginger Ted gets himself mixed up in a brawl and lands in court presided over by the friendly Governor. The missionaries, brother and sister, are there to try to get Ginger Ted deported from the island for being a menace to its morals. The more they plead, the smaller becomes the sentence the Governor intends to give. He strokes his notes out from three months to two, and then to one month's imprisonment.

While all this is going on Ginger Ted is unashamedly ogling the court room full of attractive native girls, and being ogled by them in turn. When sentence of one month is pronounced, one of these girls flies to him and protests, and there are screams of protest from all the other girls.

The significance of this scene is staggering, when one remembers the identical position of the blacksmith who is the king of the wet-nurses in the Goebbels-Goering inspiration, *Der Ammenkoenig*. Amidst the protests of all the charming village girls to whom he has been the communal bull, the blacksmith, too, is threatened with imprisonment by the decadent forces of democratic law and order, who still possess a modicum of human decency, who dare defy the spirit of Hitler, Goebbels, Goering, by interfering with their little bit of fun in the village!

We know now at least where we stand with films of the type of *The Vessel of Wrath*.

Thus we see as clearly as in a magic pool, the reflection of the minds of a very small but influential stratum who spread their ideas broadcast to the community.

To escape. To be on such an island, with plenty of booze and plenty of women, with no moral or social ties, and with the money rolling in from heaven knows where; this is very paradise.

From one island, far away from the turbulent sea of the world's troubles to another island where there are still more women, wearing garlands of flowers, in a land of milk and honey, and where you splash with them swimming in the water. And from then on to yet another island, the tight little dinky and prosperous *Fox and Rabbit Inn.*

Bliss, perfect bliss.

And so, with a sigh, to bed.

XIX

AND so to *Second Best Bed*. Once there was an inseparable partnership, Tom Walls and Ralph Lynn. Now there is only Tom Walls.

Not only that, but as if to emphasize the Fuehrer motif that runs through *Second Best Bed*, Tom Walls is the producer, the director as well as the leading man in this film. King of the castle.

The title of the picture is slightly misleading, for there is not only a second best bed, but beds of every shape and size, and beds in every situation.

The signature tune to this film could well be: 'He shall have beds where any she goes.'

There is the one you start with, the one known as the Legal and General. There is a bed in the servant's room, and a bed in the protégée's room, a bed at the manor, a bed in London and a bed in Monte Carlo. There is no escaping them.

And there is not one single suspicion of an idea in the film having the remotest contact with real life. Again, as in *The Vessel of Wrath*, the heated sex symbolism, petticoats. Flesh-fitting lingerie, paraded for no reason attaching to the story. Innumerable scenes about dressing and undressing, listening at doors to a highly coloured dialogue between a man and a woman: 'Oh! you brute,' etc.

Pyjamas, creeping and peeping, and again peeping and creeping and snooping. As in the Laughton picture, several references to bottom spanking, and a hair brush held aloft about to descend to perform that operation.

Tom Walls as the squire has his own troubles with a flighty, highly-strung wife, and he adds to them by taking under his wing a working girl who alleges that she has been the victim of a sexual assault by a man who happens to be the village football idol.

An abysmal ignorance of ordinary workaday life and basic human psychology is betrayed by what follows in the film. The girl is of the traditional English stage and film domestic servant type. Nevertheless, she is made to ogle and to apply her lip-stick with the ostentation of a street-walker.

She has come to the squire for protection, can you guess why? Although her story has the ring of truth, that the chap had her in his car and then flung her into a ditch, all the villagers are supposed to be in an uproar, and are in full cry after her, just like a pack of hounds after a fox, a visual mental image with which the smart set are so very familiar.

And the reason? They are all supposed to be yelling for her blood, because their football idol is their local god, and the girl is considered an idle hussy. The god must be elevated, and his detractor, frail womanhood, must be chased through the streets, harried and persecuted.

Football before humanity.

These are the sentiments attributed to the common, ordinary decent people, in whom in real life the first instinct is that of sympathy for any one of their kind who has fallen by the wayside. Here is a picture of the English villager as seen through the eyes of the smart set!

Social feeling, sympathy, the social instinct are the root and basis of human life. To have lost sight of that fundamental principle is to confess an inability to voice the thoughts and feelings of the vast majority of the population, and a total ignorance of elementary human psychology. We can never hope to remedy the poverty of ideas in so many English films until they are rid of the artificialities that may appeal to those living in an artificial world of their own.

It would be well, at this point, to contrast the way we treat crowd psychology with the way it is handled in a recent American film: *Fury*, directed by Fritz Lang.

Exiled by the Nazis, because he had committed the crime of having had a great-great-grandmother who was a Jewess, Lang arrived in Hollywood at a time when a tremendous wave of communal feeling was sweeping across the U.S.A. Such films as *Scarface* and *I am a Fugitive from a Chain Gang* had already had a few years to simmer into the public consciousness, and had already translated themselves into action in the real world. Firstly, as a result of *Scarface*, gangsterdom was being cleaned up, and secondly a movement for the abolition of the chain gang system was launched, so that to-day the chain gang is no more.

The great slump of 1929 had a widespread social effect in America. For millions of people the highest standard of living ever achieved had vanished as in a dream, like Eddie Cantor's City of Ali Baba. The agitation for work schemes, for social insurance, for new and wider Labour organization; the ex-servicemen's mass sitting down on the steps of the Capitol at Washington, and the struggle centring upon the New Deal, were all being reflected in pictures like *Black Fury*, *Riff-Raff*, *Black Legion* and *Mr. Deeds Comes to Town*.

This was the community into which Fritz Lang landed. From all the subjects that he might have chosen out of this bubbling cauldron of ideas, he chose to pillory an aspect of American life which had not yet been seriously tackled—lynch law.

The story of this, his first American film, *Fury*, concerns a young worker at a petrol filling station (Spencer Tracy), who, whilst driving a car in the country, happily thinking of his approaching marriage, is stopped by a search party, and is arrested on suspicion of being the murderer for whom they have been on the look-out. (Remember the innocent victim in *Dr. Caligari* and *The Man with the Flower in his Mouth*?)

The victim, in this case, is quite certain that he will be free in a few hours, since the whole thing is a mistake.

But it doesn't pan out that way.

One or two sadist-minded individuals in the community, at first quite casually, start talking about the capture, and assume without a second thought that the captive is the guilty person. The conversation takes place in a drinking saloon. When people start to loosen their tongues, surmise and insinuation begin to spread until what started as a false theory, is translated in the minds of hundreds as a fact. The basic social instinct with which we are all imbued becomes twisted. The few manage to stir the many into a frame of mind which prepares them for the job of lynching.

The sound which started as a whisper in a saloon, increases to a murmur, until stage by stage it has become a roar of fury, and an organized attack is made upon the prison in an attempt to kill the innocent victim of circumstance. The victim escapes by the merest chance.

Here we see clearly how the anti-social nature of lynching grows from the sadist propensities of certain perverted individuals under the influence of alcohol, *and is spread in the very name of the social good*.

The whole action is a clear recital of the development from cause to effect. In *Second Best Bed*, by contrast, the crowd scenes have no sociological or psychological basis whatever; the crowd situation is created arbitrarily to suit the fantastic plot conceived by some writer. Nothing in the crowd scenes of *Second Best Bed* could have happened anywhere, in heaven above or on earth below.

But in *Fury* you see the story started on a firm foundation and being built up, brick by brick, before your eyes. You see that from the fuddled minds of saloon habitués come the seeds from which anti-social movements spring, movements which fraudulently invoke the name of the social good.

And here is something of extreme significance. Fritz Lang himself and thousands of his countrymen were victims of organized crowd fury, in almost exactly the same way as the victim of unreason in his first American film. The story of *Fury* is a microcosm of the Nazi movement in Germany—the same origins, the same motives and pretexts.

Again we see that, consciously or unconsciously, what has been experienced in real life will find its outlet in some form of expression, if the medium and the social opportunities present themselves.

And so in their own way, films like *Second Best Bed* wittingly or unwittingly are a reflection of what is uppermost in the minds of certain select upper strata.

Let us take three recent English films as a group, we will see how clearly this thesis is substantiated:

South Riding, with Edmund Gwenn and Edna Best;
The Housemaster, with Otto Kruger;
Convict 99, with Will Hay.

Here is an extraordinary state of affairs. The above three films, together with *The Vessel of Wrath*, all arrived at about the same time, each contained the idea of the schoolroom in a greater or lesser degree.

In *The Vessel of Wrath*, there is a mixed native school of children and adults, all being made to sing the most unnative song imaginable: 'Gathering Nuts in May,' all in unison, like automatons, to the conducting beat of the schoolmistress. The schoolroom equipment is quite poverty-stricken: just forms, a teacher's desk and a black-board. No objects, no pictures, no maps.

In *South Riding*, the scene is much more prosperous Yorkshire, where you would expect to see a more cheerful-looking classroom. But no, the same severity, and very little modern equipment. And there is the same predominating idea of education, that is, the Fuehrer principle enthroned at a high desk, in the person of the teacher who rules a cowed subject-state of children, all in fear and trembling of what the teacher is going to do or say next.

In the classroom occur two incidents which reveal the queer ideas about democracy which seem to prevail among the select. It so happens that the squire of the village has a young daughter whose education has been neglected because the mother is in a lunatic asylum and he himself is financially unable to send her to an aristocratic school. Ultimately he is prevailed upon to send her to the parish school.

The teacher, knowing all this, is sitting at her desk one morning, handing back the essays the children have written. When she comes to the one written by the squire's daughter, she calls the child before her, and holds her up to ridicule by reading out to the class examples of her bad grammar and spelling mistakes, to the little girl's utter shame and humiliation.

Perhaps this is to show that there is no ill-feeling, and that a teacher can be as refinedly cruel to a squire's daughter as she can be to another, a poor girl, who is next for the pillory. Remember, that this teacher has been appointed by the local committee from a number of other applicants, and is supposed to be very up-to-date, and from London.

The poorer girl who comes to the desk is one whose story the teacher knows equally well. This child has to spend her time out of school acting as little mother to a family living in the most appalling conditions in a caravan among other similar derelicts at a spot called the Shacks. The teacher tells her, and in front of the whole class, that her essay was the best, but what about all these blots and dirty grease spots?

'Was it fish and chips?' asks the teacher.

'No,' answers the child. 'Just chips.'

There is a sad deficiency of human feeling and psychological understanding when two such incidents are offered us with the idea of recommending this supposedly benevolent, kindly teacher to the audience.

Everyone knows Will Hay in the part of the comic schoolmaster of Narkover School. He is supposed to be parodying the Public School, although, in practice, he shows that a weak, irresponsible schoolmaster won't do at all, and so he helps to strengthen the conviction that the Fuehrer schoolmaster is really the only type worth supporting.

In *Convict* 99, he sets out to take charge of a school for backward boys to 'knock some sense into them.' By accident, he finds himself in the position of a governor of a prison instead.

He starts his first 'reform' by introducing the committee system run by the prisoners themselves, and before you know where you are, he is out-voted, and rapid changes take place in the prison.

For the prisoners, breakfast in bed is served by warders, who adopt the mock mannerisms of Ritz Hotel waiters. There is beer and whisky, horse racing, betting, football pools, stock-exchange gambling, and the introduction of women into the prison. The same conception of bliss as in *The Vessel of Wrath*.

There is also a staged bank robbery led by the Governor himself, Will Hay, from the consequences of which he escapes by the skin of his teeth.

You see the idea? See how ridiculous a prison would

Four typical episodes in SOUTH RIDING, produced by Alexander Korda and Victor Saville, with Edmund Gwen and Edna Best

(*United Artists*)

be, if we followed the ideas of those agitating prison-reform cranks. Obviously, as Will Hay has shown, the best way to run a prison is to run it as a prison, not as a benevolent institution. You are led to suppose that only one reform, the prison committee idea, was responsible for bringing the whole system to caricature. It follows that if you give the prisoners an inch, they will take an ell, and then where will discipline be? And where will our civilization be?

Ah, some will say, but it is all meant in fun. No doubt; but in the Middle Ages there were people who saw fun in mocking hunchbacks, and in teasing and persecuting the mentally feeble. What is there funny about a prison, especially to the prisoners?

School—Prison, or Prison—School. The basic idea is discipline of the Fuehrer kind and no nonsense about it.

Here is an example of a joke from *Convict 99*. Will Hay meets a one-time pupil, and asks:

'How's your father?'

'He was hanged this morning,' is the answer.

'Ah, well, he had a nice day for it,' says Will Hay.

But the fountain-head and epitome of the formal, mediaeval, scholastic method of education, the subconscious elevation of the Fuehrer principle, which is receiving so much advocacy in English films, is to be seen in *The Housemaster*.

The opening shot gives the whole game away, *as does the very first sound*, the swish, swish of a descending cane heard off-stage, a sound which is the very motif of the picture. The camera pans round from a sombre interior in a Gothic ecclesiastical building to a scene where the swishing performance has just been concluded upon a young fellow.

The hypocritical old idea is suggested that 'it hurts me more than it hurts you to have to do this.' In this school, which is obviously one that caters for the offspring of the aristocracy, the boys, ranging from about twelve to eighteen years of age, are being conditioned to a maddening, unquestioning obedience, until there comes a breaking point and some of the boys mutiny by breaking bounds. But only a section of the school is able to join the insurrection, and so the revolt is broken, authority remains as firmly established as ever, the rebelling boys get it in the neck, and the schoolmaster who had displayed a little more humanity than the rest is sacked.

The Fuehrer principle resides in the person of the Headmaster, a thin-lipped, ascetic-looking clergyman who runs the school as arbitrarily, as feelinglessly and as ruthlessly as if he were driving a steam-roller. Certain of the things he orders to be done in the school show neither rhyme nor reason, except as the exercise of his own overweening egotism.

The problem is solved by the intervention of the Prime Minister. The Headmaster is given a sound kick upstairs into a Bishopric of Outer London. This resembles the similar kicks upstairs that so many Cabinet Ministers receive when, having made a mess of one job, they get hoist into another.

The more humane schoolmaster becomes Head, the boys cheer, and now it is the turn of Outer London to get a taste of the Number One egotist.

Thus the real problem at the school is successfully evaded.

Looking at the schools in every one of these English films, you would never suspect that for the past century many great educators have been at work, or that the technique of modern psychology had come into being. Such people as Montessori, Froebel, Decroly, Kirkpatrick and Dewey might never have been born. Freud, Pavlov and other eminent psychotherapists of the last fifty years might never have been heard of; for the schools you see in these films are unchanged in form, method and spirit from those of the Mediaeval Church under feudalism.

Such schools, in the long run have the effect of spreading the idea that authoritarianism is necessary and admirable. It is a thousand pities that this should be so, because it is quite evident that our film makers have no such deliberate intention. Our film makers, in fact, do strive to make pictures that will entertain, elevate and educate, that is to say, pictures that will evoke the greatest possible response at the pay-box.

Unfortunately, such efforts are largely negatived by the disruptive social philosophy that underlies the majority of their productions. We will examine one or two more English films and the general trend in English film production to show that it is the wrong social philosophy which is at the root of the trouble, very little else. There exists a very wide gulf between the mind of the general public and the minds of our film executives. If this gulf could only be narrowed down, the result would be an immense stimulus to the film industry.

Start with a firm, strong foundation, a sound social outlook, and you are on the way to building up a film which will be a credit to you. With a sound basis to start with, everything is added unto you. The right outlook will determine your choice of the right story to start with. The treatment is far more likely to be right. If the psychology is properly understood, your players will get into the skin of their parts. If that kind of spirit is engendered in the studio, everyone connected with the technical side will be infected in the same way, and your film will be a winner both in prestige and at the pay-box.

One of the first requisites to a sound foundation, to the correct social outlook, is a recognition of the fact that the vast public is eternally sound in its ethics and in its judgments, and that it demands something that rings true in ordinary every-day human behaviour, something

167

based upon psychological fact. In real life and under ordinary conditions, men behave decently and with some consideration for other human beings. In real life, people seldom go in for humiliating children, as in *South Riding*, they never hound a fallen woman, as in *Second Best Bed*, or booze themselves almost into decay as in *The Vessel of Wrath*; and although egotists in authority, like the Head in *The Housemaster*, do crop up, the people are about sick to death of that type, and they are little pleased to see him patted on the back as in this film.

The public are far more disposed to see the Hitler type humbled in the dust. They are far more likely to applaud the way Charlie Chaplin used to handle the over-weening Jack-in-authority in the old days.

XX

FILMS, as we have seen, are the reflection of the social scene, as surely as *The Cabinet of Dr. Caligari* was the reflection of the ruin that was Europe in 1919. They are, however, also projections of future trends in the social scene. Coming events cast their shadows before.

We would not need to feel so deeply concerned with the type of school being shown in English films, were it not that we have the experience of Germany to illuminate a clearer path, to help us from floundering into the same dangerous swamp in which, unfortunately, the Germans now find themselves.

The school that cast its shadow before, before Hitler came to power, was the one in *Maedchen in Uniform*, which was very widely shown in this country. This film was made about 1930, and consciously or unconsciously it is a harbinger, a portent of what was about to take place in the social and political field in Germany.

As the title indicates, the picture is set in a school for girls which is run with extreme rigidity, conformity and terrible uniformity. The school is one for the daughters of Prussian officers who have drilled into them a spirit of almost unbearable discipline.

The Headmistress, tight-lipped, wearing tight collar, and with her hair done in a tight bun, might be the exact counterpart of our friend the Head in *The Housemaster* or a female Prussian General. The situation in *The Housemaster* is repeated; the unpopular Headmistress is set against the sweet and popular schoolmistress. Like the boys in *The Housemaster*, the girls at this school suffer every form of major and petty repression.

The innate, lively good spirits of young girls, living in segregation, are given no outlet. The food is mouldy, school entertainments are only given by certain selected pupils once a year, and the harmless adolescent hobby of cutting out pictures of male film stars from fan magazines and sticking them in their wardrobes, is forbidden.

To this school comes a sensitive, adolescent girl, Manuela, played by Hertha Thiele, who, like the two girls in *South Riding*, has no mother. This young girl finds herself out of it in the school atmosphere, and is drawn to the kindly schoolmistress, who, amid all this rigidity and the forbidding barrack-like walls, offers her a little human sympathy and consolation.

As any psychiatrist would expect, this feeling towards the schoolmistress develops into a morbid sex-obsession. Since none of the girls have any opportunity of acquiring a balanced view of life or sex, the love-life of Manuela finds outlet in this fashion, with the inevitable consequence that the film ends on a note of tragedy.

The young girl, with all the promise of life before her, becomes unbalanced through the force of social disharmony, and makes a desperate attempt to commit suicide.

We have here an indication of the atmosphere of intellectual Germany when Hitler was knocking at the door. A social problem is offered to the German public as an individual problem, to be solved by the individual, socially destructive and utterly reprehensible method of suicide. *Maedchen in Uniform* presented a microcosm of Prussian life, and you could take it or leave it. No attempt was made to explain how Prussianism came into being. There was very little blame attached for what had happened, and that little was put forward very inoffensively. And no solution was offered, except the impossible one

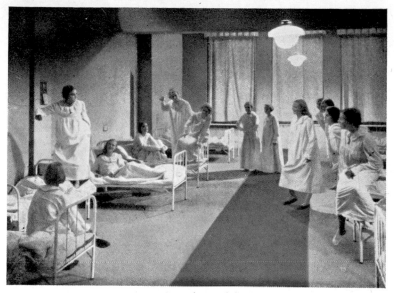

MAEDCHEN IN UNIFORM, directed by Leontine Sagan
The uniformity of pre-Nazi Germany

BOYS TOWN, the Metro-Goldwyn-Mayer production with
Mickey Rooney
The varied individuality of Roosevelt America

of self-destruction, or the equally impossible idealist way out of leaving it to a change of heart in the Head-mistress.

We shall have occasion to examine other pre-Nazi films to show that the mood of the intelligentsia was one of throwing up of hands in despair. At a time when the German people were harassed by economic stress and the claims of rival politicians, one of whom offered all the lying promises of a heaven on earth, cultural leader-ship had abdicated, leaving the solution to be worked out by the abandoned and distraught people, *all in their own several ways*.

In pre-Nazi Germany, we see in *Maedchen in Uniform* the fatalism which portrays an abhorrent, crushing authori-tarian Prussianism, and is helpless to do anything about it. Prussianism shrugs its shoulders, simply says 'Very well!' and goes on its way as before. In English films, there appears the fatalism which accepts the method of authorit-arianism, and smilingly pats it on the back as the only and inevitable manner of bringing-up the young.

Only in the American film is there no such fatalism. As we shall see in an examination of *Dead End* and *Boy of The Streets* and the trends which such films indicate, there is a straight look in the face at reality, a determined feeling that what man has twisted man can straighten out, a desire to transform the social instincts of children from the gang spirit to the communal spirit, a realization that children have the right to be treated as self-responsible individuals on equal terms with adults, to achieve their citizenship. They must not be driven to a terror-stricken obedience as in the case of the drummer-boy in Korda's *The Drum*, who stands before a General sagging at the knees with fright, and who is made to breathe an intense sigh of relief when the interview is over.

All the evidence goes to show that we in England have not, and the Americans most certainly have, learnt the lesson propounded by Ekk's *The Road to Life*. For this film portrays the application of the best known educational methods, the fruits of the most widespread study of child and adult psychology. From the very first shot to the final fade-out in this picture, there is never a single authoritarian slap, let alone the appearance of a cane as in *The Housemaster*; never the slightest hint of the humiliation of children in front of other children as in *South Riding*, no Jack-boot Prussianism as in *Maedchen in Uniform*, no regimented singing of 'Nuts in May' as in *The Vessel of Wrath*, and no heartless jokes as in *Convict 99*.

Maedchen in Uniform, both in itself and as a portent, was a finger-post to the Road to Death. The Road that leads to Life is the same road that leads to healthy films and a vigorous, healthy and prosperous film industry.

XXI

IN the English films we have examined, you may have noticed one outstanding peculiarity common to them all: a certain unmistakable attitude—shall we call it a certain stance? You get the feeling of people standing on stilts or on some elevated position, and being very condescending. This attitude occurs in the majority of English films, but it becomes more apparent in films dealing with or touching upon schools, because it is more sharply defined.

This posture of looking down, and 'talking down,' from an artificial height is the characteristic which distinguishes the English film from the American. Life to the Americans has always been real. Their Constitution dealt with fundamental human realities. Hence their culture did not and could not acquire the method of speaking to the people from a height.

The cinema is in closer proximity to the nature of truth, life, sincerity than any other medium because of the inherent quality it possesses in common with life itself—movement. It will therefore favour that country, that social philosophy which tackles its problems with the nearest approximation to truth.

The success of the American cinema derives from the truth that social life is a social process, and a film can only be truly successful if it follows the essential movement of that process, if each craftsman is prepared to put his strength into the communal effort towards achievement.

The relative unsuccess of the English film is due to a

173

certain amount of rigidity in social life, in the ideas of superiority, aristocracy, exclusiveness and elevation which inevitably bring about distortion in what is being looked at below.

But this distortion is so easily remediable. All that is necessary is to get off the perch and mix with the people, live amongst them, get some idea of human psychology in the real, not from arbitrary imaginings.

It is also very necessary to put aside all thoughts of the 'I am' in the studio, and for all to work as one; and above everything it must be remembered that a high-powered medium like the cinema only serves to show up more vividly the social, cultural and ethical concepts of, say, 1888.

For it must be said with regret, judging by so many of our films, that English culture seems to have been frozen to the pattern of not later than 1888, and this is to put it as generously as all the evidence will allow.

If the films we have already discussed are not enough to show this, let us take a look at one of Mr. Korda's productions, *The Drum*. In this picture, which must have cost at least £150,000, we get the latest word in the mechanics of cinema, brilliant Technicolor, perfect sound, lavish sets, expensive cast and crowds, and every evidence to show that so far as technical equipment is concerned our studios are equal to any in the world.

But in this story of the North-West Frontier, every gesture, every gag, might have been lifted intact out of the *Boy's Own Weekly* of 1888, down to the last gallant officer, the last soldier caught in an ambush, the last fluttering flag. Psychology and ethical standards also fit in with the same date, as in *The Housemaster*.

The officers are such nice gallant upright fellows, but the men are always bawled at (as in 1888). The officers may have their wives with them, but the men can do without (as in 1888). From the fact that wireless is mentioned in the

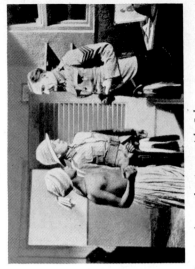

Four stages in THE DRUM, an Alexander Korda production, with Sabu

(*United Artists*)

course of the film, one gathers that the action takes place in 1938, but the only way the Residency keeps contact with the outside world is through a white man, presumably an officer, disguised with turban, darkened face and black beard, who noses around amongst the natives whom you see walking aimlessly as if they were on the stage at His Majesty's (as in 1888).

One of these spies comes dashing in dishevelled, and with his last breath (as in 1888), tells of a revolt in Tokot. The officers discuss the situation in great seriousness around a wall map. The problem is acute. Tokot is four days' march from where they are, will they be in time to suppress the revolt? (What about the Air Force? Sh! this is 1888.)

You then see the first stage of the problem being solved. In the twilight of the following morning, the massive gates of the walled Residency open slowly, and the gallant kilted lads are seen marching out in perfect line and step, each with rifle and pack, headed by the fluttering flag and the glorious martial drums and bag-pipes (as in 1888).

In keeping with the current conceptions of human rights in 1888, there is sadism, cynicism and a contempt for human dignity packed tight into the picture.

The Governor passes a bar-room cynicism to an officer on his recent marriage, *in front of the officer's wife*. The officers bark at non-commissioned officers, and both grades talk to natives as if they were dogs. The non-commissioned officer bawls at the men and insults them gratuitously, just because they are men living segregated from women. This is supposed to be humour.

The men in turn humiliate the drummer-boy, and the drummer-boy treats the dark-skinned boy, Sabu, with contempt, until he finds out that he is some kind of Prince, and even then he talks to Sabu with sickly condescension. As Shakespeare put it: 'Every dog in office is obeyed.'

If what we said about the American film is correct, that the success of a film generally depends upon its approxima-

175

tion to the truth, then if there is any basic reality in *The Drum* it would surely evoke sympathy and enthusiastic patronage amongst the people with whom it is largely concerned, the people of India.

After all the proof of the pudding is in the eating, is it not?

Let us see. The following appeared in the *Evening Standard* on Saturday, September 17th, 1938:

'THE DRUM' BANNED

Madras, Saturday.

Following disturbances in Bombay the Madras Government has banned Alexander Korda's film 'The Drum' featuring Sabu the Elephant Boy, despite the action of Moslem censors, who ordered the elimination of several sequences before passing it.

Exchange.

Even with slices cut out of *The Drum*, it would appear that the Indian people would have none of it.

The moral is obvious. So is the remedy.

XXII

NEARLY all first feature and many second feature films in England have been made from books. This in itself is not enough to explain the inadequacy of English films, for a number of very successful novels have been turned into very successful American films.

A book is a description of life in words. It is a *tête-à-tête*, as it were, between a writer who sees life in a certain way and the reader, who, sitting comfortably at home in his armchair, has to draw upon his own imagination and an acquired gift of reading to see the picture which the writer intends to convey.

A film, unlike a book or a play, however, is not a description of life, it is a direct representation of life, it is life itself as nearly as any imitation of life can be. Scientists have long been intrigued with the idea of creating life in a laboratory. The talkie film is the nearest and truest approximation to synthetic life we have reached so far.

The success of the American film, it is worth repeating, is in its close approximation to the nature of life, to movement, to action as well as thought, to its three-dimensional roundness.

The relative backwardness of our own films is explained precisely because, for one reason and another, we have failed to grasp what the Americans seem to have realized in their bones.

The staple output from the English studios at the moment, in the second feature class, is the detective or so-called thriller film. A good many of these productions are based on stories already successful as books. Many of the Edgar Wallace stories have been filmed both as first and second feature films, and the work of Director Alfred Hitchcock falls into this category.

In most of the second feature detective pictures which are being churned out, a description of the problem is conveyed to the audience in words, the development of the story hinges upon words, and at the end of it all, when all the red herrings have been gathered together, one of the chief characters will deliver a homily to one or more fellow characters, and will explain how it all happened and how it came about, again in words and more words.

In plan and outlook this type of film follows the book almost exactly. Thus it is neither one thing nor the other, neither a film nor a book.

Another unreal characteristic about these films is that they are made to appeal mainly and almost exclusively to one instinct only, the investigatory reflex, in much the same way as the films of Tom Walls appeal to the sex instinct and very little else.

Since an audience is made up of human beings in whom all the instincts reside, a film which occupies itself with one instinct has no sufficient relation to life and therefore never can and never does come alive to the audience. Such a film has to fall back on words to help it along, and this dependence on words for holding the thing together removes the film still further from reality. For life is expressed in action.

Even the films of Hitchcock suffer from the inability or an implied unwillingness to recognize that life is more, very much more, than the investigatory reflex; although it must be stated that Hitchcock is able to tell a story in cinematic images without having to depend entirely upon the word.

But every one of these films is a deliberate shying away from every aspect of social life except one, which reduces the general appeal and cultural importance of these pictures. And cultural importance is something which is eventually synonymous with Box-Office importance.

In most American films, whenever the mirror is held up to crime, the situations fit much more closely into the social scene, and there is a real attempt to convey the motives and the true psychology of the criminal.

Films like *Scarface*, for instance, in which Paul Muni achieved one of his first great successes, started a series of gangster pictures in America which spurred the American people into action, *and they did clean up gangsterdom*. *Scarface* may therefore be termed a classic, because one of the tests as to whether a poem, a play or a film is a classic is whether its emergence helped to advance the social process.

In their handling of sex problems, the Americans are infinitely nearer to psychological truth, as we shall see.

We have pointed out that if you start with a firm, solid basis, a social outlook derived from standing on terra firma and not from walking about on stilts, you can hardly make a bad picture, for everything will be added unto you. But if you persist in looking at the world from an elevation and through a lorgnette, then everything is subtracted from you. The situations in your film will fit badly and will have no sufficient relation to life, and the psychology is bound to be false.

In the field of film production in this country Mr. Alexander Korda's organization is obviously in the lead. We will therefore take another of his recent films for examination, *The Divorce of Lady X*, regarding it not merely as an individual film but, since things tend to follow a leadership or a trend, as an indication of what is happening in English film production generally.

Again, as in *The Drum*, we get the last word in lavish sets, excellent Technicolor, perfect sound, every evidence to show that no money or pains were spared to entertain and amuse us. But all this avails nothing if a film is built upon a shaky foundation, an unreal approach to life. You may get away with it in a book or even in a play, but the cinema is far too powerful a searchlight and X-ray in one; and so, in *Lady X*, the lack of any common link with what we observe in ordinary life is pitiful to see.

The Divorce of Lady X starts off, appropriately enough, in a fog. A highly-polished young man is travelling in a taxi in the West End of London, crawling slowly through the fog, which is so very thick that he cannot possibly reach his destination that night. Near Park Lane he dismisses the taxi and puts up at a very elegant hotel nearby, after a little palaver with the manager who explains with polite regret that he has nothing else except a complete suite.

In the ballroom of this hotel there are sounds and sights of revelry reminiscent of the night before the Battle of Waterloo. The ladies are dressed in crinolines nearly all alike, and the gentlemen are dressed like Wellington's hussars, looking very gorgeous. However, in the middle of the dancing there is a tattoo on the drums and a tap on the cymbals. Announcement. Ladies and gentlemen, owing to the very thick fog and the suspension of traffic, those who would like to be put up at the hotel for the night may apply at the reception desk—or words to that effect.

From this moment onwards, the picture becomes the most fantastic collection of psychological improbabilities.

Psychological mistake Number One: The moment the announcement is made, the women surge around the reception desk in one vast crinolined crowd, noisily clamouring as though their very lives depended upon getting somewhere to lie down. The hussars, peculiarly enough, have all disappeared. You are never told what happens to them; suddenly the place is all ladies. No group of women of any class at any time or place could possibly have behaved like the bunch here depicted. The whole idea is a soap-bubble.

Mistake Number Two: The manager, accompanied by about a dozen ladies seeking accommodation, politely knocks at the door of our young man, who has just acquired the suite, and politely asks if he will give up part of it for the night. Contrary to the very roots of ordinary instinctive human behaviour, and although he is supposed to be a person of education and breeding, *the young man says no!* He prefers to let elderly women sleep on the billiard table!

Mistake Number Three: The women and the manager take no for an answer and disappear, but one young lady, played by Merle Oberon, stays behind in the corridor. She cannot possibly know what kind of man this may be, who is so immersed in himself as to lose all sense of decent social behaviour. She has never seen him, and yet, all wide-eyed innocence, she decides to burst in on him alone.

Can you imagine any girl anywhere, outside an English film, placing herself at the mercy of a man she has never seen, and who has obviously behaved like an utter boor?

Mistake Number Four: The girl foists her presence upon the young man, who at first is resentful. Then there occurs, for fully twenty minutes of the film, a sparring and an ogling and an angling, an opening and shutting of doors, a peeping and a creeping, suggesting the false idea that here are two innocent children. You remember how the idea of innocence is suggested in the case of Ginger Ted. It's the same here.

In subsequent scenes, time after time, the phrase is emphatically repeated that: 'Nothing happened,' which obviously evokes the suggestion that something did happen.

Mistake Number Five: Although these two are total

181

strangers to each other, the young woman proceeds to take all the best for herself, the bed, the pyjamas, the book, the first claim on the bathroom and the breakfast, all in the spirit of petty selfishness previously displayed by the young man.

A film that starts with five major psychological errors before it is fairly well on the go, can be relied upon to keep it up until the very end—and it does.

Here is our young man, who happens to be a barrister, standing before the judge in court, dressed in his wig and gown, that is to say unassailable, a person whom you cannot answer back on pain of being indicted for contempt of court. Here he stands using the assembled in court as his audience, to give voice to his opinions on the 'worthlessness' of women. According to this self-appointed judge, this unassailable Fuehrer, women are:

mercenary, stupid, brainless and hopeless, for ever wondering which part of their bodies to paint next.

Also:

The sooner men take out the whip again the better.

The perversity of thrusting such sentiments upon half the population is only matched by the colossal stupidity of this scene, when we remember that one of the first requirements in any court of justice anywhere is *relevance to the case*, especially in England, where, although judges are sometimes a law unto themselves in expressing opinion, counsel is always extremely circumspect.

Later on this same barrister is 'defending' a woman in a divorce case in which she is said to have four co-respondents. He now thinks apparently that he is defending women when he tells the court that: 'Women are made for the comfort and solace of men.'

182

Four stages in THE DIVORCE OF LADY X, the Alexander Korda production with Merle Oberon and

Laurence Olivier

(*United Artists*)

Is this in any way different from the Nazi tenet that women are made for the comfort of the warrior?

He goes on to say that if the woman in the case really did have four co-respondents she was 'only guilty of being a woman.' He is evidently quite unaware of the kind of company he is putting himself into. In *Der Ammenkoenig* as well as in *The Vessel of Wrath* you get one man rampaging among a crowd of girls, and in *The Divorce of Lady X* one woman among four men is, apparently, just as satisfactory. You mustn't be a spoil-sport, suggests Korda's barrister; let them have their bit of 'fun,' the same message that Goebbels, Goering and Hitler convey to their audiences through the *King of the Wet-Nurses* and all the many channels of the Ministerium of Enlightenment and Propaganda.

And so right through to the end of *The Divorce of Lady X*. Incongruities, psychological improbabilities and the advocacy of every kind of anti-social behaviour, all because the film is like a house built on quicksands, shaky all over.

We shall see later in our examination of the main body of German films that preceded the Nazi regime, that they displayed the precise characteristics to be seen in a milder form in the main stream of English films to-day, of which *The Divorce of Lady X* is a fair sample. The German films were not only the reflection of the current social consciousness, they revealed that paralysis of constructive thought which ham-strung the German people, immobilized them, and prepared them with a halter round their necks for the coming of Hitler.

If the subjectivism that showed in every one of their films for fourteen years had not been spread around, if instead a healthy outlook had been engendered, the patent irrationality and falsity of the Nazi doctrine could never have succeeded in gaining acceptance. Hitler never conquered. The people just gave themselves up.

If in England you start the public advocacy, through the most powerful medium in the world, of one kind of social anarchy and anti-social behaviour, such as the snatching of other people's beds and other people's wives, how long will it be before you take the next logical step, the snatching of other people's property and jobs on the cock-and-bull excuse of 'Jews'?

What is the significance of this advocacy of anti-social behaviour in English films?

For consider the avalanche of murders and thefts in second feature films. Consider the humiliations in *South Riding*, the beating and authoritarianism in *The House-master*, the unconscious heartlessness in *Convict 99*.

Consider:

I'll spank you till you can't sit down.
Women are made for the comfort and solace of men.
The sooner men take out the whip again the better.

How is it that these characteristics, which have never appeared in English films before, are now coming upon us in full flood?

We can say from the start that Mr. Alexander Korda and Mr. Charles Laughton, in their own persons, are entirely innocent of any deliberate intention to further this trend. We know that both have the deepest interests of the English film and the English scene at heart. We know that there is not a single responsible executive in England's film world who would wish to see our social life deteriorate. It is therefore of the highest importance that this trend should be brought out into the light of consciousness.

We have in this country the finest technical resources, and some of the world's best craftsmen and players. It remains, therefore, for those in responsible positions in the film industry to reverse the trend which we have seen to exist before we are all over the cliff.

The trend can be reversed and our films can be made enjoyable and widely acceptable in this as well as in every country in the world. It can be reversed by discarding the lorgnette and looking at the world from the viewpoint of the people.

It's as simple as that.

XXIII

IN order to confirm and deepen our understanding of the thread of subjectivism so clearly to be traced in the English film to-day, we shall find it extremely illuminating to survey the development of the German film from its inception before the war, through the post-war years to the present day.

This examination may be helpful in strengthening a desire to arrest a tendency that certainly proved dangerous for Germany and for Europe.

The film, as we have seen, is the most dynamic cultural medium that has ever appeared in human history. It is a reflection of the social scene through the minds of those engaged in film production. It has this in common with every other preceding cultural medium, that it is not only a reflection of the present, but a preparation for the social epoch which is about to appear.

Through every phase of human evolution, this mental preparation for future action, the process we call culture, has taken place; and it has preceded every great new historical epoch. The works of Voltaire, Rousseau and the French Encyclopaedists prepared the way for action in the French Revolution, to give a well-known example.

Action is the core of life, and in men action is preceded by thought. In every period in history, men of intellect have related their thought to the objective world except and until about the end of the nineteenth century, when for the first time upon a widespread scale the idea began to gain ground that thought could exist for thought's sake, art for art's sake and culture for culture's sake.

This belief that culture and 'art' were ends in themselves, this separation of intellect from the so-called 'lower' activity in the mundane world, betrays a desire among a section of the intelligentsia to rest on their oars, to enjoy the fruits of liberal humanism bequeathed to them by the Renaissance and the French Revolution without reference to the future movement of society, in very much the same way as the pampered son 'enjoys' the wealth of his father who had to accumulate his fortune by getting down to it, and facing up to the real world.

A strong tendency set in, leading away from the objective world towards inner contemplation, introspection, subjectivism; from the unity of thought and action towards the separation of thought *from* action—thought above and action below.

This notion that there is such a thing as a division between the so-called higher and lower activities in human society achieved its Nemesis after only about half a century of development, with the coming of the Nazis, who represent the logical peak of subjectivism. Nazism took false intellectualism at its word. Since this doctrine claimed that culture had nothing to do with the mundane world, the first thing the Nazis did upon coming into power was to stage a public bonfire of books in the squares of all the university towns in Germany.

As Field-Marshal Goering has said: 'Whenever I hear the word "culture," I reach out for my revolver.'

After that let no one be surprised that a famous English writer who for years has engaged in the apparently harmless pursuit of lovingly contemplating 'my garden,' gradually slides towards the prostrate worship of Fascism. It is an almost inevitable and logical development.

But, despite Goering, culture does not cease in Germany, it simply changes its direction, in the direction of the needs of Nazism. So we get *Der Ammenkoenig*, which is as clear an official directive for having babies indiscriminately as anything could be.

The main stream of the German film did not achieve any great importance except when three tributaries began to flow into it, the Russian, the Swedish and the Danish film. In Sweden, the Svenska Biograph Company was established in 1909 and immediately exerted a great influence upon the European cinema, which lasted until about 1929, especially in Germany.

The coming of the talkies and the language difficulty undermined the position of the Svenska Company, but in the year 1912 it was at a point of advance. In that year a new studio was built and two actors were engaged, Stiller and Sjoestrom, who soon became film directors and who did much to give the Swedish film its original poetic and literary character, for which it became world-famous in a very short time.

The Danish film industry proper began in 1906 with the Nordisk Film Company in Copenhagen. The products of this company came into great demand almost immediately. There were two subjects that proved so popular that they were made several times over. These were *The Four Devils* from Herman Bang's novel and *A Marriage under the Revolution*, based upon a popular play. The abortive Russian Revolution of 1905 had evidently made a deep impression upon sensitive Scandinavia, to judge by the success of this picture. One film, *At the Prison Gates*, sold as many as two hundred and fifty copies all over Europe.

Both the Danish and the Swedish films were usually based upon novels or plays which formed the dominant cultural trend of the time, deriving from the strong liberal humanism of the Scandinavian group of novelists and playwrights.

Altogether it is very difficult to separate the Swedish and Danish films, because they derive essentially from the same source and their development was very similar. Their dramatic intensity, the scenery, the fresh air, their poetic quality, were greatly esteemed in Germany and in France.

They were well circulated in England, but they were not so well appreciated here as they were on the Continent. The mood of industrial England was one for action, fast tempo, movement. People expected a story to come to the point. When the average story lasted only fifteen to twenty minutes in the telling, English audiences on the whole were rather impatient of the slow contemplative introspection with which the Scandinavian films were imbued. Not for us were the carefully composed shots, the wide sweep along the drive to an aristocratic Swedish mansion, the slowly opening luxurious-looking french windows, whence emerged one of the characters, deeply wrapt in thought, and in this state of contemplation, slowly walking down the beautiful, wide, stone steps, slow tread by slow tread. It is highly significant that this type of introspective picture should have found greater point of contact in Germany than in England at so early a date.

There was one truly worthy contribution that the Danish film made towards the common stock, and this was in the style of acting popularized by Asta Nielsen. She exercised a restraint and an austerity infinitely more impressive and intelligent than that of the Italian players, whose conception of acting was taken over from the bel-canto tradition of Italian opera.

Years later, in Germany in 1925, Asta Nielsen and Greta Garbo appeared together in *Joyless Street*, directed by G. W. Pabst. Throughout her screen career Asta Nielsen in film after film developed the typically European screen character: a beautiful woman, sensitive, intelligent, in the toils of an implacable fate.

How tenacious the European social consciousness must have been we can see when we consider that, from first to last, in every film in which Greta Garbo has appeared over a long period in the U.S.A., she has remained faithful to this type of character.

In the immediate pre-war and post-war days of uneasy questionings, this type of character established by Asta Nielsen was exceedingly popular on the Continent. She displayed the sensitive humanism of the North with the imagination, reflectiveness, sorrow and sympathy that is so fully expressed in the work of Björnson and Ibsen, Sigrid Undset and Knut Hamsun.

The pity of it is that this trend should have developed into morbid self-examination, twisted conceptions, despair and a throwing up of the hands when the Germans took over the lead in the European film world from the Scandinavians.

When we look at the titles of some of the films in which Asta Nielsen appeared, we see the principle again confirmed, that they indicate the mood of the films and of the social consciousness from which they sprang:

> *The General's Children*
> *The Black Dream*
> *The Strange Bird*
> *Vertigo*
> *The Power of Gold*
> *Poor Jenny*

The titles seem to express the conflict in the minds of a highly-civilized people, sensitive to the beautiful scenery of their own native land where life could be worth living, who were yet compelled to watch, in a closely neighbouring country, another great people living in tension and engaged in an arms race with England. In these films we see the menaces of power and gold and social decline for

190

FEVER,
directed by
Louis Delluc
(French)

THE STREET,
directed by
Karl Grune
(German)

THE EXILES,
directed by
Victor Sjostrom
(Swedish)

The gloom in post-war European film production in the early 1920's

an innocent people who deserve everything, but who seem to be buffeted by a heartless destiny.

Only in one other country do we find similar tendencies appearing in films, and this is in the pre-war Russia of Tolstoy, Tchechov, Dostoievsky and Gorki. The Italian film industry, which until the outbreak of the war was the strongest in Europe, was largely concerned in the development of the film from the historical, spectacular point of view. The glories and magnificence of ancient Rome, the splendour of the Italian painters and sculptors, still dominated the cultural consciousness of Italy.

There was also the prestige enjoyed by Italian opera. From these sources the Italian film drew its characteristics. It recreated the past in motion pictures with a vast sweep and grandeur. People thrilled at being able to look at the historic past for the first time. The cinema made history live for the common people, and the public appetite for films like *Cabiria* and *Quo Vadis* was truly enormous. But once the main aspects of treatment, spectacle and feature length of film, had been absorbed by the American cinema, Italian influence began to decline and gradually ceased altogether in Europe.

On the other hand, the pre-war Russian cinema, like that of Scandinavia, flowed directly into the post-war European film. It was based on the stories of the Russian novelists and on the Russian theatre, which utilized the naturalistic and advanced dramatic technique of Stanislavsky and the decorative genius of Bakst in the Moscow Art Theatre.

Touriansky made films of *Mozart and Salieri* and *The Brothers Karamazov* with the actors of the Moscow Art Theatre. The salient features of these films were the careful pictorial composition deriving from the theatre, and the pessimism, darkness and introspective individualism taken over from the Russian novel, which was the expression of the profound cleavage in Russian life itself. There was

191

always that overhanging shadow of a barbaric, mediaeval, monarchical authority and an enormous bureaucracy riding like a juggernaut over the human rights of a vast Continent.

Besides those already mentioned there were other films such as *The Alchemist*, *What the Forest Said* and *The Suicide Club*. Again the titles speak for themselves.

Puppet films which conformed to the main characteristics of the Russian film were made by Starevich. They were dark, grotesque and highly subjective. One of these, *The Grasshopper and the Ant*, was shown to the Tsar in 1913. Starevich left Russia for France after the Revolution. Subjectivism can have nothing in common with a period in which millions of people are facing the real world anew, and are grappling with objective problems.

In Paris, Starevich continued to make puppet films, of which *The Mascot* and *The Ringmaster* have been fairly widely shown in England, but these films still retain the morbid, introspective manner of his earlier productions.

In contrast with the grotesque animals of one person's imaginings that we see in the work of Starevich, the lively gusto of Disney's creations, studied from real life, have swept all before them.

In the cartoon, as in the main fictional film, the Americans have shown their faithfulness to real life and their appreciation of the fact that the cinema is a co-operative medium and not suited to the expression of one mind only. With their determinist, objective outlook, they have succeeded where so many others have failed.

The immediate heirs of the Swedish, Danish and Russian reflective films were the Germans, who carried the subjective tendency so strongly marked in these films very much further. *The Cabinet of Dr. Caligari* represents the beginning of this trend, coming, as it did, from the very bottomless pit of the agony of war. The social fabric of Germany

192

SNOW WHITE AND THE SEVEN DWARFS
Walt Disney's full-length feature film   (*R.K.O. Radio*)
Note characteristic animal expressions

THE MASCOT, a puppet film by Starevitch, whose method is the opposite
of Disney's

had been so strained by the war years, by famine and blockade, by an abortive social revolution, and the national spirit had been so oppressed by the peace treaties, that the cultural life of Germany was frustrated and twisted to its very roots.

No entirely healthy cultural expression could come from such a soil. The abysmal pessimism and brooding introspection that characterized the first films made in Germany after the war, represented the mood of the German intelligentsia as a whole.

The Cabinet of Dr. Caligari represents the lowest depth of depression in the German social consciousness. In this picture you see reflected the irrationality and confusion of a society sick unto death. Germany never quite recovered from this social sickness, and as we mark the progress of the German film from year to year we shall observe that the elements of Caligarism were present in nearly every one of their major productions. At the same time, it is interesting to note that as year by year we move further away from the year 1919, there occurs a greater effort towards clarity, a struggle towards the light.

This struggle, however, did not turn out successfully. By 1930–32 the German film had sunk back into the worst form of Caligarism, and even lower, for by that time we find more than one film ending in complete depression and the death of one of the chief characters by suicide. Let us first trace the development year by year by means of the film titles.

1919	*The Cabinet of Dr. Caligari*	Wiene
	Madame Dubarry	
	Anne Boleyn	
1920	*Sumurun*	Lubitsch
	The Flame	
	Shattered	Pick
	The Golem	Galeen

1921	*Waxworks*	Leni
	Genuine or *The Bloodthirsty Priestess*	Klein
	Destiny	Berger
1922	*The Earth Burns*	Murnau
	Warning Shadows	Robison
	Dr. Mabuse	Lang
	Nosferatue (Dracula)	Murnau
	Vanina	Von Gerlach
	Lucrezia Borgia	Oswald
1923	*The Street*	Gruene
	Raskolnikov	Wiene
	Fredericus Rex	Učkicky
1924	*The Nibelungs*	Lang
	Nju	Czinner
1925	*Tartuffe*	Murnau
	The Last Laugh	Murnau
	The Joyless Street	Pabst
1926	*Vaudeville*	Murnau
	Student of Prague	Galeen
	Metropolis	Lang
	Berlin Ruttman (Documentary)	
	Faust	Murnau
	At the Edge of the World	Gruene
1927	*The Spy*	Lang
1928	*Girl in the Moon*	Lang
1929	*The Wonderful Lie*	Schwartz
	Ueberfall (Attack)	Metzner
	Secrets of the Soul	Pabst
	Diary of a Lost Girl	Pabst
	White Hell of Pitz Palu	Pabst
	Mutter Krausen	Jutzi
Talkies	*The Blue Angel*	Von Sternberg
started	*Rasputin* (with Conrad Veidt)	
1930	*Westfront 1918*	Pabst
	Kameradschaft	Pabst
	Kuhle Wampe	Dudow

1931	*Emil and the Detectives*	Lambrecht
	Dreigroschenoper	Pabst
	Brothers Karamazov	Otsep
	Maedchen in Uniform	Sagan
	Flute Concert of Sans Souci	Uckicky
	Congress Dances	Pommer
1932	*Morgenrot*	Uckicky
	M.	Lang
	Träumende Mund (with Eliz. Bergner)	
		Czinner

There were, of course, many hundreds of other first and second feature films produced in Germany during this period, but the point to remember is that the above represented the peak of German filmic expression in each year: they were the examples upon which the lesser German films were modelled, just as the lesser films in any country will tend to model themselves upon the biggest film winners emanating from that country.

The list commences with *The Cabinet of Dr. Caligari*, and it is a misfortune that 'Caligarism' remains a basic ingredient in the atmosphere of the German film, until what had been prepared, unwittingly perhaps, in the minds of the German people was consummated with the appearance of Caligarism in real life, in the shape of Nazism enthroned.

Let us see how it happened.

Starting at the head of the list, it will be observed that the darkness of *Dr. Caligari* is set against what may at first sight appear a brighter trend in *Madame Dubarry* and *Anne Boleyn* made by Lubitsch, but a moment's reflection will suffice to show that these two films are as subjective as *Dr. Caligari*.

In *Madame Dubarry* the central character is seen, horrorstruck, upon a scaffold in front of a guillotine, a crowd below shaking their fists in execration. *Anne Boleyn* is the well-known tragedy of a person losing her life at the whim of a king. Thus you have in both these pictures an unconscious interpretation of the German scene of the year before, when millions of people had had their lives crippled or destroyed as if they had been the playthings of Kaisers and Princes.

Sumurun and *The Flame* follow the same Lubitsch trend as far as decorative externals and costuming are concerned, but the underlying introspection and unconscious self-pity are unmistakable. *Sumurun* tells the story of an eastern potentate, also with power of life and death over his subjects, and *The Flame* is set in the Europe of about 1870. Notice the significance of such titles as *The Flame*, *The Earth Burns* and *Shattered*. They have much in common with Karel Čapek's play *R.U.R.*, which ends with the world in disaster.

With *The Golem*, *Genuine (The Bloodthirsty Priestess)* and *Destiny*, we are again back to the authentic *Dr. Caligari* trend. *The Golem*, based on an old Central European legend, is a graven image that comes to life to avenge a people. In every one of these three pictures is suggested a common underlying motif: poor, helpless, self-pitying man in the clutches of a destiny that deals him cruel blow after blow, that he cannot fathom, that he cannot even see. And as in *The Cabinet of Dr. Caligari*, there are streets of queer twisted gables, darkness, fog, clocks, chemists' retorts and human skeletons.

If it is permissible to describe the Caligari and the Lubitsch trends as thesis and anti-thesis in the early German film, we may say that *Waxworks* represents the synthesis of these two influences, for in this film you see them merged. *Waxworks*, like *Dr. Caligari*, starts off in a fair-ground. The fair-ground is a symbol which is often to be met with in markedly subjectivist films, not only in Germany but in every country in the world, including America. A notable U.S. example is *City Streets*, directed,

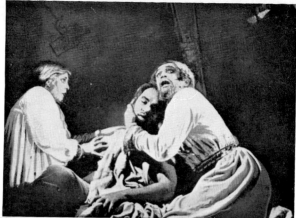

Conrad Veidt
as Ivan
the Terrible

Werner Krauss
as
Spring-heeled
Jack

Emil Jannings
(on right) as
Haroun-al-
Raschid

WAXWORKS (German, 1921), directed by Paul Leni

as was to be expected, by a European, Reuben Mamoulian. In a fair-ground everything is moving, many things are chancy, people are whirled around by a force not controlled by themselves—at somebody else's will—and they end up dazed.

In the *Waxworks* fair-ground there is an exhibition tent owned by a character who has the same queer stooped appearance as Dr. Caligari himself. At night (it is always at night), a young man approaches him and offers to write stories about the different characters represented by the different wax figures in the exhibition. With an old-fashioned lantern in his hand, throwing strange shadows about the waxworks exhibition, the proprietor shows the prospective author first a figure of Ivan the Terrible, then of Spring-heeled Jack, who is a kind of Jack-the-Ripper, and finally of Haroun al-Raschid.

Again we see subjectivism personified in an all-powerful, fantastically sadist monarch and in the equally incredible, ruthless murderer, Spring-heeled Jack, who is the same type as Caligari's assistant, Cesare.

The anti-thesis to these two is the semi-comic, bizarre character of Haroun al-Raschid, played by Emil Jannings.

The author retires to his desk, lifts his pen and writes the stories of these three characters in turn. As he begins the figure of Ivan the Terrible comes to life. The scene dissolves and you see Ivan the Terrible, played by Conrad Veidt, in the Kremlin at Moscow: domes of the most bizarre shape and angle, and gloom everywhere. You see him practising the most cruel sadism. You see his utter callousness, his deception of the people, his claim to the bride of one of his courtiers, and finally his pitifully mad end, when he eternally turns over an hour-glass upon which his name has been written by an enemy, for fear that if the sands run out he will die, in the manner his astrologer has predicted.

As this episode ends, the author wakes up with a start,

to find himself in a long tunnel that twists in all directions, with all kinds of cubist formations appearing and dissolving. He runs and staggers back horror-struck as the round-faced, expressionless, unthinking figure of Spring-heeled Jack moves upon him relentlessly. But this episode appears to have been a bad dream, too, for he wakes up with a start once more and finds himself confronted by the waxworks proprietor holding the costumed wax arm that had become detached from the figure of Haroun al-Raschid. He asks the author to write a story to explain how Haroun al-Raschid lost his arm.

Who can doubt that these episodes in *Waxworks* and the hundreds of films that appeared in a similar vein, were the expression of the social subconscious mind? For consider what had been happening in Germany. Karl Liebknecht and Rosa Luxembourg had been murdered, but although their death was mourned by millions of people it was never seriously investigated, and the murderers were never brought to justice. Foreign minister Rathenau is murdered. Political murders—the 'Fehme' murders—were everyday occurrences, but their perpetrators seemed to be protected by some unknown power. Hitler, following his first, abortive *putsch*, was mysteriously released from prison after a few months, and was able with impunity to warn his opponents that 'their heads would roll in the dust,' and to rejoice his supporters with promises of 'the night of the long knives.' Did authority connive at these things, or was man incapable of exercising any real authority? Were these happenings simply the portents of a hideous and reasonless destiny which nothing could avert? Such was the atmosphere of the Weimar Republic. Was it any more sane or reasonable than the nightmare world of *Waxworks*? . . . .

The author begins again to write as the figure of Haroun al-Raschid comes to life, and the scene dissolves to the courtyard in the palace in Bagdad where Haroun al-

Raschid is seen playing chess with his courtiers, with the Grand Vizier in attendance.

The whole of this episode is enacted as if in forced comedy, a fantastic charade. To see this part of the film to-day is to see a people trying hard to laugh boisterously around a sick-bed. In this last episode the author is the humble baker who has a very handsome wife.

Haroun al-Raschid is a tyrant of the same despotic calibre as Ivan the Terrible. He, too, exercises the power of life or death over his subjects. Nevertheless, the story is toned down to be a little more acceptable to the spirit of comedy. Haroun al-Raschid is in the habit of going about at night incognito to 'solace the lowly and comfort the lovely.' Upon the recommendation of the Grand Vizier, who describes the baker's wife to him with many sly winks and comic gestures, Haroun sets out to visit her while the baker is away from home. The same idea of the ruler's prerogative as in the Ivan the Terrible episode, but carried out in comedy form. That which seemed most lovely and sacred, the treasure of life itself, is ruthlessly commandeered by the sadistic monarch. The baker has only this one treasure, but Haroun al-Raschid, who has everything, seeks to deprive him of it.

Directed by Robison, *Warning Shadows* represents again the escape trend seen in the work of Lubitsch, in that it is set in the eighteenth century. It is a most vivid portrayal of a man eaten up with jealousy and tortured by the thought that his wife may have been unfaithful. The jealous husband, the wife and the three suspected lovers are seated round a banqueting table when a travelling showman presents himself at the door and is allowed to come in to entertain those assembled.

The entertainer takes out some silhouette figures from his carpet bag, candles are extinguished, and in the manner of the re-enacted murder in *Hamlet*, the story of the jealous husband, the wife and the three suspected lovers is given in shadow play upon the wall. The shadow performance merges in a very curious way to a dream-play of the real characters, at the end of which the husband is on the point of running a sword through his wife in a fit of jealousy, while she is bound to the table. At this point all the characters gradually awaken and discover with relief that it was all a dream.

How else can the coming into existence of a production like *Warning Shadows* be explained except as the reflection of the social subconscious of a nation consumed with doubts and fears?

Observe the nature of the films that follow in the list given. Notice that right until the end of the silent period, pictures are made with one central character who is either a split personality, a Jekyll and Hyde, or a person who pretends to be what he is not, or one who is the sport of an inscrutable fate. In the first category we have already seen Dr. Caligari, Cesare, Spring-heeled Jack and Haroun-al-Raschid.

There is also Dr. Mabuse, who is both a doctor and a criminal, Nosferatue, at once human and a vampire, Lucrezia Borgia, who is both the head of a reigning house and a wholesale poisoner.

The Student of Prague is the story of a young man assailed by doubts and fears in an atmosphere of gloom and trees waving in a storm at night. He sells his shadow to the Sinister One for gold, and becomes also the possessor of supernatural powers which give him such skill with the duelling sword that he kills one opponent after another, spreading fear among his fellow students. In the end his shadow is returned to him, but his joy ends with death as he shoots at his own reflection in the mirror.

The story of *Faust*, the film made by Murnau, is too well known to need repetition. The spy in Lang's film is another character who is not what he pretends to be on the surface, and is responsible for all manner of treacheries.

Lang's *Metropolis* deals with a fantastic and terrifying world of the future, but there is also a human being made synthetically in a laboratory, who, like Frankenstein, becomes uncontrollable.

The sly hypocrite who pretends to be a saint, Tartuffe, created by Molière, is played by Emil Jannings with infinite depth of sinister cunning.

The Last Laugh is a picture that reaches the utmost limit of self-pity. And it also represents the Fuehrer principle *in excelsis*, for in this picture there is no other important character at all from beginning to end except the proud and resplendently uniformed hotel commissionaire, who, because of old age, falls from grace and becomes the lavatory attendant.

The pre-occupation with self which is the chief characteristic of the jealous husband in *Warning Shadows*, is turned in a slightly different direction in *The Last Laugh*. Here the ex-doorman is seen going through all the sufferings of morbid introspection and wounded pride because he, *He*, once so proud in his glorious bemedalled uniform, the centre of admiring attention, has been dealt such a cruel blow by an unthinking fate, and is now obliged to bend low and scrub floors in a lavatory.

This part was uncannily well played by Emil Jannings. Is it not clear that subjectivism, which is the anti-social pre-occupation with self, finds one of its compensations in a childish penchant for uniforms, black or brown, with or without buttons?

There is an unmistakable link between this kind of unhealthy pre-occupation in German culture and the subsequent establishment of the Third Reich. Is not General Goering the highest expression of this aspect of pathological subjectivism? Are not his uniforms the subject of Homeric laughter right round the world?

In *Fredericus Rex* you get the Fuehrer principle together with escape into the eighteenth century once more.

You get self-pity in *The Joyless Street*, sadism in *Ueberfall*, the sense of dazed loneliness in *The Diary of a Lost Girl*. In *Vaudeville* you see Emil Jannings again concerned with self-adulation, but this time he shares the exercise with another, a woman, with whom he experiences all manner of love trials and tribulations against a circus background. The heights of 'splendid isolation' to which he had climbed in *The Last Laugh* will never be repeated. Such an achievement occurs only once in an epoch.

At the Edge of the World and *The Girl in the Moon* are films preoccupied with universal disaster and with escape. The escape motif dominates *The White Hell of Pitz Palu* and the story of *Pandora's Box* is well known. In *Secrets of the Soul*, as might be guessed, you get introspective doubts and questionings of the most vivid character imaginable.

Towards the end of the silent period, a film appears with a strange new development, an ominous and terrifying augury of what was about to happen to the people of Germany. This is *Mutter Krausen*. The original title, deliberately ironical, was *Mutter Krausen's fahrt ins Glueck*, which may be colloquially translated *Mother Krausen's Journey to Heaven*. This film appears to have been sponsored by a group with Left Wing sympathies, for it has all the marks of a sincere desire to present the case for the poor and downtrodden. But, as we shall see, this desire was sadly mis-directed, with the consequence that the effect of the film upon an audience was the exact opposite of the one intended.

Mutter Krausen is a widow in the poorer district of Berlin, prematurely aged, face deeply lined, eyes expressive of years of patient suffering. She lives in a sparsely-furnished room in a block of flats surrounded by people on the very edge of subsistence. The last few months of her life are traced in the film.

The humiliated doorman degraded to the position of lavatory attendant

Emil Jannings in THE LAST LAUGH, directed by Murnau

(*U.F.A.*)

During this period, every kind of personal and family misfortune that could happen to a working-class widow happens to her. As in every German picture we have looked at, the story is told through this one person, the central character, who is like the anvil upon whom the hammer-blows of fate fall relentlessly with devastating effect. We see from this that even the progressives in Germany found it impossible to extricate themselves from this method of presenting a social problem, a method which seems to have gripped the minds of the intelligentsia like a vice.

But the progressives in this picture excelled themselves, for, as the film nears its close, Mutter Krausen places her head in the gas-oven and ends her life.

Mutter Krausen journeys to heaven.

The effect of a suicide upon an audience, when it is shown upon the screen, is devastating and lasting. You may forget every other circumstance of a picture, but the actual, living portrayal of a person's self-destruction is something that leaves an indelible scar upon the mind.

In *Mutter Krausen*, the German intelligentsia, floundering in a sea of subjectivism themselves, can think of nothing better to do than to present to a harassed, nerve-wracked and therefore highly suggestible people the idea of self-destruction, in this living dynamic form, the film.

The intelligentsia, it seems, had not realized the essential nature of the cinema. The medium was new to them, and they unthinkingly brought to the film the personal, individual outlook of the individual working at his craft, the painter, the novelist, the composer.

That this new social medium required a different approach had never occurred to them. In addition, they carried on faithfully the tradition of Caligarism upon which the whole German film industry seems to have been based. In doing this, in playing with this toy, in relieving the oppressions of their own subconscious, they were like children playing with dynamite.

With this, the first suicide to appear in a realist form in a German film, the progressive forces of Germany had taken one of the first steps towards their own extinction. For following this film, and just before the coming of Hitler, there appear still more vivid suicides in the yet more vivid medium, the talkie.

Der Träumende Munde, with Elizabeth Bergner, ends in a suicide. *Maedchen in Uniform* ends on the brink of suicide. And the progressive film, *Kuhle-Wampe*, beats the lot. Made by co-operative effort and with voluntary workers assisting, this film, instead of ending with a suicide, begins with one.

The German people were indeed being well prepared for January 1933.

The essence of Caligarism is the triumph of the subconscious, of anarchy, of something which has no point of contact with ordinary social behaviour.

In 1919, a section of the intelligentsia who were dreaming aloud had placed in their hands, for the first time in history, a medium which was in fact a Frankenstein which would destroy its creators. Hundreds upon hundreds of technicians and directors who had been engaged in the perpetuation of Caligarism in the minds of the German people now find themselves scattered in exile over the world, victims of that Cesare of Caligarism that they unleashed throughout the fourteen years of the Weimar Republic.

There were streaks of Caligarism in certain post-war schools of the Russian and the French cinema. There were even traces of it in the English cinema, and more than a few traces of it in the American cinema. But no other country has such an unvarying record of the bizarre, of twisted amorality, darkness, recurring shadows, the self-examination and the self-pity that Germany can show with such overwhelming persistence.

In England, these films could only find an echo of response when they came in contact with the same wavelength in a very small section of London society. One or two showmen in working-class districts, willing to try anything once, put on *The Cabinet of Dr. Caligari*. In many cases it was withdrawn after the first matinée performance. The healthy-minded audiences, with their healthy objectivity, would have none of it. There is something deeply significant in the fact that none of the German silent films, not even *The Nibelungs*, made any impression upon the average English audience. In Germany, however, these films circulated among all classes.

Despite the fact that a good proportion of the cinema offerings in Germany were of American origin, with the clean clear air of the prairie about them, and with their objective gaze upon the world, the American film seems to have made no impression upon the German films of self-obsessions through all the long years.

The Germans, however, did have a certain influence upon the American film, not only in technique of camera angle and lighting, but in subjective outlook.

XXIV

WE have said earlier that the average audience will never feel inclined to copy the anti-social behaviour of a screen character, the vamp, the Western bad man, the society villain or the gangster. This is true because the real nature of these characters, their anti-social nature, is always presented as objectively real, and however far-fetched the situations may sometimes become, they have their being in a self-corrective real world.

As in the real world, anti-social behaviour carries with it its own retribution. In almost any American film there is a healthy balance between social and anti-social behaviour. That balance exists also in English films.

However subjectivist and self-conscious an English film may be—and most of them are—nothing has ever appeared in this country which was so devoid of any roots in the real world as were the early German films.

What was happening in the German cinema was simply this: the individual subconscious, which is anarchic, amoral, senseless and feelingless, which has no social ties and no moral obligations, was by continuous and persistent suggestion perpetuated as a living picture of the world on the broadest social scale. The anarchy, the complete anti-social self-wilfulness of the individual sub-conscious, was carried to the screen, and metamorphosed into a *living social reality*, to the minds of millions of people, who, through pain and suffering, had become invalids, ready to absorb into their own consciousness the message of Caligarism. The death that is spread abroad

206

by an unthinking Cesare, the relentless foreboding of death that is embodied in the moving figure of Spring-heeled Jack, concepts which envisage no counterbalance, no retribution for evil committed, have no counterpart in the English and American cinema, or in the cinema of any other country.

While such films were doing their work on the German social consciousness during the middle period of the Weimar Republic, young men in group formations and dressed in brown shirts were beginning to march through the streets, singing:

> *When Jewish blood spurts under the knife*
> *Everything will be well.*

Caligarism was stretching its limbs for action in the real world.

There is nothing in history to match this propagation of a gospel of unmitigated despair and destruction upon so vast a scale. When allowance is made for every exception it may still be said that throughout its history, and in all its forms, the Drama has balanced evil with good, and that its prevailing tendency has been to depict the ultimate triumph of the social good over the social ill. Caligarism, the portrayal of evil without redress, the cult of evil for evil's sake, is a new and terrifying phenomenon in the history of mankind.

Its importance can scarcely be over-estimated. For if it may be accepted that no form of expression is without significance or wholly without effect upon the general consciousness, how much more is this true of the cinema. Those sinister and grotesque shadows upon the German screen could be mechanically duplicated to an unlimited extent. They went into the crowded working districts, into the country towns, into the villages: and to the packed audiences seated in the darkness they were a reflection of the world about them, a philosophy of life; worst of all, an insidious and distorted expression of the fears and horrors hidden in their own minds. This was the mental food they were offered; this was the entertainment of the people. To grasp the significance of this is to understand many of the things that have happened in Germany since those films appeared.

In England and America to-day, film producers have the most magnificent opportunities men have ever had. To know what has happened in Germany and why it happened is to set about eliminating that ingredient in the English and American film, that element which, in its undiluted form, contributed to the establishment of Caligarism in real life. That ingredient is subjectivism, in all its anti-social forms. Even a small trace of it in a film tends to create that state of mind in a people which may lead them along the road that Germany has so tragically taken.

On the other hand, the elimination of every suspicious trace of *unconscious subjectivism* before a film is put into production will give health to the film and joy at the pay-box, for as the effect of the early German film on English and American audiences has shown, the healthy millions prefer the good and the sound to the spurious, the selfish, the dark and defeatist. Give the millions what is good and you can't go wrong. Let us study the needs of the customer and not be led away by the deceit and decay of spurious intellectualism, that ruined the social life of a great nation and made its film industry dependent on the rubber stamp of Dr. Goebbels' crazy 'Filmprufstelle.'

The reaction of the average *healthy* audience is always right. In the film industry, social good sense and good business go hand in hand.

XXV

BEFORE going on to an examination of the basic nature of the German sound film, let us look at the post-war films of France, to see what was happening during the time the German silent films were being made.

It is a commonplace that like conditions produce like effects. We find, therefore, that up to a certain point the French and German film resemble each other.

But beyond that point the French film displays a clearer objectivity, and is not so wholly concerned with introspection and despair as is the German film.

The reason for this is easily understood. In post-war France the impact of war upon the social consciousness was relatively less disastrous than upon Germany. The French suffered neither blockade nor defeat. The end of the war saw their territory free from the enemy.

Whilst in Germany there was utter desolation of spirit, there was at least a feeling of hope in France that a long period of peace was about to set in. Nevertheless, the torture that France had endured, the destruction that was everywhere, the deeply felt loss of loved ones, left its mark upon the social consciousness, and the sense of catastrophe was strongly expressed in the early French films at about the time the war ended.

In the same year that *The Cabinet of Dr. Caligari* was being made in Germany, Abel Gance was turning out *The Zone of Death*, *The Right to Live*, *Mater Dolorosa* (*Mother of Sorrows*), *J'Accuse* and *Tenth Symphony*. He then made *La Roue* (*The Wheel*). This title has the same importance in the symbolic expression of the social consciousness as the fair-ground. *The Vortex*, a play written in England by Noel Coward about the same period, may be placed in the same category of subconscious symbolism.

In the early 1920's, Louis Delluc made three films with these significant titles: *Thunder, Fever, Flood*. Each was expressive of pathos, dissatisfaction with life, illusion, the feeling that all is vanity. There was the same attitude of throwing up the hands in despair that we saw in Germany.

One point of great interest may be noted. The French films of the *Dr. Caligari* type, the type that reflects the deepest trough of social despond, did not arrive before about 1921.

The Germans knew the fruits of war when the war ended, but it took several years for the first flush of victory and elation to evaporate from the French, before they began to suspect that the peace was possibly only an uneasy interval between one war and the next.

The difference in the nature of the social consciousness between Germany and France at the immediate cessation of the war may be gauged by the difference between *The Cabinet of Dr. Caligari* and the French serial film *Judex*, which came at about the same time. Directed by Louis Feuillade, it featured René Creste as Judex, the redresser of wrongs, who always escaped from the tightest situations after the most terrific struggles.

This serial was very popular with the French public. Judex was the male prototype of the woman wonder in the American serial of the type of *The Exploits of Elaine*. The American films circulated widely in France, and the healing influence of the Chaplins and the Westerns did very much to keep the French people from slipping into the greater depths of morbidity that had been reached in Germany.

Despite the fact that France had been invaded for nearly

four years, the impact of war was less severe upon France than upon Germany. The French had suffered no diminution of national pride. They had never been obliged to undergo the *ersatz* food and the semi-starvation which the Allied blockade had laid upon Germany. And so we find that in spite of the state of world war, the French were sufficiently buoyant to produce such films as the *Judex* serial and its predecessors such as *Two Little Kids* and *Chante Coq Ultus*. Yet very soon the sense of catastrophe, the frenzied questionings, the doubts and introspections, were to be reflected in the French film.

It was in 1921 that *La Roue* (*The Wheel*) was made, an amazing production, exceedingly long, which cost more than two and a half million francs. The story of *The Wheel* is of an engine driver who rescues a little girl from a train disaster in which her parents were killed. When the girl grows up both the engine driver and his son fall in love with her, but she is eventually married to another man, an engineer.

Catastrophe succeeds catastrophe. The engine driver goes blind. His son and the engineer husband are killed, leaving the blind father and the adopted but now widowed daughter alone. Maiming, disaster, frustration everywhere. We're all being swung around on this mad wheel of a world, and if we land on our feet whole, then we are lucky indeed.

Much of the work of other French directors portrays the same unconscious symbolism; the same reflection of the social state of mind. Here is a representative list of titles:

Germaine Dulac made: *Enemy Mothers*
                                    The Mysterious Geo
                                    The Tempest of Life
                                    Souls of Madmen
                                    The Happiness of Others

Mercanton made:	*The Torrent*
	Bouclette
L'Herbier made:	*L'Homme Du Large* (*Balzac*)
	Eldorado
	Don Juan and Faust
	Prometheus is a Banker
	L'Inhumaine
Baroncelli made:	*The Squall*
	Le Père Goriot (*Balzac*)
	Champi-Tortu
	The Dream
	The Midnight Carillon
	The Unknown Woman
	Island Fishermen
	King of the Sea
	The Return to the Land

In addition to the films already mentioned, *Thunder*, *Fever*, *Flood*, Louis Delluc made *Silence*, *La Fête Espagnol*, and *Black Smoke*. Without exception all these were films that betrayed a certain subconscious despair at the misfortunes of frail man, who, pitted against elemental forces and the madness of his own kind, seemed to have no means with which to defend himself.

The Russian *emigré* directors who had settled in France were in the grip of the same influence. In addition to the grotesque puppets of Starevich, we find films with titles such as:

> *Tempests*
> *A Child of the Carnival*
> *The Prosecuting Attorney*
> *House of Mystery*
> *Le Rouge et le Noir* (*Stendhal*)
> *Casanova*

In *Le Rouge et le Noir*, Mosjoukine, the handsome Russian actor, played the hero with much galloping through woods, revolutionary uprisings, duels, orgies and fights in taverns. In *Casanova* the same actor did battle with twelve enemies at once. Here is a remarkable difference between the subconscious expressed through the Russian *emigrés* and the conceptions of the German directors.

The Russians, despite exile and a sea of trouble, saw themselves fighting back, against a real enemy. There was none of that fatalistic and relentless killing that occurred in the *Student of Prague* for instance, when the student's arm in the duelling field is guided by some malevolent and supernatural force which destroys all who oppose it.

Other films made in France during this period are worth mentioning:

> *Le Vertige*
> *Le Diable Au Cœur*
> *Money*
> *The End of the World*
> *Crainquebille (Anatole France)*
> *Sense of Death*
> *The Shadow of Sin*
> *Towards The Light*
> *Jeanne D'Arc*
> *Crazy Ray*

Thus we get ingredients similar to those in the contemporary German film: fear, disaster, gambling with life, struggling against titanic odds, at the mercy of unseen, malevolent forces. But we do see a change towards a brighter outlook, towards social satire, and this makes its first appearance in *Crainquebille* directed by Jacques Feyder. In this picture Dr. Mathieu has a nightmare in which he sees a court-room filled with a sea of eye-balls looking down at the poor bewildered costermonger, Crainquebille. The judges are shown flying about in the shape of enormous birds, and the diminutive defendant is overshadowed by a colossal policeman. Here we see subjective symbolism for the first time brought into the service of social satire. *Jeanne D'Arc* in France may be compared to *The Nibelungs* in Germany. It was an escape from the worst effect of the post-war disillusion by going back to the story of an heroic Frenchwoman who, by her leadership, had saved France.

But it is *Crainquebille* which is of special interest to us, because it marks the point at which the French film was about to deflect its course from the path of Caligarism towards a clearer objective and an infinitely more healthy outlook. We can say that up to the moment when *Crainquebille* appeared the French and German film were both travelling upon the same road, but whilst the German film remained the faithful slave of Dr. Caligari, and landed the German nation into Nazism, the French film in branching off towards the path of social criticism was greatly instrumental in shaping the outlook amongst the French people which resulted in the formation of the Front Populaire. And just as we see a continual struggle within the French film, with its ever shifting relation of forces between the two ideological trends of subjectivism and objective reality, so we see later in real life the spectacle of young men strutting about dressed in the uniform of the Croix de Feu, worshipping at the shrine of an ego and a "leader," while at the same time the extremely powerful Popular Front movement was developing.

From the time *Crainquebille* appears, objective social criticism and social satire become more and more apparent in the French film. They hardly appear in the German film at all.

At the same time there is no sign that the French film has ever been able to shake off completely the depressing influences which were a legacy from the immediate post-

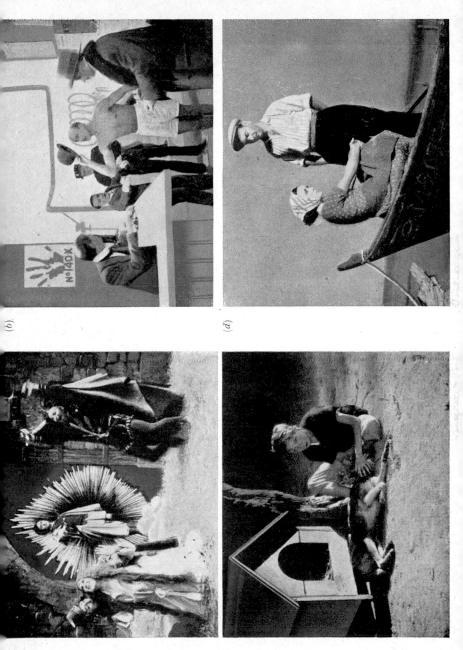

FOUR FILMS OF THE FRENCH SCHOOL

(a) FAUST, a Méliès production of 1905 (b) LE MILLION, directed by René Clair
(c) POIL DE CARROTTE, directed by Duvivier (d) TONI, directed by Jean Renoir

war years. In the same way, and for the same reason, France has been unable to shake off the subjectivism which still clings to the French body politic, and which strives to reach to the top in the way it did in Germany.

As a further illustration of the new branching off tendency towards a healthy objective social satire, we cannot do better than describe the first film made by René Clair, in 1924, with very few technical resources at his disposal. It was called *Paris Qui Dort*, but the title under which it became known in this country was *Crazy Ray*.

This picture opens by showing the caretaker of the Paris Eiffel Tower sleeping in his quarters right at the top of the Tower. He gets up in a leisurely way, stretches himself slowly and walks out on to the balcony to gaze upon a Paris which presents a most amazing and unusual appearance. The time is close upon mid-day, and yet everything in Paris is at a complete standstill.

The young caretaker, greatly perturbed, descends the Eiffel Tower and finds everybody and everything petrified, standing or sitting just as they were at a certain moment about three o'clock that morning. One old man is seen standing like a statue in the act of looking through a dust-bin. Another is an early morning reveller, leaning against a window-sill, with a fixed look of inebriation on his face. Yet another is standing on the edge of the Seine, hair dishevelled, about to throw himself into the river. Further on we see a thief with a watch and chain in his hand and a gendarme in hot pursuit—like a group statue. Most disconcerting!

Amid this city of deadness, he suddenly hears faint noises which increase as he comes across a small party of people who, like himself, were fortunate enough to escape this general immobility which has descended upon Paris. They welcome him as if he were a long-lost brother, and he is as glad to see them as they are to meet him. They have arrived that morning in an aeroplane, and like the caretaker, at the top of the Eiffel Tower, they must have been high enough up to escape whatever it is that has immobilized the rest of the city.

They all join forces and make the best of their opportunity, indulging in great revelry. All the restaurants are open to them, everything is free, money and jewels are to be had for the taking.

This condition of Paris is due to the work of a crazy professor, whom we see working in a comic laboratory with crazy retorts, glowing valves and levers. By pulling one of these queer levers towards him he sends out a ray which petrifies Paris on the instant. By pushing the lever in the opposite direction, all Paris starts up again from the exact point at which it was transfixed.

Between the world stopping and starting in this manner, the "live" group go through many entertaining adventures.

But it all ends well, because at the end all the gadgets of the mad professor are destroyed in a general mêlée between himself and his friends after a heated argument, and that is the end of the Crazy Ray.

In this picture we see an extraordinary resemblance to, and yet a strong divergence from, the German sub-conscious conception of Dr. Caligari, the malevolent. The crazy French professor exercises a similar power over the world, but he does it in a light-hearted manner and in a way that places fortune in the hands of a favoured few. Another point worthy of notice is, that the professor's power is derived from something *you can see*. The valves and levers may be burlesqued, but at least they are something intelligible.

The power of Dr. Caligari, on the other hand, is ruthless, uncanny, inexplicable, and mad to the end.

Observe the subjectivism of the opening shot in *Crazy Ray*; the one observer at the top of the tower, isolated from the rest of the world. He meets a party who are equally fortunate in having escaped the malady which has befallen the rest of the world.

He even sees the would-be suicide, but this incident is given a light-hearted twist when he thrusts a bundle of notes which he has picked up into the man's rigid hand. When everyone becomes alive again upon the withdrawal of the Crazy Ray, the would-be suicide, instead of taking the plunge for which he has been standing poised, notices his suddenly acquired wealth and dances with joy, thus making of the incident a decided bit of social criticism: that it is only the want of money which causes some people to think of suicide.

We see how clearly the two philosophic trends are unconsciously entwined in this one film. In all Clair's subsequent silent films, notably in *Les Deux Timides* and *The Italian Straw Hat*, we get the same curious intermixture, in the first the subjectivism of timidity and in the second, a small ingredient of sex intrigue at the beginning but in the main an excellent satire upon the habits and little foibles of the French middle class.

The subconscious of the later French silent film is expressed in some form of way-out of trouble, even if it is only the fantasy of suddenly acquired wealth. In the German subconscious there is hardly any way out at all, to judge by their earlier silent films; and their way out in the later silent and early talkie films is a socially reprehensible one. The disaster of inflation seemed to have crippled their idea even of the power of money.

By the time we come to the end of the silent period in both countries we see that the films that represent the two opposing peaks are illustrated by *Mutter Krausen* in Germany and *The Italian Straw Hat* in France.

No further comment is needed.

XXVI

AS we enter the era of the talkie in Europe we find
that the German and French films still continued on
the same paths along which we found them travelling at
the end of the silent period. If anything, the addition of
sound made the suicidal tendency of the German film
more pronounced than ever.

The French film, on the other hand, takes on more and
more the appearance of a projection of the Front Populaire
which was to appear in a few years, a Joseph's coat of
many colours, a patchwork of varying tendencies.

The examination of these two major tributaries, the
German and the French cinema, will be of great value to
us when we see their effect upon the American cinema,
which is the main stream of the world cinema. The trends
in Europe will offer us many lessons on how to correct that
disconcerting disharmony that seems to have been making
itself felt in many English and American productions,
especially those released about the period of Autumn 1938.

By using the main tendencies in the German and French
films as a kind of sextant with which to find our bearings
in the American film, we will be able, to some extent, to
measure that distinct wobble which has developed noticeably in the last year. This wobble only requires to be made
plain, to be brought to the level of consciousness, for it
to be corrected, for it is well to mention that 1936–37
showed a greater objectivity in the American film, a
greater cultural maturity and strength, than it ever possessed before. How to get the American film back on this

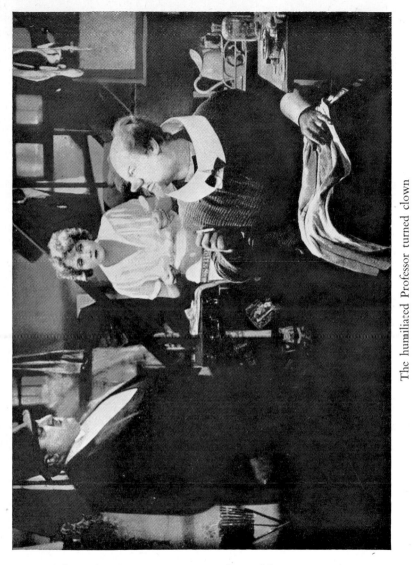

Emil Jannings in THE BLUE ANGEL, directed by Von Sternberg

(*U.F.A.*)

path is a problem the solution of which will provide the answer to the question of what is a good film, and what amounts to the same thing, good Box-Office.

One of the first German talkie films to be shown in this country was Pommer's *The Blue Angel*, directed by Sternberg.

If one takes a look at Central Europe to-day, after the Munich Agreement and its sequel, one can see it all in microcosm in this picture *The Blue Angel*. You get the shadow thrown across Europe no wider than a strip of celluloid, but with the heartlessness, the amorality, the lack of humanity that was to be projected into real life in a few years' time.

Recall that heart-broken professor (Emil Jannings), who falls in love with a selfish, calculating cabaret performer played by Marlene Dietrich. Recall the jeers and the horse-play of the students as they mock the poor old man; these students who deny to their teacher his own way of finding happiness and affection.

Recall the utter humiliation brought down upon the head of the old professor as he walks about as if in a daze, bedraggled and besmirched. Recall the sense of degradation this old man suffers when he is obliged to go round hawking photographs of his own ex-love amongst jeering café habitués, until he seems to be cruelly robbed of half his reason.

Note the characteristic so common in nearly all German films, the absence of a balancing retributory factor. In a French, English or American film some kind of balance is always to be seen. In an American film there is hardly ever such a thing as evil in the abstract. But *The Blue Angel* remains true to type. The professor makes no manly attempt to stand up to his persecutors. The boys, with no sense of shame or pity, jeer, and the café patrons jeer; but that's how the world goes, according to *The Blue Angel*.

No compassion. No balance. Nothing is set right at the

end of the picture. You are left limp in your seat with dismay. Caligari still stalks through the German film as he soon will through the social scene.

The Germans were still greatly absorbed in the contemplation of the split personality, in, for instance, *Rasputin*, the monk with the uncanny influence, who pretends to be a saint, has great influence at the Russian Court, and has a great time with the ladies.

The Brothers Karamazov follows faithfully in the Caligari trend. Feodor Otsep, who directed, had found his true spiritual home in Germany, where he could indulge his subconscious to his heart's content.

But surely a film with so excellent a title as *Kameradschaft* should show a little more hope for the future, a grand theme—*Comradeship*—the greatest, noblest story in the world—The Brotherhood of Man.

Here was an opportunity for something on the grand scale, here was a way of getting out of Caligari's clutches.

From a technical mechanical point of view the film was a pointer to future developments in technique, but the German film tradition is still adhered to, subjectivism still holds sway.

The story is set in a mining community on the Franco-German frontier. French and German miners are working on a single seam of coal on opposite sides of the frontier, deep down below the surface, when a disaster occurs on the French side, and the German workers crash through the frontier posts in a lorry to the rescue of French miners in distress. An excellent theme—the comradeship that transcends all artificial man-made boundaries at the call of humanity. But how is this theme handled?

The picture opens up with three German workers dressed in their best, intent upon spending a little leisure in a café on French territory. They take their seats in an atmosphere of French gaiety and dancing, and order beers.

One of the men approaches a French girl for a dance. Her escort resents the advance and there is an immediate bristling up and showing of teeth. It takes all the efforts of the other two Germans to prevent the incident from becoming a free-for-all fight. They retire to their own seats grumbling and grousing.

Thus, though the story is about comradeship, the audience gets its back up from the start, especially in Germany or France. The old Faust or Jekyll and Hyde conception of one man being two, is extended to show that mankind as a whole is like that; but whereas writers and playwrights for untold generations have always shown us the good side of a man first, the Jekyll first, followed by the Hyde, Pabst reverses the process by showing us the ugly mood of men first, to put us into an appreciative humour, presumably, for what is to follow.

But why show this incident at all?

The reason will be clear in a moment. When the disaster occurs on the French side, we are shown the German workers at first greatly perturbed, but incredible as it may seem, when one of them proposes to organize a rescue party, someone in the group says no, and there actually arises a polemical discussion as to whether to go or not! Of course, such a discussion under such circumstances never did or could happen; of course the workers do organize a rescue party and go to the assistance of the French miners.

But imagine putting this second negative idea into the minds of the audience. To save life or not to save life. Let's talk. Let's discuss. The old intellectualism comes to the surface in the twentieth century dynamic medium, the film. Fair's fair. We must have a discussion. Wobbly shakiness must be brought out, put into a film and broadcast, so as to leave the German people just as wobbly and undecided in the face of an approaching enemy. The German intellectuals have certainly done their unconscious work well.

But there is more than this wobble in the film. The pompous managing director of the German mine, too, has a calm talk with the managing director of the French mine over the telephone, and tells him how sorry he is. He will do what he can. *He* will do it! The German miners approach the managing director and, with cap in hand, tell him of their decision to go across with equipment. The managing director magnanimously consents. Thus all the formalities and the correctitudes are observed, though life is in danger, though every minute counts. Fair's fair. Let's stop on our way to pat the managing director on the back.

There is, too, a strong trace of the old pre-occupation with the individual mind. During the rescue operations, deep down in the mine, a French worker is seen in a state of collapse. As the German rescuer in a gas mask and rescue uniform approaches, the scene dissolves to the subconscious imaginings of the Frenchman who sees himself back in the trenches during the war years, grappling in a bitter life-and-death grip with a German soldier. This negative idea is bound to have had a derogatory effect upon a German audience.

A few weeks after the rescues, a joyous celebration is given when French and German gather together in the greatest friendliness, and speeches are made by representatives of both sides calling upon them all to sink their differences and to live in brotherhood in the future.

But while this is going on above ground, something else is taking place in the mines below. The frontiers are being re-established by officials in uniform.

Introspective intellectualism again fails to realize the dynamic nature of the film medium, and thinks it can afford to indulge in a little irony. While the workers celebrate, we see the point at which the German and French mines meet below ground being carefully blocked off with iron bars and concrete, to form a closed barrier.

Officialdom in the shape of a German Frontier officer on the one side of the barrier, and a French officer on the other side, politely click their heels, stamp certain papers, and exchange them. Then they salute, the formality is complete, and they depart. And there stand the iron bars, set in concrete, separating a people.

This incident, intentionally or unintentionally, has a most depressing effect. It has the same effect as the Prussianism of the old Headmistress in *Maedchen in Uniform*. It has the effect of putting in the mind of the audience yet another doubt to take home with them: of what avail is all this self-sacrifice to save others, international brotherhood, humanity and comradeship, if all that comes of it is, that the frontiers are once more sealed with cement and iron bars by heel-clicking officials on both sides? But, some may say, that is how it happens in real life. Supposing it does, must it therefore be perpetuated in the *minds* of the public? Should not a film about comradeship end on a note of rousing cheer and a message of hope to the people, instead of in an intellectual exercise of irony?

Pabst's *Westfront* 1918 is anti-war in sentiment, but it, too, carries with it many negative ideas, and ends in doubt, in a great big question mark as the film ends with the general assertion, 'we are all to blame,' by the innocent victims of war.

The *Dreigroschenoper* is credited with having been inspired by Gay's *Beggar's Opera*. But *The Beggar's Opera* was written in the eighteenth century with an eighteenth-century setting, and takes place in taverns and thieves' hide-outs *above ground*. Pabst gives his film a twentieth-century London setting, all the streets are dark and dreary, and most of the action is taken down into dark, deep cellars.

Why?

For the same reason that the theme of *Kameradschaft* goes below ground, that *Westfront* 1918 goes on in trenches and dugouts. For the same reason that his *Secrets of the Soul* goes below the conscious mind to the subconscious. For the same reason that Fritz Lang is fascinated by the subconscious of the Duesseldorf child-murderer in his film, *M.*, and that most of the thieves' conferences of the Duesseldorf underworld take place in a dark deep cellar in a derelict factory.

For the same reason that Czinner's *Der Träumende Munde* concerns itself with the subconscious of a woman torn between loyalty to her husband and affection for her lover, and for the reason that causes her to part from her lover during a thick fog, go through another fog to a riverside café, write her last despairing note to her husband and drop herself into the river.

We have to forgive them, for they knew not what they were doing in thus infecting millions of other harassed human beings with their defeatism and despair.

Congress Dances, produced by Erich Pommer, appears to promise a more light-hearted view of life. In common with the first talkies in U.S.A. and in other countries, the German film burst into song. 'Live, laugh and love, Laugh love and live.' But actually we are back full circle to the immediate post-war years when all was Caliphs, Emperors, Kings and Tsars. This time, in *Congress Dances*, the story is mainly about Tsar Alexander I of Russia who goes to the Vienna Congress of 1814. He has a double who executes his dull, official duties while the real Tsar has a good time in the company of the pretty shop-girl. Which is still another facet of the split personality obsession among the German film producers.

There is, in this film, an atmosphere of forced gaiety of the 'Eat, drink and be merry, for to-morrow we die' kind. Behind the glamorous scenes, the tuneful music, the elaborate and decorative costumes and the imposing palace interiors there is sadness and frustration. A man and a woman fall in love with each other, but because the man is a Tsar and the woman only a humble shop-girl, their respective positions deny them the right to marry. As usual in the German film, instead of the substance of a normal married life to which every couple is entitled, we get the shadow of the nostalgic looking back to a 'memory.' There had to be a heart-break of some kind.

There is one small but very significant incident in this picture. In spite of a published decree against throwing flowers at the Tsar of Russia when he travels through the streets of Vienna, the shop-girl (played by Lilian Harvey) throws a bouquet at the Tsar and is put into prison, where she is sentenced to a number of strokes with the whip. The Tsar arrives in the nick of time to prevent the sentence from being carried out. But just before he arrives the shop-girl is placed in the cell where the punishment is about to take place. Here you see the fellow whose task is to do the whipping setting about his present job with a carefully studied air of professional *élan*. With hardly suppressed glee and mock gentleness, he first firmly places the woman over the whipping-horse, fastens a belt over her to hold her down, and with a gloating and rubbing of hands and excited anticipation takes down the whip and handles it like a true and trusted servant. This whole performance is reminiscent of some incredible monster dripping at the mouth at the sight of its prey.

Lasting only two or three minutes, there is more concentrated sadism in this short sequence than there is in an average year's output from Hollywood. All very good propaganda for the future rule of the rubber truncheon and concentration camps, and none the less propaganda for being unconscious and unintended.

There is a similar incident, brief but ominous, in *Morgenrot* (Dawn). This film is about the submarine war from the German side. An enemy ship is sighted in the distance, orders are given, a torpedo is placed in position for firing. When the order is called out to fire, one of the sailors in charge of operations affectionately and smilingly pats the torpedo and in colloquial German says something like: 'Good luck, old boy, go on your way, and have a good time.'

That the German intelligentsia had no idea of what they were really doing, may be seen from the 'progressive' film *Kuhle Wampe*. Here was a film, sponsored, written, directed and financed by persons who were, every one of them, men of sympathy for the common people, sensitive and humane, and in their every-day lives anti-Nazi to the core. Here you would expect some kind of directive, some guide to social life, some attempt at least to get out of the slough of depression into which the rest of the German cinema had sunk.

But no. Fully three-quarters of the film is taken up with the most destructive, negative ideas imaginable. You are left too limp with dismay at the end of it to pay any attention to whatever message of hope the director has up his sleeve in the last quarter of the picture.

First you get headlines and figures in newspapers, showing millions of unemployed increasing month by month. This sequence dissolves, and you see a group of Berlin unemployed, hungry and cold, anxiously looking through the situations advertisements in the early morning editions. Then you see them on their cycles, travelling from place to place and being turned away. No hands wanted.

Right. That should be enough of the negative side to go on with, should it not? What is the film being made for, if it is not to offer a corrective, a balance to the social scene? If you must start off with a negative aspect, is not what we have already seen a big enough dose?

The reply is *no*. Our German left-wing intellectuals are determined to plug you with depression until you are almost fit to drop, unable to stand any more.

At the end of the day's job seeking, a mournful proces-

THE JOYLESS STREET, with Greta Garbo
A silent and a talkie film, directed by G. W. Pabst, illustrating the pre-Nazi path of despair

KAMERADSCHAFT

(*Nevo-Film*)

sion walks dejectedly home wheeling their cycles to the tune of mournful music played by a street musician. With this music as a background, Franz, an unemployed young mechanic, returns home tired and dejected, utterly depressed. He seats himself at the table, with his mind far away. Father has been reading out loud an item in the paper which tells of further official reductions in unemployment benefit. Father, Franz and his sister Anni sit round the table whilst the mother serves the food in an atmosphere of gloom. Above the fireplace a motto, freely translated, reads: 'Don't complain about the morrow—Love andWork go hand in hand.' Irony.

The talk is of nothing but the lack of work, rent in arrears, public assistance, bailiffs, eviction. The discussion leads to taunts from the father: 'Those who want work, those who are not lazy, can always find work.'

This leads to a quarrel, and the father walks out in disgust to chat with his cronies at a pub. Franz remains at home brooding. The sister and mother have to leave the house for a while. Franz remains alone. He raises himself slowly from the table, and with a look upon his face as of one already dead, slowly walks to the window, contemplates a flower on the sill, takes off his wrist watch, and with a last look round drops himself into the street.

A woman's piercing scream—and all is silent for a few moments. Nothing has been forgotten to make this scene as effective as possible, so that the will of the German people to face the world may be immobilized and paralysed. If there is a grain of constructive thought anywhere in the rest of the film its effect is less than nil, once this suicide has left its scar upon the mind.

Still the film goes on its relentless way. You are not spared anything about the suicide. Neighbours rush to the scene, ambulance and police arrive. The ambulance doors shut and away it goes. A few children gather in the street in a group and look up. One of them says pointing: 'It

227

was not from that window, or that one, but from that one over there.' There is a picture of a sorrowful woman neighbour standing in a mood of depression and saying:

The loveliest years of his life—one so young.
He had all life before him.

These words still echo as the picture dissolves to cornfields waving in the breeze, a babbling stream, a sunset through the trees. Franz will never see all this again. One can see how all-absorbed the intelligentsia were in introspection and morbidity: they seem unable to wrench themselves away from the consequences and accompaniments of a suicide. It must all go in to harrow your nerves to shreds.

But before the point and purpose of the film is achieved more trouble and sorrow is piled upon the heads of the characters. The family are evicted from their home. Whilst the furniture is being piled up in the street, you see a picture of a lawyer in cap and gown in a court-room who mumbles through the warrant relating to this eviction case. As he ends each paragraph or turns over a page he reads: 'Im Namen des Volkes.' 'In the name of the people.' More irony.

Fritz, a chauffeur in employment, is Anni's young man. The family is pursuaded by Fritz to go and live at Kuhle Wampe. Fritz borrows his master's car to transport the family to this place, which is a colony of campers near a wood outside Berlin, where Fritz and other workers manage to get along, living in tents throughout the summer.

The ideas derived from the method of the literary craftsman writing a book are now even more clearly put into the film, with depressing effect. The pros and cons, the doubts and hesitations, to marry or not to marry, the why and the how of every-day social behaviour may be legitimately thrashed out in a book, over pages and pages of reading where all the aspects, objective and psychological, may be piled up and examined by the reader at his leisure. But to employ the same method in a film is to court disaster. A book gives you a chance to exercise your imagination and to tone down first impressions in your own mind. A film like *Kuhle Wampe* gives no chance for the imagination to do any toning down anywhere.

The unmarried Anni, after a while, finds herself pregnant. Fritz is then seen talking to his work-mate, who advises him to marry her. But Fritz says he would rather have his freedom. Fair's fair. Even in a left-wing film, the negative ideas of sexual anarchy are permitted a platform.

The literary method is employed slavishly when you see Anni drooping at her condition, whilst the father, who has already lost a son, glowers over her and in his brutish way even suggests abortion. But despite all this wobbling, uncertainty and lack of firm approach to the subject, all this whether or not, they decide there will be a wedding.

And the wedding is celebrated in an enlarged tent at Kuhle Wampe, with crates of beer, sausages and cake. Again we are spared nothing of what happened or could happen in such circumstances—the beer-swilling taking effect, the drunken song, the drunken brawl, lurching, belching, bottle smashing, Fritz going off in dudgeon, and Anni left forlorn in her trouble. And nearly all of this action is given in the darkest manner, in the pitiful light of the camp or outside in the night-blackness.

What a way of presenting the Berlin working class! What a calumny! The Berlin poor are not, and never have been, like this. The heartless father and the wobbling selfish lover are monstrous distortions, and even if they existed they had no business to be put into the dynamic film medium, when the people of Germany were looking to the intelligentsia for some kind of positive, healthy, constructive lead.

For three-quarters of its length, the film thus deals with this one family. What happens next? The young people are shown joining in the activities of a Youth Sports organization. You see them indulging in all kinds of sport and races, the idea being to show that active co-operation in sports may teach them to co-operate in other spheres of life and thus improve their position.

But what happens to the older people, what is the solution to *their* problems? No answer. The older people are left out of the picture, completely forgotten. So far as they are concerned there is the same shrug of the shoulders that is implied in *Maedchen in Uniform* when the film ends in near suicide. Take it or leave it. That's that. That's how the world goes. You were in despair at the beginning of the picture, you are in the same state at the end, whilst the Chelsea of Berlin has been amusing itself making a 'progressive' film.

The picture ends with the youth marching home to a brave song. A group of them get into an underground train, and in one of the compartments a respectably dressed middle-class person reads out aloud from a newspaper that they are burning ship-loads of coffee in Brazil.

Fair's fair again. Would you credit that this sequence, which ends the film, finishes up in a cascade of words and still more words, and that someone who is apparently a Nazi sympathizer in the crowd, is made to say: 'Wenn wir Kolonien haetten . . .' 'If only we had colonies, how dandy everything would be!'

And so to the final fade-out, discussing, playing with their sub-conscious to the bitter end. The intelligentsia are unconsciously preparing for their own fade-out.

Just before Hitler came into power a film was smuggled out of Germany called *The Last Testament of Dr. Mabuse*. The split personality of Fritz Lang's silent days is back again, more powerful than ever, cunningly scheming, and finishing up with a dashing and a smashing and a burning, all the results of the workings of a mad but cunning brain. *The Last Testament of Dr. Mabuse!* Indeed, The Last Testament of the German Intelligentsia.

The fire in the American *In Old Chicago* ends with a vision of hope and reconstruction. But the fire that ends *The Last Testament of Dr. Mabuse* leaves everything in chaos and without hope, and it happens through the inscrutable workings of a mysterious 'mind.'

The Last Will and Testament of a destructive social philosophy.

XXVII

IT is indicative of the tendency that distinguishes the German from the French film of the talkie period, that by contrast with the German *The Blue Angel*, the first among French sound films to be shown in this country was *Sous les Toit de Paris* directed by René Clair. There is in this film a distinct air of a happy band of brothers settling down to make a picture with a spontaneity and joy which seems to lessen as the responsibility of making a film begins to weigh more heavily in successive productions.

In *Sous les Toit de Paris* we find none of the depression and the personal degradation to be seen in *The Blue Angel*. At the same time, there still exists an element of introspective subjectivism in the all-pervading darkness and the shadows of the background. From the uncertainty of life in the back streets, with its sharp vicissitudes and its skating on the thin ice of criminality, there emanates a strong feeling of sad disillusion, in spite of the fine sense for social comedy which is associated with the name of René Clair.

The title, too, *Under the Roofs of Paris*, has a subconscious significance similar to the cellars in the German films and titles like *Pandora's Box*. Things are not what they are on the surface. There is something hidden and unusual going on down below, just as there is something ominous contained in Pandora's Box.

René Clair did a great deal to show the rest of the film world that there existed a much more imaginative way of using sound in a film than had hitherto been suspected, and traces of his influence began to be visible in the American film a year or two later.

The element of comedy and healthy social criticism is to be found in every one of his subsequent French productions. In this connection, where will you find, in the work of any one German director, a list of titles with the bouyancy and healthy outlook of *A Nous la Liberté* (For us—Liberty), *14th July* (the date of the fall of the Bastille), *Le Million* and *Le Dernier Milliardier* (The Last Millionaire)? In the last-named film he takes a severely satirical hit at the pompous Fuehrer principle, showing to what a ridiculous pass the logic of this principle may bring people.

It is this healthy spirit evidenced in the work of René Clair which serves as a kind of forecast of the unity of varying social trends which was soon to find its expression in the Popular Front. Had a little of this outlook been present in the German film during the Weimar Republic, the scales might well have been turned by just that little which would have prevented the Nazis from coming into power.

Suggestion and auto-suggestion is just as effective upon the body politic, upon society generally, as it is upon the individual. But that suggestion has an effect ten times greater when presented in the living, moving picture at a cinema with subdued lights, while people are sitting in cushioned comfort and warmth, with their power of absorption at its maximum.

Clair's films were greatly effective because of this power of healthy suggestion. The part-subjectivism in his first film, *Crazy Ray*, which as we have seen was allied to objective comedy, became less in his succeeding films. There was so much which was normal and human and infectiously social in his portrayal of character, and in his style of humour, that by the time he came to make *Le Million* much of the darkness noticeable in *Sous les Toit* was dispersed. Friendliness, lightness, hope and social

233

living were reflected in its optimistic sequences, even though it dealt with a millionth chance of happiness in the winning of a first prize in a lottery.

Clair offers us no solution to the social problem, but in propagating hope among the French people he did his share in keeping them bouyant, resourceful and healthy in their social attitudes.

Thus the French cinema continued on its path, combining objective reality with varying degrees of intellectual introspection, although nowhere was that subjectivism so deep or so pernicious as that which reigned supreme in Germany. This intermingling of trends, expressive of the social scene in France, became as closely allied to the actual outcome of future social events as was the first expression of man's culture, the dance, when it preceded the battle or the hunt.

There is no mystery about it, nothing occult. The course of culture is the same, effect follows cause, and cause brings new and wider effects. That the objectivity of the French film, and not only the film but French culture generally, has its effect, may be seen from the fact that, when the Popular Front was first formed, it was accompanied by a social movement on an unprecedented scale. The legislation put into effect to satisfy the demand of a united and awakened people was likewise little short of astounding in its scope. This social movement, in turn, had the effect of bringing the French film to an even higher plane. The peak of its development was reached in one of the most remarkable films ever made, *La Kermesse Héroïque*. But this film was only the high spot of the general upward movement in the French film industry, for in the year 1936 the French had doubled the number of films exported, compared with the average for a good number of years.

During the same period German films for export declined in number with every succeeding year of the Third Reich. In the German home market attendances at cinemas also suffered a considerable decline. This is paralleled in the steeply declining appeal of the Nazi newspapers. The films with the rubber stamp of Dr. Goebbels' Filmprufstelle were, and are, no more attractive to the German people than Dr. Goebbels' newspapers or Dr. Goebbels' radio, to which you must listen when the Great One speaks, on pain of imprisonment.

The French film, on the other hand, found new strength in drawing inspiration from the unity of the people. It flourished as it had never done before. A remarkable side-light upon this is that *La Kermesse Héroïque* ran for over six months to record houses at a London cinema when it was first shown in England, and there followed a great many more French films which found enthusiastic acceptance among ever-widening audiences in London as well as in the Film Society movement in the provinces.

Let us take a few representative films that have appeared in England to afford us a cross-section of what has been happening in the French cinema. There were:

Poil de Carotte	Duvivier
La Maternelle	Epstein & Levy
The Virtuous Isidore	Deschamps
L'Atalante	Vigo
The Golem	Duvivier
L'Equipage	Litvak
Pépé le Moko	Duvivier
Marchand D'Amour	Greville
Crime et Chatiment	Chenal
Bonne Chance	Guitry
Roman D'Un Tricheur	Guitry
La Vie est à Nous	Renoir

The development of the two main tendencies, starting from the early 1930's may be illustrated in the difference between *Le Million* and, say, *Poil de Carotte*. Poil de Carotte is a little red-haired boy around whom the entire film revolves. The picture is full of self-pity and ends in tragedy, and it provides a strong contrast with the social comedy of *Le Million*, which shows you a facet of lower middle-class life, with no one person ever occupying the entire centre of the picture.

Nothing could demonstrate more clearly the close connection between a cultural expression and the next step in the social scene, than a comparison between *Kuhle Wampe* produced in Germany just before Hitler, and *La Vie est à Nous* directed by Renoir in France only a few years later. This film was made under left-wing auspices in much the same way as *Kuhle Wampe*, and was distributed in France as frank left-wing propaganda. A single young man becomes unemployed, and, for a good length of the film, wears himself out in the search for work. On the point of collapse, he is assisted by a communist to regain his strength and is introduced to the activity of a party branch. As in *Kuhle Wampe*, the lesson of the left can only be imparted apparently through the subjective method of individual misfortune at its last gasp, but, unlike *Kuhle Wampe*, is there only a small dose of this treatment and *there is no suicide*. By comparison with the tidal wave of catastrophe in *Kuhle Wampe*, this comparatively short incident in *La Vie est à Nous* is like a breath of fresh air.

Even in France, the communists are apparently unable to shake themselves free of subjectivism and introspection. For another facet of this trend is the failure to realize the nature of the film as a medium when Marcel Thorez, one of the leaders of the Party, is shown in this film making a speech that seems to last for hours, with no filmic illustration other than the figure, face and background of the speaker. There is more talk and still more speeches in the same vein by other party leaders like

Vaillant Couturier and Marcel Cachin, and a group of schoolchildren are made to discuss economic problems.

It is strange that in presenting their own case, the producers employ the wordy, heavy, ultra-serious and introspective German style of *Kuhle Wampe*. Fortunately, French realism, buoyancy and satire will out in spite of everything when it comes to attacking the opposing side, especially the dictators. You see Hitler, for instance, making one of his famous speeches, but with a certain amount of tinkering with the sound track he is made to bay like a hound with extraordinarily farcical effect.

A point of importance arises in comparing *La Vie est à Nous* with *Kuhle Wampe*. In the French film a problem is stated, and the opponent forces, whom you see presented before you, are saddled with the responsibility. There they are in front of you, something objective, something to attack. There is no foggy abstraction about it. In *Kuhle Wampe*, on the other hand, in the true *Caligari* tradition, no one appears to be responsible for the tragic situation in which the characters find themselves. A young man commits suicide, and there is no enquiry, nobody is blamed. There is an eviction, but you never see the landlord and none of the neighbours raise a finger to do anything about it. Some abstract principle seems to be doing the evicting.

But in *La Vie est à Nous* the problem, despite a lot of introspection, is not in the abstract, but fully concrete and in a real world.

XXVIII

THE French film, on the whole, has followed the same ebb and flow movement as in the Russian cinema. The healthy and the less healthy trends have been far more inextricably entwined in France than in Russia, and the decline has been steep.

The French film industry reached its topmost peak of relative objectivity and clarity with Jacque Feyder's brilliant *La Kermesse Héroïque*. This film was made when the Popular Front in the real world was sweeping forward like an irresistible wave. And yet the curious situation arises that although *La Kermesse Héroïque* reflects the consciousness of a people, buoyant, assertive and resourceful, the setting of the picture is in the Middle Ages and the resourcefulness is expressed through an emphasis on sex. In its other aspects, however, the picture portrays life, and presents one of the most vivid reproductions of the Middle Ages ever made. To obtain this effect, Feyder has gone to the roots whence every good craftsman will find inspiration—the people. He shows the life, the bustle, the market-place and all the apparent higgledy-piggledy of mediaeval commerce in a Flanders city. You are right back in the past with never a thought that what you are watching was ever enacted in a film studio, which speaks volumes for the high degree of co-operation that must have actuated all those engaged upon the production.

You see this city in Flanders, a country lying on

cross-roads of Europe, whose inhabitants will be all too familiar with the routine and habits of warfare and the consequences of invasion. The news spreads that the Spanish army is approaching. The women of the town, knowing full well the fate that awaits the women of an invaded town during the passage of an army, resolve to save the community by making a virtue of necessity. They form a committee of welcome led by the Burgomaster's wife, which goes out to meet the invaders as they are about to enter the town. The women receive the soldiers with gifts and with hospitality in their own homes, and the army, charmed by the warmth and cheer of their hostesses, goes on its way next morning, leaving the town and its inhabitants unharmed.

The action of Feyder's picture is carried through in a satirical vein of comedy, but observe how closely in one respect and how divergent in another *La Kermesse Héroïque* reflects the social reality of the then advancing Popular Front. For in this picture no one character undertakes to solve the problem as if it were an individual issue. It is a problem that affects the whole community and it is resolved by collective action. The action reflects the forward advancing sense of co-operation among the people of France, but the means employed are the ideas of an earlier cultural form, the literary traditions of De Maupassant, Balzac and many others reaching back to Rabelais.

It may be very well for private individuals to indulge in the personal satisfaction that these literary traditions afford, but that these traditions are out of keeping with the social nature of the cinema, will be made evident when we touch upon the later pictures that have stemmed from the success of *La Kermesse Héroïque*.

For years before the peak of *La Kermesse Héroïque* was reached, films were appearing leading towards it, along an upward path. Two such films which are characteristic of the pre-*Kermesse* period are *L'Atalante* and *Marchand D'Amour*. In both of these, you see people in love who are honest, passionate and sincere. As in real life, they are not only in love, but make their living at their jobs, in *L'Atalante* as humble barge dwellers and in *Marchand D'Amour* as workers in a film studio, directors, players and technicians. Consequently there is not the same degree of psychopathic sex obsessions and other aspects of subjectivism that are now to be found in the French films of the post-*Kermesse* period. Nevertheless, neither *L'Atalante* nor *Marchand D'Amour* were very successful despite the objectivity of the background and the sincerity of the love moods displayed by the characters. The reason is easy to understand when we realize that the cinema is a ruthless taskmaster. It is not only relentless in revealing any physical exaggeration. It is just as intolerant of any overstressing of one side of life at the expense of the other aspects of human experience.

Life is balance as well as movement. Upset that balance in a film, and the picture loses in vitality as an approximation to life, it will fail to evoke a full response in the audience. The overbalance of the love interest in relation to the rest of the story brings about that well-known reaction, the feeling of having had too much of a good thing.

The foundation of a successful picture is, as ever, a balanced social outlook.

There still exists, more especially among French and English film producers, the habit of making pictures which concern themselves with one instinct only, it may be the business of love-making in one picture, or the business of satisfying the investigatory reflex in another. But there are clear signs that the patience of the public is nearing exhaustion. Such films will soon be as dated as the silent pictures that indulged in the bel-canto style of acting.

Astonishing in its vividness is the close resemblance between the declining character of the French film product from the topmost peak of *La Kermesse Héroïque* and the corresponding decline in the influence of the Popular Front in France.

Whereas the feeling of the German intelligentsia in 1919 was expressed and then perpetuated in the notion that the world was run by some occult Fuehrer-Caligari who was mad, and the rest of the world were passive victims, the feeling of the French intelligentsia about the world of 1939 is expressed and perpetuated by Sacha Guitry's *Roman d'un Tricheur*, *The Story of a Cheat*, that it is the Fuehrer-Cheat who prospers, and the rest of the world, to use an expressive Americanism, are suckers. This is a film in which Sacha Guitry plays the leading part. He is also the producer as well as the writer of the script, in the totalitarian manner of Herr Luis Trenker. His satirical presentation throws a searchlight upon certain parasitical modes of life. Not only have we a cheat who cheats as a profession, but almost every other character in the picture is an anti-social, self-centred individualist. The nearest approach to a normal human is Monsieur Charbonnier, who had lost an arm in the war and gambles heavily in order to forget. Guitry exercises a very slight degree of social criticism, but his film lacks what the average, healthy American film usually possesses, a normal, socially active person against whom the figure of the cheat could be balanced. Sacha Guitry displays great virtuosity in the presentation of character, but the various incidents reveal a certain perversity of taste which derive from the Romantic cults, the bizarre, the abnormal, joy in the socially reprehensible, a desire to achieve paradox out of every situation. The basic character of the French film generally, since the days of Feyder's silent *Crainquebille*, is particularly evident. As the cheat reaches the end of his pictured recital, all the characters of his imaginative past come to life, and they pose and laugh at him amidst cacophonous music in an eerie atmosphere reminiscent of the asylum courtyard in *The Cabinet of Dr. Caligari*.

The total nett result is, that the cheat in this picture, whom the Americans would contemptuously regard as 'a heel,' is patted on the back with the same sense of smug satisfaction accorded to the Fuehrer headmaster in the English *The Housemaster*.

La Kermesse Héroïque seems to have had the effect of inducing other French producers to go all out on sex, with the result that the French film is almost in a state of chaos, a bedlam of double-crossings and suicides, *belle dames sans merci* and perversions, 'the human beast' in *La Bête Humaine*, and nostalgias in *Carnet du Bal*, *Double Crime on the Maginot Line*, with the accent on the 'double.'

Corresponding to the *Maedchen in Uniform* that preceded Hitler and *The Housemaster* in England, we get *Prison sans Barreaux*, *Prison without Bars*, all with similar characteristics. Misty fogs in the pre-Nazi *Der Traümende Munde*, misty fogs in *Quai des Brumes*, a spate of suicides in the pre-Nazi German films, a spate of suicides in the present-day French films. And some of these films are being dubbed with English sound tracks for our consumption, while others are being translated into English film production.

That confusion of thought among the intelligentsia of pre-Nazi Germany, that degenerate type of liberalism which seems to have spread like infantile paralysis and affected even Soviet film production is startingly evident in the French *Double Crime on the Maginot Line*.

The *naïveté* of the cock-eyed intellectualism which in Russia permits a kulak to get away with the murder of a useful citizen, and the counter-revolutionary Cadets to run away with their arms with a 'boo,' is seen in a glaring light in this French film.

In the American *The Confessions of a Nazi Spy*, the spies are shown as the rats they are, a detestable social menace. But in *Double Crime on the Maginot Line*, this low form of life is an object of commiseration, and the last epitaph on the spy (spoken by his brother-in-law, the French commanding officer of the Maginot Line!!!) is this: 'We must be just, he was a man and a good officer.' Yet there is not a single incident from beginning to end to indicate the faintest reason for such a judgment!

In heaven's name, how can a serving officer in the Reichswehr, who in the interests of Hitler obtains a commission in the French Army, spies out the secrets of the Maginot Line, attempts the killing of the Commander-in-Chief, succeeds in murdering two French officers, and escapes retribution by suicide, how can such a one be 'a man and a good officer'? Good for whom? Do words still retain their original function of conveying meaning? In which country's interests is it that this despicable character should be praised in that manner? In the interests of the people of France?

One only needs to glance at the social scene in the upper reaches of political life in France, to notice how closely the frame of mind which creates *Double Crime on the Maginot Line* fits in with the polite courtesy which is accorded to Herr Abetz the Nazi, and the treatment meted out to Lucien Sampaix the journalist, a citizen of France, imprisoned for daring to expose the enemy spies of the French people.

In life, the idea determines the action. Unless the French start an immediate and thorough spring-cleaning in the

French film studios, there can be little hope of sanity for France or for Europe.

Happily, the sense of realism that the French possess is bound to re-assert itself in the end, and the present indulgence of the French cinema in catering mainly for the urbanized intelligentsia, will prove but a childish phase that will pass.

XXIX

THE establishment of the Nazi regime in January 1933 marked the beginning of a new development in German film production. Since everything that the German film had been unconsciously preparing through the cult of Caligarism had come to fruition in real life, the old Dr. Caligari of the fair-ground no longer has the same task to perform, and so with the appearance of Herr Hitler as Chancellor of the Third Reich, Dr. Caligari dissolves from the German film to re-appear in the Nazi film as the much more pliable servant in the hands of Dr. Goebbels.

Henceforth Dr. Caligari will take his orders from the Ministerium of Enlightenment and Propaganda and the Filmprufstelle. Dr. Caligari is too valuable a servant to be permitted to follow his creators into exile. There is much to do in a Reich where the people are offered guns they do not control, for the butter they are not permitted to eat.

Dr. Goebbels is in a position of very great power. He has at his disposal State resources, a skilled and extensive personnel. He is able to command new themes and new subjects desired by the Nazi regime for the process of 'enlightenment and propaganda' for the German people. He has the wealth of the State behind him, but he cannot overcome or subdue the power of the cinema as a medium. Before its cold eye for the truth, Dr. Goebbels and his department shrivel into nothingness. The cinema is as relentlessly on the side of truth as ever.

No matter how life is presented to suit the Nazis, the cinema, like a powerful X-ray, penetrates every disguise and every camouflage, and it betrays the cock-eyed angle which comes from looking at the world from a pinnacle.

The Radio has a similar power, for however Herr Hitler may protest, raising his voice to a strident scream, that he is no coward, the Radio betrays the voice of one who is mortally afraid of the Frankenstein he has set free and which he feels may get out of control.

The way the Nazis expose themselves in *Der Ammenkoenig* is almost childish in its innocence. Try as they may, they cannot disguise their aims, their desires, their wish-fulfilments. They cannot disguise the need of a Nazi State for the breeding of children on a stud basis. They cannot hide the callousness with which they disregard the most elementary rights of the individual to the normal joys of parenthood. In film after film that they have made since coming to power, the same sort of self-exposure goes on.

A Nazi film appeared in England recently called *Der Herrscher* (The Ruler). In this, Emil Jannings is the prosperous head of an iron works, who in one version commits suicide and leaves his entire fortune to the State: a flat-footed hint to the German people to renounce all pleasures in this world and sacrifice themselves upon the altar of the Fuehrer.

But if everybody in Germany were to do what the iron-master is officially patted on the back for doing, only the Fuehrer would be left to 'fuehr' himself, *nicht wahr?* This picture is amusingly revealing of the Nazi leaders' innermost thoughts, for the biggest backers of Nazism before and after they attained power were Germany's greatest iron-masters Von Thyssen and Von Krupp. If these powerful iron-masters would only take the hint offered by *Der Herrscher*!

Before the Nazis came to power, the German film showed you suicide as a way out of your own trouble. Dr. Goebbels now shows you suicide, not as a solution for the individual, but as a way of keeping Herr Hitler in funds. Things are much better in the Third Reich now; you die for a cause, unlike the old intellectuals who died whilst brooding over their sub-conscious.

The Emperor of California is another Nazi production seen in London. To be Emperor from the coast of California to Manhattan—that is something like an ambition!

Can anyone deny the self-revealing nature of such titles as *The Emperor of California, Der Herrscher, The King of the Wet-Nurses, The Old King and the New King*, all stories of kings who do the things the Nazis would like them to do?

Disguise themselves and squirm as they may, the Nazis cannot hide from the searchlight of the cinema. Their outlook is exposed in the very way their films are made, for this is how the credit titles for *The Emperor of California* read:

Story	Herr Luis Trenker
Script	Herr Luis Trenker
Production	Herr Luis Trenker
Direction	Herr Luis Trenker
Leading Man	Herr Luis Trenker

The Fuehrer principle carried almost to its limit. Herr Luis Trenker is the mountaineering actor who had been associated with Leni Riefenstahl in some mountaineering pictures in the silent days. Leni Riefenstahl's name has been coupled with that of Herr Hitler himself. Hence we see how it comes about that Herr Luis Trenker should make a film on the same lines as Herr Hitler runs a country.

In this story Herr Luis Trenker is an immigrant to California in the early pioneering days. Any kind of false presentation goes, because Trenker and Hitler say so. San Francisco is shown as consisting of a couple of wooden shacks, a barge and a tumble-down house. That's San Francisco, whether you like it or not.

From youth to old age, Trenker never alters in appearance by as much as a hair. The gods in ancient mythology were credited with eternal youth, and are not the Nazi leaders gods?

Trenker, in the opening scenes, climbs to the pinnacle of a high steeple, and comes face to face with a vision which tempts him to life. This vision tells him to go forward and fight for his ideals. But after Trenker has been defeated, towards the end of the picture, the vision re-appears and tells him he is a fool not to give up when his cause is obviously lost.

The immoral moral of this picture is, that it's all very nice to have had great ideals in the past, but now all that is over, and you may as well make up your mind that Hitler has come to stay. The Nazis betray their sense of insecurity when they try in this sort of way to reconcile the people to their leadership.

Here we have three sample Nazi films. In one you are asked to breed children indiscriminately, in another to work all your life building a fortune and then to hand it to Hitler and commit suicide, and in a third film, if you are not prepared to accept the Nazi moral, at least to keep quiet about it lest worse befall you.

The titles of films, as we have shown, are fairly indicative of the content and the social mood in which they were conceived. What is the mood of the Reich after nearly six years of Nazi rule? Well, let the Nazis themselves reply. In addition to the films named we have seen in England, *Die Letzte Rose* and *Der Zerbrochene Krug*. The *Last Rose* and *The Broken Jug*. Comment is almost superfluous.

The Last Rose of Summer with faded, drooping, decaying petals, and The Broken Jug which can no longer hold water, let alone the good Patzenhofer beer of long ago. Our own Albert Chevalier, famous coster comedian, once hit off that mood to a T: 'Wot's the use of ennyfink? Why nuffink!'

This is the mood to which the cult of subjectivism has landed a people.

PART TWO

THE AMERICAN CINEMA

Men are not prisoners of fate. They are only prisoners of their own minds.
                    PRESIDENT ROOSEVELT, April 14th, 1939

XXX

OVER one hundred and fifty years ago, England was stirred from end to end by a pamphlet—*The Rights of Man*. Its author, Tom Paine, described what he had seen in the distant continent of America. He told with all the enthusiasm of one who had himself fought under George Washington what the new America portended for the future history of mankind.

He told the story of Archimedes, who, in explaining the laws of leverage to his pupils, exclaimed:

'*Give me somewhere to stand and I could lift the world.*'

America is precisely that part of the world historically destined to assist in lifting the rest of the world in the manner that Tom Paine predicted. The only point in which he erred was in the time factor. He thought it would take only a few years—but that is not important. What is important is that he was right in essentials:

> *What Athens was in miniature, America will be in magnitude. The one was the wonder of the ancient world; the other is becoming the admiration, the model of the present.*

Tom Paine could not have foreseen that the admirable constitution whose birth he had witnessed, and which was one of the greatest steps forward in man's history, could be manipulated for private ends by certain groups of unscrupulous people. But historically, this development corresponded to the necessary industrial development which was to give the U.S.A. the highest standard of material prosperity in the world.

Tom Paine was right in the long run and in essentials, for after the zenith of industrial expansion had been passed in 1929, and the production of wealth had come very near to total collapse, as soon as the momentary psychological depression had passed, the whole vast continent of Americans were again capable of re-examining the position from first principles, as in the very earliest days of the American Constitution.

It was this firm adherence to first principles that had enabled America to become a continent where all the ideas and cultures and ambitions that flowed from Europe melted and merged and re-formed to build brick upon brick upon the solid foundations of the truth that men are indeed born free and equal. Free from the mediaeval notions of aristocratic superiority of any one nation, the energies of all sorts of men from all over the globe were given the greatest play, and America became what it is— a vigorous people enjoying the highest standards of life in the world.

The cinema, we have shown, exposes the false, the obscure, the socially pernicious. Nothing can be hidden from its gaze—every camouflage, every wrong attitude will be revealed. In the main, the American cinema is successful because the Americans have hardly any inclination to adopt an air of alleged superiority over other human beings. It happens, of course, that a proportion of U.S. films do not adhere to the American way of looking at things. There is no such thing as a 'pure' development. The presence of an aristocratic element and the constant influx of Europeans contributes to a certain mixing of the American film product, with productions of the type more common in Europe.

When the Great War ended, the sorrows of the Earth

had made their strong impression upon the minds of men in both continents. The darkness that hung over Europe like a cloud came through the darkness of the mid-European film. In Germany, a Lubitsch unconsciously presents the trials and sufferings of a world through the trials and sufferings of an individual, through an Anne Boleyn and a Madame Dubarry. Other European film makers gave themselves up to twisted introspections and the fascinations of the split personality.

But the story is quite otherwise on that continent which had built securely upon the Rights of Man. The social consciousness of America enabled a D. W. Griffith to mirror the agonies of the world with a nearer approximation to the truth than the mid-Europeans were able to conceive it.

Griffith saw the calamity, not as the tribulations of isolated individuals but as a calamity affecting peoples. The titles of his films indicate his concern with the plural rather than the singular: *Hearts of the World*, *Broken Blossoms*, *Orphans of the Storm*.

In the work of Griffith at the end of the war there is a reflective element reminiscent of the Scandinavian cinema just before the war. In Scandinavia, the consciousness of the issues in Europe was conditioned by the Scandinavians being observers rather than participants. From a neutral stance in a neutral country, they saw the war clouds gathering at a distance: but they were near enough to the scene to feel a pessimism that imbued their films with reflective gloom.

The Americans were further away, and so were able to be more objective in their attitude. This, and the strong sentiments drawing their inspiration from the Rights of Man, gave the American film that quality which distinguishes it so markedly from the European product, especially in the immediate post-war years. The strength of the American film was in its power to infuse audiences all over the world with hope and with a belief in humanity.

In the U.S. film, Man was still historic Man who had shaped things to the service of mankind, who had subdued the elemental forces of Nature to his purpose, who had mastered Fire, Flood, Famine, Tempest and Pestilence throughout the centuries.

In its broadest aspects, the merit of the American film lay in its proud assertion of Man's supremacy, in the assurance that Man was at the controls.

The de-merit of the mid-European film lay in its abnegation, its pitiful prostration in face of Man's alleged helplessness before *Thunder, Fever and Flood*, and the alleged unknown and inexplicable, the split 'mind.'

In the German films, Man was either the helpless sport of destiny or the victim of the sub-conscious. The only characters who achieve success are heroes like Siegfried in *The Nibelungs*, who becomes powerful through bathing in the blood of a dragon, or *The Student of Prague*, who becomes proficient in the business of killing as a result of an arrangement with the Sinister One.

Nevertheless, both these characters come to a violent end, for Siegfried has a vulnerable spot on his shoulder, and the Student dies in redeeming his own shadow from the possession of the Sinister One. Man is still the plaything of an implacable fate, even if he has all the luck of a hero in German mythology.

In the face of such ideas spread by the Europeans, the curative influence of the American film with its brisk hope and cheer and normality swept through the world like the fresh air of its own native prairie.

As in the case of the European film, it is only necessary to pick out the salient representative productions of America to gain a good picture of the nature of the American cinema and the course of its development. The main trends in the American cinema, as of any country,

254

may be quite easily followed from the most prominent films it produces.

In externals, in such things as lighting, photography and sets, the U.S. film was as clear, bright and sharply distinct as you would expect from a gaze which took in prairie vistas and exciting opportunities.

America was immense and young. Europe was ancient and cramped. America drew men to the conquest of illimitable spaces where no hereditary principle had yet laid its shrivelled hand upon the soil. In Europe, on the other hand, ideas of property, especially landed property, drove men to dig cellars for the sake of economy.

Hence the American cinema gave us the clear gaze of objectivity and the wide sweep of the Western prairie, whilst the European gave us introspection and cramped dark cellars.

In the American film the photography brought out the characters in bold relief, there was nothing blurred, gloomy or expressionist until European influence began to make itself felt. The external characteristics of the American production, whether it was a super-film or a pot-boiler, conformed to these qualities of space, freshness and brilliance.

It was not only native in its spaciousness, lighting and happy objectivity, but also in the feeling that there was no need to make a fuss about petty property, since the potentialities of the good life were there for all men to grasp. But most important of all, the American film was American in its tempo, its personnel and its philosophy; in short, it was imbued with all the youthful vigour of American civilization itself.

When we come to examine the human, the philosophic aspects of the post-war American film, we cannot do better than take as one example the work of D. W. Griffith, to afford us a cameo of what it looked like in its entirety.

The philosophy of D. W. Griffith was to the American cinema what the philosophy of the days of George Washington was to the American Constitution. It was in fact the reflection of the American drive to get down to bed-rock and the fundamentals of human life. *Man's Genesis* was among the first of his one-reelers when he started in pictures. The audacity of such an attempt with such limited means is almost breath-taking. There is no doubt that this disregard of difficulty was the very spirit of pioneering America.

When, later, he attains independence in the production of a picture, Griffith takes on nothing less than the birth of a nation!

In his next picture, the indomitable Griffith attacks the subject of intolerance on a universal and historical scale. Griffith, the giant, striding across time and space, hardly realized how far ahead he was travelling beyond the mass comprehension of his time. Neither America nor any other part of the world was yet ready for the advanced outlook contained in *Intolerance*. The great innovator was now to feel the financial curb in the luke-warm reception accorded to this film.

Henceforth, his pictures, whilst they still retained that indomitable universal vision, were rendered through one set of characters. His best-remembered productions are *Hearts of the World*, which showed the life of ordinary folk behind the lines during war-time, and *Orphans of the Storm*, which, again, was a reflection of his concern for ordinary people during great historical upheavals. This picture had the French Revolution as its background.

When the Great War ended, Carl Laemmle and very many others in the U.S.A. were deeply concerned with the effects of blockade and inflation upon the German people, and were arranging shipments of food for their relief. Griffith made a film on the plight of starving

Europe to which he gave the satirical title *Isn't Life Wonderful?*

Among his last great silent films was *Way Down East.* The high point in this picture is reached when a frozen river in Alaska breaks up into shifting ice-floes, and a girl, played by Lilian Gish, is saved by a man who jumps from one floe to another, to reach her as she is lying unconscious on one of these floes. He snatches her up and carries her back to the bank, just as she is on the point of being hurtled over the waterfalls to her death.

European novelists have treated the story of the breaking up of a frozen river as a symbolization of the shifting and melting fortunes of human beings. The significance of Griffith's treatment of this subject is, that the effects of a catastrophe may be averted by energy and daring in the American tradition of determinism.

It is worth noting that until European influence becomes noticeable, in no American film do we find that throwing up of hands in despair so characteristic of the mid-European silent cinema.

The reason for this is clear. It is because the American Constitution itself came not by the throwing up of hands, but by the throwing out of tea-chests into the sea. Thought. Determination. Action.

The reflective element in the work of Griffith never degenerates into subjectivism, but this too is characteristic of the bulk of the American output from the end of the war to this day. Despite the many European authors, directors and playwrights who had infiltrated into the U.S.A., their influence has been quite unable to shift the force and direction of the U.S. outlook, thank goodness, or to affect the basic nature of the U.S. film.

Among the few Europeans who have exercised a healthy influence upon the American cinema is Charles Chaplin. The world loved Chaplin because Chaplin belonged to the world, the real world. Chaplin brought from England to America his sympathy and his kinship with humanity.

The other Europeans, the Stroheims and the Sternbergs with their aristocratic 'von' pre-fixes, the Sjostroms, the Stillers and Viertels, brought the defeatism and the introspective intellectualism of Europe along with them. Chaplin, on the other hand, was himself a man of the people. He knew what reality was really like. Through sentiment, inclination and humane feeling, he had much more in common with the American idea as reflected by a Griffith or a Mary Pickford, than with the predominating European outlook. Charlie, in his own way, is just as expressive of the indomitable nature of man as Griffith in his more serious mood. There is nothing submissive or cringing about Charlie when trouble comes his way. It is this quality of assertiveness which has endeared him to the world, just as it partly explains the popularity of Mary Pickford and the films of Griffith. It is this quality which brings Chaplin nearer to the type of the universal man than to the European.

The subjectivism and the concomitants of the 'Great I Am' idea came in with the European directors. What distinguishes these directors from the Americans is their accent upon the sense of property, the fetish worship of uniforms, *objets d'art* and lavish architectural backgrounds. The accent of the native American director is *in the main*, not altogether, upon human beings, human relationships, human values, the only true values.

In Europe, property, objects, things, are harder to come by. Hence the everyday mental pre-occupation with obtaining *things* has created a widespread over-emphasis upon the sense of property which when carried to its extreme degenerates into fetish worship.

Take the work of one of the most prominent European directors in the American cinema in the 1920's, Erich von Stroheim.

Bette Davis in DARK VICTORY   (*First National*)

Erich von Stroheim in MADEMOISELLE DOCTEUR, a Trafalgar Film
Company Production   (*United Artists*)

An American and an English example of the Germanic preoccupation
with self

As an actor, Stroheim played the part of the Prussian officer in *The Four Horsemen of the Apocalypse* and played it extremely well. A year or two later, he writes *The Wedding March*, directs, and plays the lead in it, but this is not by any means the only way in which the Fuehrer principle is expressed, for his uniform in this picture is the most dazzling you ever saw.

His bull neck deliberately emphasized by his tight-fitting military collar, his bearing, his monocle, his heel-click and his military cloak, is as Prussian as anything could be. His manner of looking women up and down is the manner of a Prussian cavalry officer looking over a horse.

That Stroheim remained a hard-bitten European to the end is evidenced by his extreme over-emphasis on things rather than upon people. As a director, he achieved a reputation in Hollywood for being needlessly extravagant. Miles and miles of film would be shot in order to show a chimney smoking in just the way he wanted. Polished floors and glittering heavy chandeliers inside ornamental palaces, uniforms for the men and the most extravagant dresses for the women. Money no object. That is one aspect of subjectivism, a forgetfulness that things cost money, and that money is something people have to sweat for, even in the land of opportunity. The obverse side to this is in his making of a long, long film with the significant title *Greed*.

This film is a study of morbid obsession. The conception, the story, and the Caligari treatment and direction, could only have found encouragement in Central Europe. To imagine that such a film with such an atmosphere would ever find an echo in America, shows to what extent the elevation of morbidity will blind people. *Greed* cost, and lost, a lot of money.

Among the last of his American productions, Stroheim made *The House of Strangers* and *The Crime of*

Dr. Crespi, and later in England *Mademoiselle Docteur*. Enough said.

Compare Stroheim's record with that of Chaplin. Never in a single film that Chaplin has made has he any property. Charlie is not concerned. His bowler hat and stick are merely his emblems of bourgeois respectability; he is always interested in people.

That Chaplin in his own life accumulated a great deal of money and is now a very wealthy man is a facet of his realistic outlook, in not only making money but being sensible enough not to squander it in the manner of so many to whom success has been like heady champagne. What matters to us is the significance of his stubborn disregard in every single one of his productions for any sense of property. It proves clearly and decisively that Chaplin is far more interested in human life than in things.

Compare Stroheim's monocled sizing up of a woman, his faint cynical smile, with the tender reverence of Chaplin as he looks at a woman. In this respect Chaplin does not share the American attitude of treating woman as an equal, but neither does he possess that peculiar Mid-European outlook expressed by a Lubitsch—women as playthings, as property, with an under-scoring of cynicism. Moreover, Chaplin's attitude to women displays his greater kinship with the universal man; it is his expression of man's eternal worship of the Madonna principle, gratitude and reverence for the goodness and sweetness of life.

It is no accident that Chaplin, Griffith and Mary Pickford are always grouped together in every discussion on the earlier American cinema, for these three have gone to the very roots of human experience. Griffith goes back to the beginning of man in almost his first one-reeler, and like Chaplin, but in his own way, expresses his reverence for the Madonna principle in *Intolerance*.

Mary Pickford endears herself to millions of people not only because she re-asserts the rights of humanity for one half of the world's population, but because she is the Madonna principle personified both as the Mother and the Child.

No better example can be cited than Chaplin's *Modern Times* to show how concerned he is with the lives of human beings. With his own sense of satire he indicts the whole conception of present-day industrialism, that man must abdicate his proud position of being master of the machine to become instead the helpless slave of the machine.

In this picture Charlie is as assertive as ever in bringing the idea to its logical absurdity. Shakespeare in his own day was never more pointed in his references to the error of men's ways than is Chaplin in *Modern Times*, and signs are not wanting in America that men have taken the hint and acted upon it. When you see Charlie at a conveyor belt, performing one gesture all day long, screwing nuts until he almost goes nuts himself, you may laugh, but that is how many men do spend their lives in gaining a living. In itself the conveyor belt system is not all that is evil; but what happens to the nerves of the operatives when the supervisor pushes the control forward and sets the belt travelling at a much increased pace?

You get the answer when you see Charlie dashing out into the street, still holding his tools in his hand and twitching and screwing as if he had St. Vitus Dance. He meets a woman wearing buttons on her coat shaped like nuts, and the woman has to dash away when she meets the queer look in his eye as he twitches towards her.

Chaplin is never as unrealist as so many intellectuals who admire the advances of science in a general way. He does not enthuse over the technical wonders of television sets, for Chaplin is consistently quite uninterested in things

261

except as they affect human beings. Chaplin feels there will be time enough for enthusiasm when men learn how to use things properly as well as to make them.

In the meantime, in *Modern Times*, he shows the television apparatus suddenly flashing on to the wall of the work-shop the picture of the foreman who bullies the men on to hurry with their work: speed and more speed. In the interests of maximum output with minimum waste of time Chaplin sits at the machine screwing nuts, whilst the automatic feeder slaps food into his mouth, automatically pours liquid down his throat and automatically wipes his moustache for him.

This resentment expressed in social satire, in comedy form, at the indignity imposed upon man was later to be translated into real life. *Modern Times* and one other little film, only a one-reeler, Disney's *Three Little Pigs*, were the ideological straws that presaged great social storms. 'Who's afraid of the big bad wolf?'

Within a year or two a trade union movement of tremendous vigour and determination occurs in the U.S.A. under the leadership of John L. Lewis. An intense anti-Hitler sentiment is created throughout the American continent, and the Rights of Man are re-asserted as passionately as in the first days of the American Constitution. Was this a coincidence? Not at all. It is no more a coincidence than that the negative, senseless destructiveness of the pre-Nazi film should be followed by the Nazis setting light to the Reichstag or destroying synagogues and torturing a whole people.

The satire that runs through every one of Chaplin's pictures is expressed even in their titles. *Shoulder Arms*, made in 1917, is a military command, but militarism as an end in itself is treated as a farce. *The Gold Rush* was a gold rush—but not for Charlie, or the likes of Charlie. *The Circus* is symbolical of the vicious circle of poverty, of the ups and downs of life. *City Lights* refers satirically to the standards of a very rich man who is only humane when he is drunk—all lit up. And of course Charlie shows us exactly what he thinks of modern times in *Modern Times*. Chaplin's superb flexibility and the richness of his comedy have hardly ever been surpassed.

XXXI

CHAPLIN departed from his usual style in 1923 to make *A Woman of Paris*, a film in serious vein in which he did not participate as a player. He was the first in films to show a woman of the *demi-monde* as just a woman, neither degraded by her mode of life, nor elevated in a haze of romanticism. The maturity of his presentation made a very deep impression everywhere. Like Griffith's *Intolerance* it was ahead of its time, and the American cinema did not catch up with *A Woman of Paris* until about three or four years later.

Chaplin's universality found its opportunity in America. He is reflective in his outlook and in his natural desire to do something about it. He finds himself at home in a country where the gift of thought followed by action has given that country a lead in the field of the cinema. Thought allied to action forms the balance that life itself demands. And the success of Chaplin's films shows the validity of that principle in the cinema. In *A Woman of Paris* he was not only an innovator in the delineation of character upon the screen. In this film he brought the technical side of film production to a higher plane; he had anticipated certain aspects of Eisenstein's contribution to cinema technique.

Chaplin made this picture at a time when the relationships of the sexes were being re-assessed and discussed on a world-wide scale. It will be instructive to examine how the native American compares with the average European approach to this problem.

The Europeans brought to the American cinema their subjectivism with its offshoots, cynicism in the guise of comedy in the style of Lubitsch, and in a depressing defeatism expressed by directors like Sternberg, Murnau and Viertel. But however much the directors of these two schools felt like throwing up their hands in their own native manner, they never quite got away with it in America. The American atmosphere was too strong. The American character still predominates.

An analogous position has arisen in England since the talkies came in. No German, French or Viennese director has ever been able to make any impression on the basic character of English films, except in the most superficial way. In his native France, Jacques Feyder creates a master-piece, *La Kermesse Héroïque*, in England the result is *Knight Without Armour*!

The social and ideological background against which the different types of women screen characters evolved immediately after the war must be taken into account. The war was over. Millions of young people who had been living under a sense of doom both in U.S.A. and in Europe, suddenly released, heaved deep sighs of relief.

In war-time no man is his own master. He cannot choose where he will stay, what he will do or when he will love. The State is master. In the new-found peace, men again had their individuality returned to their own keeping, and so they determined to live to the fullest possible extent.

From the bewildering immensities of a world war in which one individual seemed of as little account and as vulnerable as a fly upon a window-pane, young people now found intense relief in a re-action towards self. Dancing, cocktails and parties, pleasures of every kind, Freudian psychology, introspections and questionings of every previously accepted standard were widespread.

265

The American screen women who mirrored the social scene may be placed in three groups. In the first we get Mary Pickford, the Gish sisters and the Talmadge sisters. These represent the basic American woman in character.

In the second group we have the European influence in Pola Negri, Alla Nazimova and later Greta Garbo and Marlene Dietrich, who brought with them a conception of womanhood distinctly opposed to the basic American idea.

The third group represents a synthesis of the two influences. Here we have Clara Bow, Gloria Swanson and Marie Prevost.

Again we find that the mood and the message of the productions in which these players appeared is nearly always indicated in the titles. Film titles are a most revealing index. Immediately after the war Mary Pickford appeared in:

The Little American, Poor Little Rich Girl, Daddy Long Legs, Rebecca of Sunnybrook Farm, The Heart of the Hills, The Hoodlum, Tess of the Storm Country, Rags, Such a Little Queen, Romance of the Redwoods, Amarilla of Clothes Line Alley and many others.

The Gish sisters appeared together in *Orphans of the Storm, Hearts of the World* and *Romola*. Lilian Gish played in *The Greatest Thing in Life, Birth of a Nation, Way Down East, The Great Love, The White Sister*, and later *Annie Laurie*.

Norma Talmadge appeared in *The Dixie Mother, A Tale of Two Cities* (1916), *Sunshine and Shadows, Helpful Sisterhood, The Battle Cry of Peace* (1917), *Cupid Versus Money* (1918), *Panthea, Poppy, The Children in the House*. Constance Talmadge played in: *The Honeymoon, Up the road with Sally, Sauce for the Goose, Romance and Arabella, Smilin' Thru*.

The opposite trend can be detected in the film titles of

the Europeans. Pola Negri played in *Passion*, *Gypsy Blood*, *Hotel Imperial*, *Woman on Trial*, *Barbed Wire*, *Three Sinners*, *Secret Hour*, *Loves of an Actress*, in the American film from about 1920 to 1924. Before then she played the *Madame Dubarry* in the German film made by Lubitsch, and in *Carmen* and *Sumurun* also for the same director.

Alla Nazimova played in the American *Salome* and *The Redeeming Sin*.

Greta Garbo, after appearing in *The Atonement of Gosta Berling* in Sweden and *The Joyless Street* for Pabst in Germany, went to America and made her appearance as the star in *The Torrent*, *The Temptress*, *The Flesh and the Devil*, *Love*, *The Divine Woman*, *The Mysterious Lady*, *Wild Orchids*, *The Kiss*, *Woman of Affairs*.

Marlene Dietrich came into the American film at a much later stage, when talkies were already in full swing, but her film titles are as significant of the Mid-European ideology as those of Greta Garbo. These are: *Three Loves*, *Morocco*, *Dishonoured*, *Blonde Venus*, *The Scarlet Empress*, *Desire*, *The Devil is a Woman*.

Now we come to the third group of women screen stars. Here will be noticed a marked difference from the film titles of the first and second group, a real synthesis resulting from the native American vigour combined with European sophistication.

Clara Bow, the Elinor Glyn 'It' girl, starred in *Rough House Rosie*, *Get Your Man*, *Red Hair*, *The Fleet's In*, *The Wild Party*, *Three Week Ends*, *No Limit*, *True to the Navy*, *Dangerous Curves*.

Marie Prevost appeared in *Man Bait*, *Up in Mabel's Room*, *Almost a Lady*, *For Wives Only*, *Getting Gertie's Garter*, *On to Reno*, *The Godless Girl*, *The Party Girl*, *The Racket*, *The Rush Hour*.

A little of the exuberance in the films of Clara Bow and of Miss Prevost is slightly toned down when it comes to the list of films in which Gloria Swanson plays the lead, but the synthesis is still there: *Don't Change Your Husband*, *Male and Female*, *For Better For Worse*, *Under the Lash*, *Beyond the Rocks*, *The American Wife*, *The Great Moment*, *Society Scandal*, *Manhandled*, *Wages of Virtue*, *Stage Struck*, *Fair Manners*, *What a Widow*, *Indiscreet*, *To-night or Never*, *Sadie Thompson*.

Side by side with the shifting standards in personal relationships, throughout the 1920's, there was a desire on the part of the people of America to learn ways of conducting their own lives according to the formalities, and of enjoying their material prosperity. Mass production of goods was climbing up to its highest point of intensification in every industry, and very high wages were becoming increasingly available. The social consciousness of the U.S.A. was dominated by a satisfaction with all the evidence of continuously increasing wealth. Everything seemed possible.

The social consciousness is therefore closely reflected in the American film throughout the period, as a glance through the few titles we have given will show.

The films became picture-books for the people on how to walk, how to dress your hair or trim moustaches, what kind of clothes to wear on every occasion, how to take a girl out, how to behave in a restaurant, how to furnish your kitchen, your bedroom, your drawing room, how to drink a liqueur, how to avoid bootleg liquor, and how to conduct a love affair.

People modelled themselves closely on the film stars, both male and female. In the days of Rudolph Valentino, young men in every town and village were to be found wearing Valentino whiskers. At the height of the Clark Gable cult, young men adopted the Gable moustache and hairdressing, the cut of the coat and the tilt of the hat, and the Gable manner of courting the female of the species.

The women, too, paid close attention to the clothes, the hairdressing and the mannerisms of the Garbo and the Dietrich, all of which is thoroughly to the good, since it was a necessary stage through which people had to pass, from a sense of discrimination in personal attire and conduct to the wider questions of the relationship of the individual to the rest of society.

The period from 1918–30 represents a stage in the American film which, in the main, laid the greater stress upon the individual and upon personal fortune. Inevitably this was the hey-day of the star, upon whom most of the emphasis was laid. The value of a picture in Box-Office terms depended much more greatly upon the star than it does to-day. The star is still a considerable factor in pulling power, but it is doubtful whether a return to the undisputed pre-eminence of the middle 1920's is possible. The tremendous historical changes that have occurred in the world in the last ten years have had a corresponding effect upon the social consciousness, and public standards are visibly in process of change.

And let it be repeated, in the long run it is the nature of the social consciousness that determines the nature of the film. The customers are always right. In a normal healthy community, they will only pay for what they want at a given historical moment, and they are learning more and more every day. The omnipotent money barons of Hollywood who think of no-one but themselves in making films are a myth. Without their finger on the pulse of the public they could not last a month.

The influx of the Europeans, both players and technicians, into the American film was conditioned by several considerations. America's films were penetrating to every country in the world, and so a seasoning of established European film favourites in the American production was not only good business but good tactics as far as the public outside the U.S.A. were concerned.

The rest of the world was very interested in things American, but the Americans on the other hand were keen on taking an occasional look at something or some-body that reminded them of their European origins. Distance in time and space lends enchantment.

The American film is quite clearly expressive of the American social consciousness. It is both active and reflective, but whenever a particular production tends towards introspection or subjectivism, whenever it departs from its true native character, it will show a distinct tendency to flop at the pay-box.

A few more titles of films made by representative American film directors will only go to confirm our thesis, and will further sharpen up in our minds the American social scene which the European players and directors were about to enter.

Action and reflection is well balanced in the work of John Ford, who made: *The Iron Horse, Four Sons, Three Bad Men, Mother Machree, Just Pals, Little Miss Smiles, Salute, Strong Boy, The Seas Beneath.*

A much greater active exuberance is displayed in the work of director Mervyn Le Roy: *Flying Romeo, Oh Kay, Naughty Baby, Hot Stuff, Broadway Daddies, Little Johnny Jones, Playing Around, Showgirl in Hollywood, Top Speed.* Le Roy began to direct more serious subjects after 1932, making such talkies as *I am a Fugitive from the Chain Gang* with Paul Muni, *The Heart of New York*, and *The World Changes.*

Director William A. Wellman displays the same basic American characteristics as Le Roy; freshness, drive and freedom from inhibition: *Wings, The Cat's Pyjamas, You Never Know Women, Beggars of Life, Young Eagles, Woman Trap, The Man I Love, Steel Highway, Dangerous Paradise, Maybe it's Love, Public Enemy* (James Cagney). A list of films that Archie Mayo directed confirms the cinema's function in spreading ideas on personal behaviour and on personal appearance: *Johnnie, Get Your Hair Cut* with Jackie Coogan, *Money Talks, Slightly Used, The College Widow,*

Beware of Married Men, Is Everybody Happy? My Man, Sonny Boy, Courage.

Again, after 1932, we notice a change in Mr. Mayo's productions towards a mood of greater seriousness: *Two Against the World, Street of Women, The Mayor of Hell* (with James Cagney), *Ever in my Heart, Border Town, The Petrified Forest.*

It was inevitable that a degree of European influence should impinge upon the American cinema almost from the very first, but nowhere is it really marked until after the Great War. The slight trickle derived from imported productions from France and Italy—the films of Sarah Bernhardt, *The Fall of Troy* and *Quo Vadis* increased greatly after the making of Rex Ingram's *The Four Horsemen of the Apocalypse*. This picture was mystical in its conception and execution. The title alludes to the four mystical figures in the Book of the Revelation representing War, Famine, Pestilence and Death. The despair that had taken hold of Europe had to find some echo in America. That echo was expressed in *The Four Horsemen of the Apocalypse*, which was made after the story had achieved a considerable circulation as a book. The film was produced as a mystical explanation of the cause and effect of the war, but it hit the mood of the moment and it became one of the biggest financial successes of the silent cinema.

The spectacular nature of the production also contributed to its success. Significantly enough the script was from the story by Blasco Ibañez, a Spanish writer. It placed Erich von Stroheim, an Austrian, and Rudolph Valentino, an Italian, in the top class as stars right away, and the film was directed by Rex Ingram, an Irishman from Dublin.

The nature of the films that Rex Ingram directed can be deduced from his titles. They are worth comparing with the vigorous assertiveness of the contemporary native American product. They are: *The Chalice of Sorrow, Under Crimson Skies, Scaramouche, Shore Acres,*

271

The Conquering Power, Hearts are Trumps, Mare Nostrum, The Magician. Although these were all made in U.S.A. they are thoroughly European in their outlook. Such films must have found some response in the American social consciousness because of the increased contact with Europe that followed American participation in the world war, and because of the general feeling about the catastrophe that had descended upon the world.

The re-assessment and the intense interest in sex problems found expression in the immediate popularity of Rudolph Valentino. There is no doubt that people found in him the personification of the male principle, the Adonis, and he attained unheard of sudden success after his first appearance in *The Four Horsemen of the Apocalypse.*

He made a great name in *Monsieur Beaucaire, The Sheik, The Son of the Sheik* and *Blood and Sand.* When Valentino died in 1926 there were many mass demonstrations of grief all over the world, and especially in New York, where his lying-in-state was followed by something akin to a state funeral. It is not likely, although hero-worship of film stars still exists, that such an unbalanced state of the people will occur again. Sex is no longer a subject of glamorous mysticism. Scenes of love-making for its own sake, or protracted kisses, get the bird to-day in almost any cinema theatre.

Stroheim also had a big break after his performance in *The Four Horsemen,* and he began making the films already referred to. In one of his last American talkies, *The Great Gabbo,* you see him as steeped in subjectivism as when he began. In this picture he is a magician-performer and a ventriloquist, a fairly modest kind of person you would think. But his picture is replete with splendour and subconscious property worship—chairs like thrones, tables like altars and gorgeous ceremonial attire all complete.

The successor to Rudolph Valentino was Ramon Novarro, who followed the same cult. Born in Mexico, he resembled Valentino in cast of features, and for many years his following among women was very great. He appeared in: *The Prisoner of Zenda*, *Scaramouche*, *The Midshipman*, *Ben-Hur*, the big Metro production, famous for its chariot race, and one of the biggest silent winners, *The Student Prince*, *The Road to Romance*, *Forbidden Hours*, *The Pagan*, *The Call of the Flesh*, *The Singer of Seville*—every title tells a story!

The German director Murnau, maker of *The Last Laugh* and *Vaudeville*, both with Emil Jannings, came to America to continue the good work. There he made *Sunrise* with George O'Brien and Janet Gaynor: the subjectivism of lone figures against misty horizons at the rise of the sun.

Joseph von Sternberg made the *Salvation Hunters* and *The Docks of New York*, extremely depressing in all their aspects. These were followed by *The Street of Sin* and *The Last Command*, in both of which Emil Jannings took the leading part. It would appear that Sternberg and Jannings had come to show these benighted Americans how to make pictures, but what happened was that they both remained as rigidly German in their intellectual subjectivism as ever. *The Street of Sin* to some extent anticipated *The Blue Angel*, but instead of being the one who takes the blows, as in *The Blue Angel*, Jannings plays the part of a dock-side rough who humiliates another weaker than himself.

But in *The Last Command* we get a supreme instance of man's stubborn rigidity to a habit. The film tells the story of an ex-White Russian General, but it reproduces the atmosphere, the spirit and the general idea of Jannings' performance in *The Last Laugh*, made in Germany three years earlier.

The White Russian General, an exile, finds himself stranded in Hollywood. He is fortunate enough to obtain a job to play a part of a Russian General in a film production. Any rational man in such circumstances would obviously be delighted to earn some money and to be able to put his past experience to some practical use: but not Sternberg's Russian General played by Emil Jannings.

Jannings' General takes the job, puts on his General's uniform, and recalls, with a great deal of moping, weeping and morbid introspection, how once upon a time he was a real General in the army of the Tsar, whereas now—pity him!—he is only a fake General acting for a film to amuse the vulgar multitude. The subsequent fetish worship and self-pity (as in the *Last Laugh* over the uniform of the doorman) is repulsive to witness.

He mopes and he gropes, dazed with the tremendous weight of his 'suffering,' over the part he has to play in his gorgeous uniform. The sorrow that this poor introvert has heaped upon his head, the imaginary disgrace is so great, that as the General gives his last command in the Hollywood Russian Army—he dies.

The Last Command was one big flop. This display of subjectivism and decay, this anarchical conception of values, was something that America and the rest of the world would have no truck with.

The work of Berthold Viertel on the whole is less subjectivist than the work of the average German director working abroad. He had perhaps a little more in common with the Scandinavian Victor Sjostrom whose productions in America were of the contemplative rather than the subjective type.

In Hollywood Victor Sjostrom continued the Scandinavian tradition of reflecting upon the elements, the wind and the sky as symbolizations of the shifting nature of social life. He made *The Scarlet Letter*, *The Divine Woman*, *The Tower of Lies* with Norma Shearer, *The Wind* with Lilian Gish, and *He Who Gets Slapped* with Lon Chaney.

All these European influences, the recital of which may sound so formidable, were however no more than a drop in the ocean in the quantity and quality of American film

Bette Davis in JEZEBEL
(*First National*)

Norma Shearer in MARIE ANTOINETTE
(*M.-G.-M.*)

Robert Taylor and Greta Garbo
in CAMILLE
(*M.-G.-M.*)

Robert Taylor and Margaret
Sullivan in THREE COMRADES
(*M.-G.-M.*)

The European influence upon the American film

production. The Americans were still making typically American films, their soundness was unshakable. The American film only became tinged with self-pity between 1930–32, when the full effects of the slump of 1929 was making its impression upon the American social consciousness; but the recovery has been quick, and there have only been slight occasional lapses since.

An interesting feature emerges from our scrutiny. Not a single European director has made a real honest-to-goodness comedy in Hollywood. This is hardly surprising since no comedies ever came out of Germany or Austria in all the post-war years. The people in Central Europe evidently had very little to be exuberant about.

XXXII

AMERICAN comedies, American song and dance films, American cartoons, American dramas and American Westerns continued to sweep on their way throughout the world. A book could be filled with the titles alone of all the Westerns that have been made and shown these many years, films that have reminded the world that movement and action is still the core of life, despite the opinions of the select.

Big Bill Hart in the early days made films with such titles as, *White Oak, Travelling On, Tumbleweeds, Waggon Tracks.* Later Ken Maynard came along with, *Texas Gunfighter, King of the Range, Come on Tarzan, Dynamite Ranch, Between Fighting Men, Fargo Express, Tombstone Canyon, Lawless Riders, Hell-Fire Austin, 50,000 Dollars Reward.* Tom Mix gave us, *King Cowboy, The Dude Ranch, Son of the Golden West, The Texan, Hidden Gold, The Terror Trail.*

There were thousands of such pictures made; fresh air, action, movement and rough justice came through all of them. The popularity of the Western all over the world has been persistent and consistent. In many places it is still the bread and cheese, the staple fare of the local cinema proprietor. The Western is cheap to make and cheap to hire, and world demand is regularly satisfied.

But the Western was very far from being the only product of the American film industry. The U.S. film provided the richest vein of humour and the loudest laughter, combined with the Douglas Fairbanks poise

Eddie Cantor in KID MILLIONS (*United Artists*)

The Marx Brothers in ROOM SERVICE (*R.K.O. Radio*)

American screen comedy

and skill in acrobatics. It has given us the comedies of Chaplin, Buster Keaton, Joe E. Brown, W. C. Fields, Laurel and Hardy, Our Gang, Harold Lloyd, Disney, Charlie Chase, Mack Sennet, the Marx brothers and Eddie Cantor.

The Marx brothers indulge in comedy, musical virtuosity and vigorous social satire in films like: *Coconuts, Animal Crackers, Monkey Business, Horse Feathers, Duck Soup, A Night at the Opera, A Day at the Races.*

It is significant of the character of the U.S. musical that two of the first Eddie Cantor productions were entitled *Whoopee* and *Palmy Days*. The exuberant confidence, the poise and the fine physique of most of the men and all of the women is unmatched anywhere in the world, native products of a high material civilization.

There was a short period between 1930–32 when the American film entered a transition stage, resulting from the tremendous shock of the 1929 slump upon the American social consciousness. One aspect of this transition is the deliberate and emphatic auto-suggestion contained in *Whoopee* and *Palmy Days*, and the other is a descent into an indulgence of self-pity which was quite un-American in character. The films of the latter type that were being produced were still following the old habit of giving the individual outlook in which the characters lived and loved in a synthetic world as hitherto, but with this difference, that the characters were beginning to find themselves in all kinds of trouble. This mood, however, was rapidly displaced, and America regained her buoyant independence and her wonted social outlook of facing the world with determination.

Broadly speaking, before 1930, the U.S. film was a reflection of American satisfaction with the world. Between 1930–32 it displayed the consciousness of one trying to recover from a bang on the head, but after 1932 there is a distinct change again towards a vigorous re-assertion of the social principle, coupled with a determination to conquer difficulties in the American manner.

During the period of lapse, 1930–32, we observe in the appearance of such films as *Street Scene*, *City Streets* and *Back Street*, a resemblance to similar titles appearing in the German cinema at the time of crisis and inflation, *The Joyless Street*, *The Street* and *Night Without Dawn*.

The subconscious significance of the street in such titles seems to lie in the constantly moving traffic with its apparently unrelated people and unrelated vehicles. The street, leading to an infinite number of destinations, suggests and reflects the subconscious feeling of infinity and dazed helplessness.

Street Scene was photographed very much in the manner of the play by Elmer Rice, upon which it was based. This film was made very early in the days of the talkie, when the photographed play, complete with stage dialogue, was in vogue. It dealt with an unfaithful wife, a jealous husband, a gossiping neighbourhood, the murder of the wife by the husband and the break-up of the family.

Gloom, self-pity and subjectivism, all conveyed by dialogue.

Back Street, produced by Joseph M. Schenk, deals with a subject which would find no response in the America of 1939. It is a very unreal story of a wealthy man who has both a wife and a mistress. He keeps the latter in the background, back street that is to say. The mistress is a woman whom he has loved for many years, but he marries another woman because his position in the business world appears to demand it. Despite the marriage he continues the liaison with the first woman for years without the wife ever finding out anything about it, although everybody else hints and smirks.

The unreal suggestion is conveyed that a woman will, at the request of her lover, retire to a back street, and sacrifice her whole life in devotion to such a man, remaining resigned in the name of 'a great love' for twenty years after his marriage to the other woman. She continues to suffer and to dote on him, living upon his small monthly allowance.

Towards the end of the picture this elderly rich man has a stroke of paralysis, having had a quarrel with his grown-up son about the mistress, and after a good many harrowing bedside close-ups, he dies. The soulful mistress, suddenly aged several years in a day, sits at a table in her own apartment with the photograph of her dead lover in front of her, fades away and dies too.

In one of the musicals of the same period *Puttin' on the Ritz*, the chief character (Harry Richman) goes blind. He cries out 'I am blind, I am blind, I am a blind fool.' (This because of complications in his recent past.)

Thus both these films end in quite unwonted self-pity. Both are escapes into illness, in one paralysis, in the other blindness. Both ways afford a way out of the difficulty of fending for oneself. It is no coincidence that this type of film appears almost immediately after 1929, when seven hundred banks closed their doors in the U.S.A. and when the economic life of one hundred and thirty million people was shaken to its foundations.

City Streets was directed by Reuben Mamoulian, and the principal parts were played by Gary Cooper as a young fellow employed in a circus, and Sylvia Sidney as the daughter of a racketeer. Sylvia Sidney is innocently sentenced to a long term of imprisonment for complicity in a murder with which she had nothing to do, and for which her father's gang are really responsible. Gary Cooper is persuaded by her father to become a racketeer in order to save her. She is compelled, however, to do the full term, and when she comes out of the prison she is desired by 'the big fellow' at the head of the father's gang.

'The big fellow' plots to get Cooper, his rival, out of the way. After a good many tight-corner escapes Gary Cooper outwits his would-be assassins. With Sylvia Sidney in the front seat beside him in a car he takes the racketeers for a crazy ride into the country and drives close to the edge of precipices, until the would-be assassins are persuaded to hand over their guns.

He then allows them to get out, miles from anywhere, and the happy two go off to make a new life for themselves in another part of the country.

The film is full of the symbolism that meant something in the recent silent days: statues of sleek black cats, caged birds, a fair-ground and shooting-gallery, a long misty expanse of seashore with lapping waves and so on. Mamoulian evidently had not given much thought to the function of symbolism, useful perhaps in the silent medium, but comically dated when sound makes possible all the commentary necessary.

The photography in this picture is dark and Germanic, but at least the hero and the heroine do get away with their lives, which means that in a little while we shall be getting the old silent winner, *Smilin' Thru*, re-made as a talkie with Sidney Franklin directing, and Frederick March and Norma Shearer in the leading parts. America was getting over the first shock of the slump and was Smiling Through. In *Smilin' Thru* there is a blindness motif, but there is at least a logical reason—one of the calamities of war.

XXXIII

THE year of the great slump in America is an historical dividing line of a fairly marked character in the history of the American film. An accelerated process of change had been going on just before the slump came. Signs of an impending economic upheaval were beginning to become visible, and with this uncertainty hovering over the minds of the people, attendances at the cinemas began to drop off very badly.

People had learnt all there is to learn about external fashion and modes of behaviour. With money becoming tighter and jobs becoming more difficult to hold on to, they had no further patience with the type of picture where the characters seemed to get their living miraculously. The flow of nickels and quarters into the pay-box began slowing up. When cinema proprietors are obliged to hand out tea-sets a bit at a time, as an inducement for patrons to come into their halls, then things *are* in a bad way.

Hollywood suffered a severe financial shake-up, but among the first of the producing companies to feel the draught were Warner Brothers, who, in a mood of desperation, launched into talkies and landed into a fortune.

Thus it was the first rumble of the impending economic disaster which was at the root of the great change in the film industry, not only in the change from silent to talkie, but in the development towards a much higher quality and richer content in the film itself.

There was one other important contributory factor which assisted the change from silent to talkie. It is known that various systems of talkie equipment had been bobbing up almost since the beginning of the film industry, and a practicable commercial system of combined sound and picture recording was available a good many years before Warner Brothers took the plunge and made their first semi-talkie, *The Jazz Singer*.

The United States was the largest single market in the world, and the home market for pictures. The population had been divided into language groups almost as diverse as those on the continent of Europe, although English was the language which all were endeavouring to master.

Immigration into America on a mass scale ended about 1914. After this strict quota regulations were introduced and the number of immigrants was limited. By 1928, fifteen years had elapsed since the great influx, time enough for at least elementary English to be acquired. The children of immigrant days were now grown-ups, possibly fathers and mothers, who had themselves been to school and who spoke and behaved like true American citizens. By 1928, when talkies were introduced, the language position in the United States had changed completely and radically. There was now one huge homogeneous market for the English-speaking talkie film.

The same spiral progression which we noticed at the beginning and during the subsequent progress of the silent film is clearly observable in the development of the talkie, but on an infinitely higher plane and at an infinitely greater tempo. From quality to quantity, and when satisfaction has been reached, again from quantity to a higher quality.

In precisely the same way as audiences, twenty-three years earlier, had thrilled to see *The Great Train Robbery* enacted upon a white sheet, so the experience was repeated in the first talkie singing drama. Audiences were far too astonished with the wonder of it to be in any mood for criticism.

The Jazz Singer, with Al Jolson singing coal-black mammy songs, was the simplest, unadorned, unsophisticated sentimentality imaginable. Not only were audiences fascinated by this coming to life of the film, but the producers themselves seemed to have become entirely mesmerized by it, until they were shaken out of their torpor by the warning sound of the gradually diminishing chink of the nickels once more. The first talkies made so much money for the producers that for a time it seemed that the only function of the talkie was to talk.

It was talk, talk, talk. When two characters appeared they seemed to stay on the screen until they nearly talked their heads off.

There was not only the wonder of seeing shadow people speak and sing who had been dumb for thirty years, but there was the chance for millions of the world's inhabitants who had never been to New York, for instance, not only to see the place, but to become completely absorbed in its atmosphere. To hear its buzz, its street car clangs, its paper-sellers' cries, to participate in the life of a strange city as it had never been possible before. There was the fascination of hearing the sound of a door click, a telephone bell ring, the hoot of a liner and the whistle of a train. It was as near to personal travel in distant lands as it had ever been possible for the millions.

Many critics who had developed a friendly disposition towards the silent film, who had admired the products of Russia, Germany, France and Czechoslovakia, could see nothing in the advent of the crude, sentimental talkie except the destruction of an irretrievable Golden Age.

The ordinary person felt, however, that the talkie was an experience worth indulging in, and that it had far greater potentialities than the old silent medium.

The ordinary person was right.

The critics lamented bitterly the loss of their satisfactions, in montage, super-imposed photography, fades and

283

dissolves, and the movement and inter-cutting of the old silent cinematography. The momentary emphasis on speech was taken to be something that would remain. The dissentients failed to appreciate the laws of motion of every cultural medium that has ever been used since man began.

The Jazz Singer was admittedly a step backward as far as theme and content were concerned, but it was a step backward which was necessary to give added impetus to an infinite number of steps forward.

There were people who imagined that cultural growth is a progression in a straight line ahead. But the very word 'culture' refutes a conception of such rigidity. Culture is what it says it is, a cultivation of the lives of the people. It has much in common with the process of agriculture, and the analogy can be extended to explain what took place with the talkie in Hollywood.

A plant requires a *good mixed soil* kept up by fertilizers; and to maintain the vigour of crops, you must get an occasional change of seed from a different part of the country. When talkies first came in, the directors found themselves treating talkie recording as if it were a new-born child. From being free to roam about in natural backgrounds from place to place, the camera was now obliged to be placed within the sound-proofed padded walls of the studio. It was almost as if the characters in the first talkies were afraid to move about the screen, for fear of upsetting the sound equipment. Even with the coming of the first *Gold Diggers of Broadway*, the ideas on sound were derived directly from the conventional stage.

But soon, and inevitably, the soil of Hollywood was completely turned over. Hundreds of players of the silent days fell out. Fresh actors came in from the legitimate stage. New technicians who came in to operate sound, not only brought their own technical skill, but their own ideas of integrating sound into a given production.

With the best technicians from all over the world,

Al Jolson in THE JAZZ SINGER *(Warner Brothers)*

Edward G. Robinson in KID GALAHAD *(Warner Brothers)*
The theatricality of 1928, compared with the naturalistic buoyancy of 1938

with fresh ideas from every country's productions, with the growing American temper towards the unity of the people, and the growing feeling against Nazism, the quality of the American film reached new heights.

The coming of sound broke up centralized production. Each film had now to be independently financed. There were formed producer groups with their own staff of technicians. It was found that this method of de-centralization and independent control over each production as it took the floor, was the only way in which profits could be safeguarded. The increasingly sensitive demands of audiences made it impossible to continue making films on the old centralized factory system.

Producers and directors had to be given their head. This new freedom benefited not only the pay-box but also the education of the people, judging by the way in which so many second feature films are occupied with fundamental problems, against authentic backgrounds of factory and farm, to instance only one aspect of the change.

Concurrently with this development in Hollywood, there occurred in the U.S.A. the drive towards a more vigorous trade unionism, and an insistent demand for better labour conditions and social work schemes within the New Deal. To force the operation of the New Deal, mammoth strikes took place and were fought with an intensity and upon a scale unprecedented even for the U.S.A.

In such an atmosphere, the appearance of a play in New York, *Waiting for Lefty*, took the town by storm. It was a play with a message expressed with passionate feeling, a punch in every line, and the connecting thread to a series of scenes like film sequences was the story of a taxi-men's strike in New York.

One may realize how charged was the social atmosphere when at one time Clifford Odets, the author of *Waiting for Lefty*, had five plays running simultaneously in New

285

York. This phenomenon dispersed any doubt there may have been in Hollywood that there was opportunity in the infinitely wider field of communal life.

Chaplin's *Modern Times*, coming early in this movement, afforded producers a hint as to what could be done in the way of sugar-coating of varying degrees of thickness. Films were coming through seriously tackling social and economic problems. Such were *Riff-Raff*, *Black Fury* and the highly successful *Mr. Deeds Goes to Town;* the economic factor treated in a popular way, with the faintest degree of fantasy.

Highly significant of the future trend in the U.S. film was the appearance of *My Man Godfrey*, directed by Gregory La Cava, and played by an excellent cast headed by William Powell and Carole Lombard. This film was a two-edged weapon. It exposed the unreal world in which those who were fantastically rich were living, and it had a message of determination and courage for the millions whose lives had been shaken by the economic crisis.

In this picture William Powell plays the part of one who, from being a member of America's élite, is reduced during the crisis to the position of having to live like a tramp in a packing-case at a place called 'the dump' near New York's riverside. Hundreds of others are shown living in the same way at this spot.

A group of society people who are having 'fun' at the Ritz-Astoria descend upon this dump, and for five dollars induce Powell to come to the hotel and be presented just as he is, bearded and in rags, as the 'forgotten man.' The discoverer of the 'forgotten man' gets some kind of silly prize. At the end of this incredible ceremony, all those assembled, in boiled shirts and jewels, call out for a speech, and Powell responds. He tells them exacly what he thinks of them, giving it as his opinion that they are conducting themselves 'like a bunch of empty-headed nit-wits.'

Jean Harlow in RIFF–RAFF

Spencer Tracey in RIFF–RAFF   (*M.-G.-M.*)
A study in contrasts
The American talkie film enters the field of social criticism

'Nit-wits' asks an exquisite dame in all seriousness, 'what are they?'

Powell, however, accepts a job as butler at the home of a family of these nit-wits with whom he has many crazy adventures. A friend of Powell's old prosperous days pays a visit to the house, and is taken aback when he sees Powell as the butler. The two make an appointment for the following day.

Powell tells him the story, which might be the recapitulation of the story of millions of other Americans. From having everything, he found one day he had nothing.

To illustrate the story Powell takes his friend to his former residence at the riverside, the dump, and introduces him to all the boys. They all chip Powell on his prosperous appearance, and Powell says jokingly it was due to a corner in wheat. A fellow asks whether that is the corner 'prosperity is always just around.'

Some of the things that Powell tells his friend as they seat themselves upon an ash-can amidst the squalor, are worth remembering:

There's a very peculiar mental process called thinking, and while I was here I did a lot of it.
The Parkes were never taught to fight life.
It's surprising how fast you can go downhill, when you begin to feel sorry for yourself.
The only difference between a man and a derelict is a job.

America had indeed travelled a long long way from the self-pity of such films as *Back Street*, *Street Scene* and *Puttin' on the Ritz*. America was not only snapping out of it, but doing something about it. As happened on the wider social scene in America, Powell and his friend get some money and build a pleasure rendezvous on the dump, and although the solution may not be quite in accordance with orthodox political economy, they do manage to give employment to a few score of men.

Let those who sneer at Hollywood contrast the manly assertion in *My Man Godfrey* with the 'art' and the spread of despair in *Kuhle Wampe*, *Mutter Krausen* and *The Blue Angel*. Let them contrast the resulting social scene in the U.S.A. with that of Germany to-day and—ponder.

It is astonishing what an enormous field of actuality is being covered by the U.S. film since the agitation round the New Deal. Every possible aspect and combination of aspects in social life is being treated. Films on the early days of the American Revolution, on immigration, family problems, the factory, the stage, the film industry, the penitentiary, prison reform, reform schools, problem boys at school, college, University, sports, gold-mining, stock exchange manipulations and share-pushing, the press, the National Broadcasting services, Army, Navy, air pioneering, news-reel cameramen, fishing and whaling and every imaginable activity.

From *Mr. Deeds* and *My Man Godfrey* there has been a development towards a greater boldness in tackling economic and social problems. It came to a point where the side of the Spanish people was taken up uncompromisingly, directly as in *Blockade* and obliquely as in *Four Men and a Prayer*. Consciously or unconsciously, by the very tendency of the American film to take up the side of the people, we find stress laid upon *unity* time and time again.

We see it as advocacy of the unity of the family in *Four Men and a Prayer*, where four sons operate from the ends of the earth, as a unit, working to collect evidence against an armaments racket which was responsible for the death of their father. The film ends with the four vigorous brothers arm-in-arm, with their object achieved and their father's name cleared.

In *Marked Woman*, the four professional dance hostesses

288

MALA THE MAGNIFICENT   (*M.-G.-M.*)

GOLD IS WHERE YOU FIND IT   (*First National*)

Backgrounds of American films: fur-trapping and gold-mining

join forces and act as one. By so doing, they are able to secure the conviction of their gangster employer who was responsible for the death of the sister of one of them. After the gangster has been convicted, they too walk away together arm-in-arm, a symbol of that unity of action which alone can achieve the apparently impossible, the unity that will humble the apparently most powerful.

Only second feature in status, but significant, is the series of films depicting episodes in the life of The Jones family. Each film in this series, which is sponsored by Twentieth Century-Fox, is self-contained. They all employ the same cast, the same sets are in use—the house of the Jones family, and the drug store of which father Jones is the proprietor. Metro-Goldwyn-Mayer run a similar well-made series dealing with the fortunes of the Hardy family. *Love Finds Andy Hardy* is one of several that have been made in the first feature class.

These pictures are remarkably inexpensive to make, and yet the dialogue and the situations seem to be extremely interesting pointers to the trends in American family relationships and to social trends.

Situations that might occur in any normal family are reproduced with the utmost fidelity, engaging charm and high intelligence and in the most unpretentious manner. The Jones family series usually stresses the importance and the need of unity in the family, and the obligations of its members to the rest of society. In one of these episodes the father is persuaded to permit a poor boy picked off the streets by his young son to live with them, because— it comes out in the family discussions—they all feel that a good environment will change this orphan boy, who had become a problem even to the recently formed voluntary organization of Big Brothers, of which father Jones is a leading member.

That such an organization as the Big Brothers for the assistance of youthful delinquents should be mooted and

T

discussed is in itself a significant reflection of the social scene in present-day America. There is hardly any doubt that this episode of the reclamation of the orphan boy from a life on the streets could be traced in a direct line to the Russian film, *The Road to Life*.

The Jones family series is very popular with English audiences, and the greatest admiration is accorded to the mother who so tactfully and so self-effacingly smooths over every family difficulty, until things right themselves again, with everybody coming to their senses.

Families of an entirely different brew have been treated after the manner of *My Man Godfrey* in such films as *Merrily We Live*, *The Baroness and the Butler*, *Hundred Men and a Girl*, *Live Love and Learn* and *Danger Love at Work*. The American way of looking at their upper ten is fairly well indicated by these pictures, and is in marked contrast to the awe and adulation with which the élite are treated in English films, that is to say in English social life also.

In the American films, the *My Man Godfrey* type of family is shown—in isolation from any contact with the reality of life. Enormously wealthy, not knowing or caring where their money comes from or how it is spent, they each play their own lone hand, amoral and without much feeling. These are not comic characters but types that really exist. With the power of irony and satire they are turned into a laughing-stock.

Danger, Love at Work, made by Twentieth Century-Fox, affords an additional target for the ridicule of the pretentious art for art's sake cult. This picture deals with one such wealthy family, each member of which has his own pet form of crankiness. One of them even goes to the length of living a stage beyond the dilettante idea of primitive man—beard, club, leopard skin and all.

The prize specimen, however, is Herbert, who affects some form of crazy daubing. A visitor calls at the house

THE LAST GANGSTER. Edward G. Robinson portraying the gangster with
Napoleonic ambitions, as a family man   (M.-G.-M.)

JUDGE HARDY'S CHILDREN, with Lewis Stone and Mickey Rooney
The Hardy family at home   (M.-G.-M.)

to see Herbert, but Herbert is out. The friendly butler Wilbur shows him to Herbert's room, and this is the conversation between them:

WILBUR: *Oh, that is one of Mr. Herbert's inspirations, sir, he calls it 'Friendship.'*

HENRY: *Friendship?*

WILBUR: *Yes, sir. His theory in this particular painting is that knives, forks and spoons are always together, and help each other out.*
He said something about the sublimation of the inanimate. I didn't quite understand him.

HENRY: *You don't say. Well, how'd he get up on the ceiling?*

WILBUR: *He suspended himself upside down from the chandelier, sir.*

HENRY: *OH—he sus—Huh?—Remarkable!*

WILBUR: *He has another inspiration that he's painting on the door of his bedroom. I'm sorry I can't show you that, sir—naturally no one can step in there until it's completed.*

HENRY: *No one?*

WILBUR: *Not even Mr. Herbert, sir—he's sleeping in the garage until it's finished. . . .*

This is Hollywood getting its own back! And about time too!

Hollywood is capable of distinguishing the genuine from the spurious, and is performing a service by doing so. That the motive force is that of making films for profit does not alter the fact that Hollywood's historical function is a worthy one, and her importance incalculable.

The U.S. film is familiarizing the peoples of the world with much of the best of our cultural heritage in every known form of expression, and from every age. Let us take a few U.S. films at random which appeared before the end of 1937, and note some of their characteristics:

Live, Love and Learn: *References to Van Gogh, Cezanne and the French school of painting. Many quotations from the classics.*

Souls at Sea: *Gary Cooper speaks Hamlet's soliloquy 'To be or not to be,' and explains it to his companion in popular language. Tells the story of the Trojan horse and the Greeks.*

Captains Courageous: *References to the birth of sea shanties and folk songs.*

Life of Pasteur: *Familiarizes the audience with the struggles of science against reactionary authority.*

Life of Emile Zola: *Familiarizes the audience with the life of a great writer, the works he wrote from contact with real life, his association with Cezanne, and his great fight for justice in the Dreyfus case.*

As you Like It
Midsummer Night's Dream   *Stimulate interest in Shakespeare.*
Romeo and Juliet

David Copperfield
Tale of Two Cities   *Create an appetite for reading Dickens which will acquaint the reader with early industrial Britain and back-ground of French Revolution.*

The Good Earth: *Shows the Chinese reverence for learning. Shows a great people who have the same fundamental needs and desires as we have.*

Ruggles of Red Gap:	*Charles Laughton recites Lincoln's speech at Gettysburg.*
Lovely to Look at:	*Sonja Henie glides to the Dance of the Polovtsi from 'Prince Igor' by Borodin.*
Happy Landing:	*Sonja Henie again in 'The Snow Maiden' ballet by Rimsky-Korsakov.*
These stars:	
Grace Moore	*Have helped to familiarize a*
Lily Pons	*generation of jazz followers with*
Deanna Durbin,	*the works of Beethoven Chopin,*
Leopold Stokovsky	*Tschaikovsky, Verdi, Bizet, Mozart, Schumann and Schubert.*

The Hollywood film is being enriched by the impac of every conceivable culture. There is the same exciting ferment as during the Renaissance, when all that was finest in Greece and Rome was being re-discovered and absorbed. Imagine anything like the list just mentioned being offered to an audie   of countless millions thirty years ago! Yet there are people who lament the supposed decline in culture.

The position of women in American society as reflected in the film, and the effect of the film upon the world's women in turn, repays careful study. This is where the curative influence of the American film upon the minds of the world's inhabitants has been most effective and most remarkable.

Until well into the beginning of the twentieth century, women in the Old World lived in an atmosphere almost akin to toleration in what was then an exclusively man's world. Such expressions as 'Lords of creation' and 'her lord and master,' commonly applied to the man, and 'the weaker vessel,' applied to the woman, show quite clearly how matters stood in the relationship between the sexes.

The first faint beginnings of women's self-assertion came at the time of the Sufragette movement, when the music-hall, in partial sympathy, began the refrain, 'The hand that rocks the cradle rules the world,' although the law of inertia determined that the women's movement was to be bitterly opposed for a long time to come.

The backward position of women in Europe and elsewhere could only be improved when ideas from the New World began to spread and take effect. The United States of America was the fulcrum from which the lever was operated to raise in varying degrees the status of women, wherever the American film is shown.

Taking an historical perspective it could not have been otherwise. It was to America that the most enterprising and vigorous types from the Old World came. The rapid expansion against the primitive forces of nature gave them the most spectacular opportunities. With such an influx of the most active elements of the Old World, fertilizing and intermingling with the population of the New, it was inevitable that the women of this new population should develop differently from their sisters in the older civilizations.

Side by side with their men-folk, braving the same dangers, toiling at the same tasks, they bore an equal share of the hardships and burdens of pioneering, while still remaining tender and devoted wives and mothers.

They achieved a respect, a dignity and an equality in the eyes of men impossible to imagine in Europe. It is not surprising, therefore, that the American woman, conscious of her own worth and of her equality with her husband, and enjoying the greatest measure of respect, should have become the model for the rest of the world. But as we

THE GOOD EARTH   (*M.-G.-M.*)

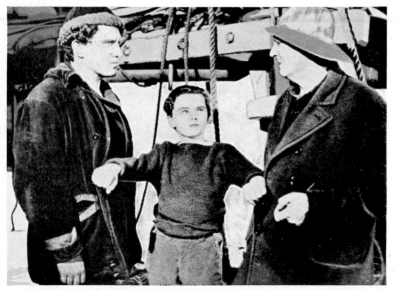

CAPTAINS COURAGEOUS   (*M.-G.-M.*)

Backgrounds of American films: agriculture and cod-fishing

have pointed out, progress is never in a straight line. It can never be 'pure,' because the new and the old ideas are continually mixing and interchanging.

We can see how this principle works in the evolution of the American woman. Despite the respect in which she was held since the earliest colonial days, her emancipation was inevitably hampered by the stream of immigrants from Europe bringing with them the mental shackles of the Old World.

The stage and the music-hall were almost completely under the sway of European ideas until the first decade of the twentieth century, and the first to take command of the film industry were the Laemmles and the Zukors, recently arrived from Europe, who naturally exerted a considerable influence, especially since they understood the then polyglot American market so well. This explains why the early story films portrayed women as shy and simpering creatures, until Mary Pickford, the prototype of the American girl, began to bring that tradition to shreds.

But despite the varying changes that have occurred since Mary Pickford, up to about the end of 1934, the film women seemed to be as like one another as a handful of peas.

All this, however, was necessary for the evolution of the screen woman as she exists to-day in all her individuality. How often were we obliged to watch the heroine go through ordeals of fire and water, with never a hair of her head disturbed, and with her make-up miraculously perfect!

Soon there was to be an end to all this 'perfection.' By 1934 a thousand straws in the wind foretold its decline. For instance, the Jean Harlow roles revealed that women could have tempers and minds of their own. An infinitely greater differentiation among screen women began to take place. Women became interesting studies. The film was enlarging its horizons, simultaneously narrowing its gaze.

For a long time after 1920, or at any rate since the beginning of the reign of Greta Garbo, women on the screen were idealized in form and feature like the Madonnas of the Renaissance painters. If you look at a Madonna and Child by Leonardo da Vinci, you will see the strong resemblance she bears to the Garbo types that dominated the screen for over a decade.

Since the majority of women in Italy are dark-haired, the Italian painters, in seeking the ideal woman type for the Madonna, would choose the rarest, the most beautiful type they could conceive, the women from the North with fair hair and fine eyebrows, whose facial contours were delicately accentuated. It is hardly surprising, then, that when the material wealth of the U.S.A. gave American women the opportunity of improving themselves, they should employ as their models two screen women who came from Northern Europe and from a strata of society that had given them the opportunity of learning how to bear themselves as if born to wealth; the two models who adapted themselves to the universally accepted standard of the Italian Madonna—Garbo and Dietrich.

A high standard of wealth and leisure gave American women opportunities for grooming, dieting, massage and hairdressing, until they had mastered every idea prescribed by the new Madonnas. The U.S.A. supplanted Paris as the leader of fashion, and American films brought American culture to every country in the world.

This was the prelude to the dissemination of the greater human values which was about to follow.

When all the lessons had been absorbed, a new period of individuality set in and broke up the uniformity of eyebrow, hairdressing and figure lines. People discovered that every kind of personality has its good points and that when every point is taken advantage of, individuality attains a charm of its own.

In externals, this brings us up to date in films.

The cult of individuality in clothes and grooming developed side by side with the growing idea of the rights of the individual in society, and the position of women particularly began to absorb the minds of the Americans.

American civilization at its height, until the slump, gave women economic equality on a material level unequalled anywhere in the world. In the Soviet Union women enjoyed equal political and economic rights with men, but their material standards were necessarily lower because large-scale industry had still a long way to go to reach the output of the good things of life that American industry had attained. But with the big slump of 1929, the position of women in America suffered a severe setback. When unemployment and economic stress began to strain the fabric of American social life, the women suffered bitterly.

Insecurity or the feeling of insecurity pervaded every section of the community, and its effect upon women began to be examined in film after film. For by this time people were hardly in a mood to indulge in any kind of enthusiasm for the super Marlene, for instance, as the devout and virginal girl who meanders through the desert in *The Garden of Allah* in a flowering marvellous veil, with her new husband, the renegade monk, living luxuriously on love.

The Garbo's Anna Karenina, Marie Walewska and Camille were meeting with less and less response from the wider masses of the people. How far the films of Garbo are removed from life may be gathered from the fact that *Camille* has been declared by Hitler to be his favourite film. This obsession with the ego, and its petty pre-occupation with its own little 'lurv,' is just about Hitler's meat.

It is an open secret that exhibitors both in America and Europe are getting restive at the effect upon the pay-box of the role of the beautiful temptress of pre-war days and long before. Marlene Dietrich in *The Garden of Allah*, *Knight Without Armour* and *Angel*, has shown us quite clearly that beauty, like patriotism, is no longer enough.

XXXIV

SIDE by side with the decline of the great queens of the screen, there began to grow up a new generation of vigorous young actresses capable of carrying serious dramatic roles of immediate social importance. They appeared in the song and dance, in comedy and in the serious films. Perhaps Barbara Stanwyck is the best example of how this new trend began to emerge in the song and dance film.

In *Banjo on My Knee* (1936), she plays the part of a servant girl who marries a fisherman whose home is in a colony of shanty boats on the Mississippi river. Notice the precise location, the clearly defined jobs and the social strata from which the characters are taken.

On her wedding-day, the dealer who buys all the fish from the shanty-boat fishermen comes aboard and demands to kiss the bride. This is a custom unknown among the fisher folk, and the young husband (Joel McCrea) knocks the fellow overboard.

The inhabitants are aghast at the tragedy that has come upon them. For in spite of an intensive search throughout the night, they are unable to find the fish-dealer dead or alive. The young husband is compelled to fly, and infrequent post cards inform the bride that he has a job as a sailor. In the meantime, the fish dealer turns up alive and well, but during the six long months it takes to convey this news to her husband and bring him back, the bride lives in the hostile atmosphere of the shanty folk. Hostility against the landswoman, who seems to have brought such unluck to their community. Her sufferings, married and yet not married, are sympathetically and directly expressed.

When at last the husband arrives home, everything is again ruined within an hour or two by his proposing to go alone to the West Indies to make a home for her. She refuses to be parted from him again, and declares that if he goes alone she is finished with him. In a violent temper, he retorts, 'he'll show her who's the husband' and rows ashore. They each make their way separately to New Orleans, at the mouth of the Mississippi, and without meeting each other, she finds a job as a dish-washer and he finds another boat. When he comes back once more, he discovers her working as a cabaret artist, but again a jealous quarrel parts them.

The hot, bull-headed husband sees light in the end and they make it up, but there is no mistaking the purport of the story. Living on the perilous edge of poverty, the life of a whole family is blighted by the attempt of the fish dealer to exercise his economic power in claiming a kiss from the bride. His male possessiveness nearly ruins their lives as well as the hopes of the bridegroom's father, who is looking forward to 'a grand baby' to continue his line.

Barbara Stanwyck portrays the bride as a woman of the people, forthright, independent, courageous and hardworking. She knows what she wants, but everything in the world seems to conspire against her getting it.

It will be seen that this type of story and these characters mark a definite change in the film world. Human rights are taking precedence over other considerations.

The position of wives and fiancées whose fate is economically linked to that of their men folk has undergone a change of treatment in the American film. Both first and second feature pictures have been showing the women's point of view.

A recent second feature film, *Danger Patrol*, distributed by R.K.O., deals with employees on the transport staff of a nitro-glycerine factory, whose ticklish job it is to handle the stuff on to lorries for delivery to oil-boring companies. These men gamble with their lives on every run, but though they receive wages well above the average, they seldom bring home enough to enable them both to run their homes and to indulge their fancy for different expensive additions to the home furniture.

Uppermost in their consciousness is the dread knowledge that the least friction, the least bump, will mean instant death. Even the strongest-nerved among them can only stand the strain for a few years. Some go crazy. Some fall victims to the dread nitro-fever. Others make their one mistake through over-anxiety. Each hopes to escape by winning riches in some gamble or other at long odds.

The womenfolk see their husbands or fathers off to work. They may have to go out on a delivery at any hour, and each trip may be the last. The women spend the hours waiting for their return in a rising fever of anxiety— a life which prematurely ages them.

Test Pilot, an M.-G.-M. production directed by Victor Fleming, is in the more expensively made first feature class. With extraordinarily fine delineation it describes the everyday occupation of men who risk their lives testing out new aeroplanes, test-pilots who want to live 'long enough to lay a floor up there in the sky, so that the world may go to bed on it.'

These men develop a swashbuckling manner as a kind of defence mechanism. Brooding would be out of the question in their hazardous life. They are all in love with the 'Miss in the blue dress up in the sky,' she who is always ready to slap her lovers in the face at the first unwary moment, and to send them hurtling down to earth.

As in *Danger Patrol*, these men spend their money recklessly, generously, and immediately it is received, and their wives and children suffer not only the successive torture of dangerous flights, but frequent need of money. With poignant sincerity these aspects of the life of a test-pilot are depicted by Clark Gable as the pilot, Myrna Loy as his wife, and Spencer Tracy as his friend and assistant.

One day, Clark Gable is flying a new machine in a race, in which the pilot of the winning machine will receive 10,000 dollars. Suddenly thick trails of smoke are seen issuing from his machine. Myrna Loy and Spencer Tracy watching from the field below are horror-stricken. With the sardonic humour that such a life demands, he turns to the wife to comfort her: 'Oh, that's nothing—it's so cold up there, it's nice to have a little fire. That guy's made of asbestos anyway.' But as the pity and agony well up, tears start from his eyes and he turns upon her bitterly: 'Well—you married him, didn't you?'

Gable wins the race in spite of the trouble, but his pal Benson, flying another machine, is killed, leaving a wife and a family of young children, with no means. Gable goes to Mrs. Benson, and on the pretext that he had arranged to split the winnings, he gives her half the prize money, 5,000 dollars; then he goes on the booze for five days, trying to forget. The wife of the dead pilot and her suffering, the agony of the wife of the living pilot who has disappeared, Spencer Tracy's patient search for him, and the re-union of the three once more, displays a reflective understanding and a complex truth that has never been matched in any other medium. Here is a film where the unity of the three friends is no less remarkable than the close team work of all the other players and the technicians who co-operated in making the picture.

The social nature of the film has been adequately matched by the social method employed in its production, and the social importance of the theme. A film of this character would have been impossible in the hey-day of the star system. The star system at the height of its development meant that story, background and supporting players had to be subordinated to one end—the virtuoso performance of the star. In *Test Pilot* we have the three big stars, and a fourth, Lionel Barrymore, as the aerodrome company manager, disinterestedly pulling together in the interests of the production as a whole. It never occurs to any one of them to shine above the other. The result is a remarkable synthesis of objectivity, and a production of the highest quality.

Test Pilot is only one of the peaks in the development of the modified star system, which started at the time of *Grand Hotel* when almost every major star in the M.-G.-M. constellation was brought into a single production, for the first time in film history. It was made in the attempt to bring patrons back into the cinemas in greater numbers after the crisis, but once this type of film had made its appearance there was no turning back.

There has been the most thorough delving into every nook and cranny of American social life. Hollywood itself, the star system and the American stage are not immune. A searchlight has been played upon much that is tragic and precarious in the lives of women in such films as *A Star is Born* and *Stage Door*.

In *A Star is Born*, in technicolor, directed by William Wellman, the world is invited to take a look at some of the consequences of the star system in terms of human lives. We see how one star rises upon the firmament as another gradually declines in brilliance, drops out of favour, and fades out in melancholy, drink and death. And we see the woman star who has to put up with every indignity to meet the demands of the star system, who too suffers deepest tragedy in the death of her man under the wheels of the Hollywood Juggernaut.

But despite tragedy, the strong, resolute re-affirmation of the rights of man, the rights of the individual to his or her own life, is asserted in the very last lines, as the picture fades to its close. In a crowded salon, with everyone offering adulation to the star, with the world waiting to hear her voice on the radio, the announcer presents her to the microphone and in his usual suave manner says: '*Here is Vicky Lester.*'

The star approaches and with bitterness in her heart calls out firmly: '*This is Mrs. Norman Mayne!*' Defiance at the system which made her a star—and a widow.

In *A Star is Born* the focus is upon the life of the big stars, but behind and around them we get a hint of the many tens of thousands of aspirants who for ever fail to catch an influential eye. It is with these aspirants that *Stage Door* is specifically concerned.

Stage Door goes further towards bitter realism bent to a specific purpose. Gone are the glamorous close-ups, the idealizing, the romanticized photography, the warm daylight from a hundred 'suns' that has lit so many thousands of pictures with the confidence that all's well with the world, that it was only a misunderstanding, and that at the end of the picture all will be happy ever after.

No, the road through the stage-door is dark and fitfully lit. It is strewn with broken hearts, broken dreams and broken bodies of girls whose only disability is to be 'beautiful but hungry.'

The very symbol of this fight for existence is The Footlights Club where a bunch of these girls live. The beginning shows a rich girl (Katharine Hepburn) taking a room at the Footlights Club as the first step to a stage career. The life of the Club is depicted, with its scanty meals, its rooms wracked with the blare of noise from the city streets, the faces of girls trying to sleep on hot summer nights patterned with the blinding, flashing, neon-lit advertisements across the road; the near respectability precariously maintained by engagements for 'dinner,' while all the time the girls are trying to storm producers' offices to get one foot on the stage. They try hard to be

A STAR IS BORN
with Janet Gaynor and Frederick March (*United Artists*)

STAGE DOOR
with Katherine Hepburn and Ginger Rogers (*R.K.O. Radio*)

tough, to keep on being tough, and their cynical wise-cracks have the bitterness of aloes and the burning pain of vitriol.

The rich girl, who aims at 'getting there' on her own, blames the girls for what she thinks is lack of initiative. She cannot understand the necessity for their mode of life. She sincerely believes that where the Great Pioneers succeeded, everybody else can succeed if they have the brains and the courage.

This girl gets her leading part all right: her wealthy father, pulling strings in secret, sees to that. But it is a part for which one of her pals at the Club had long prepared, believing that she of all people was best fitted to play it.

When the opening night arrives the rich girl has an attack of nerves and is in doubt whether to go on. It falls to the broken-hearted girl who has been supplanted to give her encouragement and final instruction. By the time the new leading lady reaches the theatre, the girl who remains behind amid the four walls of the Footlights Club has become distracted and commits suicide. The news of the girl's death reaches the wealthy girl just as she is about to step on to the stage. Now she realizes for the first time what lies behind the façade of wise-cracking in the dingy parlour of the Club.

Filled with grief, she goes upon the stage, and plays the part she was taught, but with all the intensity and the mental anguish which she is now going through in real truth. The wealthy girl is a success, but she decides to go on living with the aspirants of the Footlights Club. She realizes her success has been built upon a cemetery of hopes. As the film ends, one of the crowd of girls is lucky enough to get a one-line part, and we see them getting some forced merriment out of practising it, just as a new boarder comes in. Life goes on.

Here we come to a point of serious importance. There is a suicide in *Stage Door* and a suicide in *A Star is Born*.

Whatever we have said about the German films with their suicide complex, goes for the American. It was Chaplin who was the first to slip up on this question when he made the mistake of putting a suicide in his *Woman of Paris*. There is no doubt that this idea directly or indirectly draws its sub-conscious inspiration from Europe.

This notion of self-destruction never did or could have anything in common with what George Washington had in mind.

The mental state of a would-be suicide is a psychopathic condition, a suitable subject for examination by doctors at a clinic. Not only is it unsuitable as film material but it is socially dangerous, as Germany has proved. And if further proof is needed, what does the public say? Is there a film with a suicide in it that has ever made real money?

You may get away with it perhaps in *A Star is Born* because of other considerations, such as the novelty of colour and the public interest in life at the film studios, but in a general way, the surest way of losing one's shirt on a film production is to put a suicide in it.

In these two films we detect the first signs of a wobble in the American film, but since these have appeared other productions have come along. Some, like *Test Pilot*, have stuck to freshness and sanity and reached the heights, and a few others have developed an even worse wobble and have sunk to the depths of subjectivism. Such are *Jezebel*, *Frou-Frou* and *Three Comrades*, which we will examine in the last chapter.

Despite a few major and minor deviations from the path of common sense in American film productions, the bulk of them still stick resolutely to the consideration of true human values. Except for the suicide, *A Star is Born* dealt with the star system sincerely and fairly objectively. Now in *Mad About Music* we see the emphasis transferred from the stars to the effect of the system upon the children of the stars.

In this picture Deanna Durbin plays the part of a fourteen-year-old daughter of a famous American film star. The child is being kept in secrecy at a school in Switzerland. The glamorous, sexy star, whose very name is Box-Office, is persuaded that she cannot afford to let it be known to the world that she has a fourteen-year-old daughter. The little girl, whose father died during her infancy, and who is artificially deprived of a mother's love, invents a father to satisfy her dreams of parental affection.

This imaginary father is a great man, an explorer and a big-game hunter who sends her trophies, and from whom she receives letters in her own handwriting, which she reads with triumph to the other schoolgirls. This situation of the mother and daughter again stresses the conflict between economic necessity and the normal instinctive satisfactions to which all parents and their children are entitled, which they must have if they are to survive as normal healthy human beings. The theme is given against a background of light music, song and Swiss scenery, but the point of the story gets home.

In the Shirley Temple pictures, a seven, eight or nine-year-old child plays the part, usually, of an orphan, who, but for her quite unusual charm and talent, would be in a bad plight. Bandied about from one unwilling relative to another, these relatives are themselves assailed by the insecurities of contemporary existence. But Shirley's personal talents make her the object of exploitation by the more opportunist of them, and if at the end she comes under the influence of a home where there is honesty and affection, it is almost as if by accident.

Shirley Temple is popular everywhere, an indication that the inviolable urge, since the beginning of human society, to worship at the shrine of the Mother and Child in all its permutations of nomenclature throughout the centuries, still lives in the heart of all uninhibited normal men and women. Like the Madonna and Child principle,

Shirley Temple is the symbol of life in the bud to millions of people.

Wholesome, healthy, unaffected, unprecocious, unself-conscious and confident, Shirley Temple is a true product of the amazingly high standards of American civilization. Yet there are some who hardly even deign to look down their noses at Shirley. It shows how far away from the roots of life the cult of 'being different' will lead these people. The coterie thinks it knows better, but the coterie is mistaken.

XXXV

WE have seen how the Russians treated the subject of the problem children in *The Road to Life*. The Americans have an analogous problem. Let us look at the realistic manner in which Hollywood faces up to it.

The Samuel Goldwyn production *Dead End* opens with the camera travelling from the mountain-tops of sky-scrapered Manhattan down, down, to a spot near the riverside where the poor live in utter squalor, but where, also, several cranky rich live in a colony of sumptuous buildings, because of the alleged romantic beauty of the river-scapes.

In the midst of degrading poverty, a group of boys, about twelve to fourteen years of age, play in the streets as best they can. There is no proper home life for them, and on the streets they are chased from spot to spot by protesting liveried porters and shop-keepers. War at home and war on the streets for just room to live, strengthens the gang spirit which inevitably develops from such an environment.

As they play together, Baby-face Martin, a well-dressed gangster-killer wanted by the police, looks on. He is the adult product of one such local gang. We have seen him earlier trying to make contact with his own mother and the sweetheart from whom he has had to keep away owing to the exigencies of his adopted profession.

The mother's social feeling is unimpaired, despite the back-bending weight of poverty, and she receives him with bitter imprecations, before which he. the killer, flinches. She will have none of him.

Later, he catches sight of the sweetheart whom he had idealized for years. Instead of the lovely and innocent girl he expects, he sees her by the light of a street lamp tainted with illness from the necessity of making her living on the streets. He stuffs some money into her hand and turns away, revolted and bitter.

A fully-fledged young architect (Joel McCrea), for whom society has found no use, is painting woodwork for a living. The girl he once loved (Sylvia Sidney) is an operative in a factory. The workers are on strike and Sylvia has had to do her turn on the picket line. Lately Joel has forsaken her for a beautiful girl who is the mistress of one of the rich men who live nearby.

Sylvia is breadwinner for her young orphaned brother whom she is trying bravely to save from demoralization in the streets. But when she is at work, it means work nearly all day, and she makes so little money.

Poverty, poverty everywhere the camera goes, except on that strange luxurious block of mansions which seems to tower there like some gigantic bitter taunt.

Baby-face Martin finds himself in need of something to do, and with his henchman plans the kidnapping of the rich man's son from the flats. Snooping around, he strikes up a closer acquaintance with the street boys and gives them a few lessons in gangster tactics and technique; in throwing knives and broken bottles. That was how he had solved the problem of inescapable poverty, and now look, look at these silk shirts, the diamond-studded cuff links, the fine suit and the dough it got him.

The boys remember the lesson.

Having worked off their sub-conscious resentments against their environment by giving the rich man's son a drubbing, the boys come into conflict with the rich man himself, who happens also to be the brother of a New

310

York judge. In a scuffle with one of the boys whom he wishes to hand over to the police, this man receives a cut on the wrist with a knife as the boy escapes. A policeman arrives.

The rich brother of a judge talks to this policeman as if he owned him, together with the judiciary and the whole Police Department in the New York administration. He demands that the guilty boy be caught and punished. Meanwhile Baby-face Martin's kidnapping plot goes astray. Joel McRea, finding out in time, butts in. In a fight Joel McRea wrests a revolver from Martin's companion, a chase and gun fight ensues over the house-tops which results in the shooting dead of Baby-face Martin, and the end of a social menace, a product of this the Dead End of New York.

Dead End indicts society, even with that one gesture of Sylvia Sidney when she tilts her hat up from her forehead to show the bullying policeman how gallantly other policemen can use their clubs at women on the picket line. The finger is pointed accusingly at poverty as being the root of gangsterdom and prostitution. It is pointed at the harsh reform school system. The picture arouses the conscience of America to its responsibility for these problems.

With almost lightning rapidity comes *Boy of the Streets*, bringing an emergency answer to the problems posed by *Dead End*. A big change is needed, and, says America, there is no time to waste. The task is urgent, *therefore save lives now*, immediately, not in talk but in action.

In *Boy of the Streets*, the rich, who are depicted as being responsible for drawing rents for dwellings of the poor that are falling to pieces, are shown rolling up their sleeves and helping to clean up the sores of slum life.

Once more, in *Boy of the Streets*, you are shown a bunch of adolescent boys from slum homes; nowhere to go, nowhere to play, no money for movies and no way of entertaining themselves except by getting together and making things happen, to give pattern to their empty lives.

They squat in a disused tramway depot, and set to work to make the town services entertain them. Among them there is a young Negro shoeblack who is a fine mimic, and who is deputed to call out the Fire Brigade on various false alarms by telephone. They have a grand time enjoying the discomfiture of outraged authority, until at last their peccadilloes are discovered.

For the first time in any American film, we see in the way this Negro boy is regarded by the white boys and adults a developing change in the social consciousness which is of tremendous and heartening significance. There is never the slightest hint or suggestion that the Negro boy is at all different from any of the other boys. He is one of themselves in the gang, and is spoken to in the same tone of voice by grown-ups and policemen as are the white-skinned boys.

There is none of that patronizing condescension accorded to the dark-skinned Sabu in *The Drum*, for instance.

A young rich woman who inherits a slice of slum property in the district teams up with the local doctor who patches up the boys after an inter-gang fight. She determines to do her part to bring about a better state of affairs. She has the houses repaired and decorated, and sends an orphaned girl living there to a residential school in the country.

Jacky, the leader of the boy gang, who has become innocently mixed up with racketeers, finds himself in a gunning episode, and is brought to his senses by the exposure of the real character of his racketeer friends. The heiress, the doctor and a friendly policeman all get together to save Jacky, and, as his ambition has been to join the U.S. Navy, we see him at the end of the picture, in uniform, boarding his training ship.

312

No fatalism here. No throwing up of hands. No weeping and none of the self-pity reflected in the pre-Nazi German film. They are not concerned with who killed Cock Robin, nor are they concerned with the mediaeval pre-occupation as to what the distant future looks like.

The conscience of America has indeed been aroused when a film like this tells the rich that they have got to get busy *doing something about it now*. When the boys come of age a career must be found for them. In this picture a boy joins the U.S. Navy. Well, so long as that Navy stands on the side of the people, and with the temper of the Americans as at the present moment, that should be okay by us.

But one of the most affecting scenes in *Boy of the Streets* is the episode in which the Negro boy loses his life in a street accident. The whole neighbourhood of white people, old and young alike, who knew him so well during his life-time, are stricken with a deep sorrow. It is as if each had suffered a loss in his own family. The white boys with whom he had played, deeply affected by his death, find they have no money at all with which to buy flowers. Their decision to steal them comes to the ears of the Italian flower-seller, who thereupon places a special bunch of flowers right in front of his stall and looks the other way, so that they may steal them as conveniently as possible.

When one remembers what went on between Negro and white until a few years ago, this is indeed a straw which shows the way the wind is blowing.

Robert Burns was a thousand times right:

> *It's coming yet, for a' that,*
> *when man to man the world o'er,*
> *shall brothers be for a' that.*

It is Coming!

XXXVI

HOW can we account for the amazing popularity of the outstanding male stars in the American cinema? Names like Paul Muni and Spencer Tracy are spoken of with brotherly regard in almost every household in the country. The broad humanity, the sincere feeling that imbues the work of these actors has endeared them to countless millions. They are of the people and friendly to all people. Invariably, these two stars will be found playing parts which have the greatest social appeal, the deepest cultural value.

How fertile is the genius of a country that can produce the extraordinary diverse versatility of a Paul Muni, Spencer Tracy, James Cagney, Gary Cooper, William Powell, Eddie Cantor, and Ed. G. Robinson.

Let us take Paul Muni. A European in origin, but American since the age of about five, his complete absorption in the social principle is such that no matter what part Muni takes on, he has the extraordinary power of clothing himself in the very flesh of the character he portrays.

The utmost depths of suffering humanity mould his face as he grips the prison bars in his agony in *I am a Fugitive From a Chain Gang*.

In *Scarface* he is the very personification of that mixture of child and monster which is a gangster.

As Louis Pasteur, he is none other than the disinterested patient, stubborn scientist who bears only one allegiance—to truth, and to the alleviation of human suffering.

314

In *The Life of Emile Zola*, although a great author, he is the average decent Frenchman, who, in spite of his inclination towards a well-deserved retirement after a lifetime of struggle is impelled to take up the fight against the appalling corruption laid bare by the Dreyfus case.

One of Muni's greatest triumphs is his role in the M.-G.-M. production *The Good Earth*. This is a film of the most far-reaching significance. Coming, as it did, at a time when Japanese aggression was directing the eyes of the world upon the Chinese people, it has had its effect in creating a sympathetic link with the common people of China.

Paul Muni, playing the part of a Chinese peasant, has a dramatic task before which any serious European actor would quail. Yet he manages to carry the part through from poverty to prosperity, from prosperity to famine, and from the depths of poverty again to personal wealth. The position of Chinese women in their traditional servility to the male, combined with their own personal dignity in a life of unremitting toil, was brought home on the screen for the first time on a world scale.

The story of the film shows how a man may deteriorate when he becomes rich to the point of excess and loses all sense of balance. As in so many American films, the ending illustrates the truth that only in unity of action with all with whom one is associated, can a person find happiness, security and the satisfaction of achievement.

Spencer Tracy finds himself easily at home in a diversity of roles. In *Riff-Raff* he is a dock-side worker misled by individualistic tendencies into anti-social actions, a part rather similar to Muni's in *Black Fury*.

In Fritz Lang's *Fury*, from being a sane normal man, a garage mechanic looking forward to a settled married life, he becomes, as a result of his near escape from death at the hands of lynchers, the very embodiment of bitterness and revenge.

In *They Gave Him a Gun*, the normality of Spencer Tracy's soldier character is set against the corrupted character of the soldier played by Franchot Tone, who from using a gun in war takes to using a gun in civilian life.

The part played by Spencer Tracy in *Captains Courageous*, that of Manuel, the Portuguese sailor on a cod-fishing vessel, is the most memorable of all.

Against a background of fishing vessels riding through lashing waves and driving mists, the rivalry of competing captains to be first in port with the catch, and the singing of sea shanties, this Portuguese sailor stands out for his dignity, his humanity, his sane regard for the eternal human values.

The *Waiting for Lefty* influence is strong in *Big City*, in which Spencer Tracy is a taxi driver who with other taximen is engaged in a struggle against a gangster racket. The effect of *Waiting for Lefty* seems to have been far-reaching in America, since we meet the name 'Lefty' applied to all kinds of characters in the most unexpected places, in Westerns, dramas, and even in song and dance films.

Gary Cooper started his film career as the Bill Hart type of cowboy. In *The Wedding Night*, with Anna Sten, he played the part of an author. In a Lubitsch film we find him as a rather gawky prosperous American.

His greatest popular success, however, was in the role of the Mr. Deeds who goes to town, an apparently slow-witted rustic who has suddenly come into a fortune. But he shows that he is more than a match for all the suave, self-seeking would-be exploiters who would like to fleece him.

One feels that the sympathy he shows for the common people who have been deprived of nearly everything by the slump is not only a part of his screen character, but

The individual theme
BLUEBEARD'S EIGHTH WIFE, with Gary Cooper and Claudette Colbert
Produced and directed by Ernst Lubitsch   (*Paramount*)

The social theme
THE BUCCANEER, with Frederic March   (*Paramount*)
A Cecil B. De Mille production

that Gary Cooper himself, the man behind the character, feels the same way about it. It is the very stuff of the American social atmosphere that makes such films and such characters possible.

The Americans had learnt with great advantage from the Soviet film classics. In taking those shots of the hungry farmers from the real American prototypes, their faces lined with suffering, they showed what a slump really means, not as an abstraction or as an exercise of professional political economists, but in the plain terms of ordinary human life.

In *Souls at Sea*, Gary Cooper plays the part of Noggin Taylor, a passionate reformer out to break the slave traffic. His slow exterior belies the fire and decision that is within. A terrible incident in this film is when this vigorous, sensitive humanitarian, who never loses his head in any crisis, finds himself in a boatful of refugees from a burning ship.

They are fighting like animals for room to save themselves, although it is obvious that all will drown if the fight goes on. Coming out of unconsciousness, Noggin Taylor sees in a flash the necessities of the situation and does not flinch. He throws half the number in the boat into the sea, sixteen of them, and when they threaten to swamp the boat by hanging on to the oars and sides, Taylor grabs a pistol and shoots them one by one.

The horror of the situation to this man of the most sensitive fibre can be imagined. The suffering with which he takes command of the boat, and the hostile fearful looks of those who survive on board, is the most sober epitome of a situation that has occurred many a time in human history. To be tender-minded does not become a sword. Decision. Action. The survival of some rather than the certain death of all.

Noggin Taylor goes home to face a trial for murder instituted by the relatives of those who lost their lives. In reality these relatives have been worked upon by the slaver interests, who wish to bring the activity of Noggin Taylor, the anti-slaver, to an end by having him condemned to death; but the picture ends with the prospect of a re-trial and a chance of acquittal.

The greatest roles of each of these foremost American screen actors has in every case been that of the reflective man of action, the very essence of manhood itself.

Spencer Tracy's Manuel, the Portuguese sailor, Muni's Emile Zola, Cooper as Noggin Taylor the anti-slaver; these are men in the round, whose thought is everywhere matched with action, who are fully conscious of the part men have to play in society, conscious of their own worth and of their responsibilities to their fellows.

It is true that in the case of Zola there is a conflict of mind. Having reached success by writing and exposing injustice all his life, and feeling that it is time to retire, he is inclined at first to follow the path of pure intellectualism, reflection for its own sake; he feels he has done all he can and would fain be left in peace. But, as he examines the facts of the Dreyfus case and realizes the terrible nature of the festering sores that are infecting the body of the French Republic, the man in him rises to action. From being an old man hankering for comfort and an easy chair by the fireside, he is roused like a lion to the old spirit of his youth, burning with indignation at the wrongs men do to men.

Men are only worthy of the name when they are firmly balanced in their thinking and doing. Men who have heads but no bodies, like the apostles of the 'mind,' or those like the Nazis who have bodies but no heads, are caricatures, whom history has destined for the dust-bin.

Consider the remarkable versatility of a James Cagney, the tough guy, who takes the part of a boxer, a gangster, a G. Man or a racing motorist as occasion demands, with the greatest ease.

Yet in one of his films, *Something to Sing About*, he shows us an entirely new James Cagney, one we had never seen on the screen before, a band leader, a song and dance man, a film star who guys the Hollywood routine with all the flair of a born comedian and a born dancer, who seems to out-do Fred Astaire at his own game. There is no one in Europe with such snap, speed and skill, who is at the same time capable of attuning all these gifts to the triumph of the social principle.

Eddie Cantor is one of the most popular screen comedians in the world, but he never does anything that is cruel or unkind. There is never in an Eddie Cantor film the type of joke that scores off the weak, the unprosperous, the taxi-man, the charwoman or the maidservant. So much of kindness and good feeling is there in this little man, that in his short stay in Britain, lasting only a fortnight, he managed to raise the colossal sum of £100,000 for the refugee children of suffering Europe.

In his *Ali Baba Comes to Town* we get a picture of the U.S.A. to-day in thinly veiled allegory. It is a well-known device, used quite commonly in the Middle Ages, to relate the story of your own times as in a dream. This time the story is twice removed from reality by the dreamer dreaming that he is dreaming.

But the stuff of the dream is unquestionably related to the New Deal and all the innumerable questions that are agitating the minds of the people of U.S.A.: the principles of Democracy versus Fascism, work schemes and so on. At one point in the story, Ali Baba Eddie Cantor arrives at the house of a man who has a magic carpet, but no one remembers the magic word that will make it fly. Eddie steps on to it and in conversation with the owner casually mentions the word 'inflation.' Up goes the magic carpet with Eddie still upon it, banging his poor head upon the ceiling, and keeping him up there between the ceiling and the carpet. In this predicament, Eddie searches in his mind for the counter-word and remembers to say 'deflation.' Down comes the carpet, and Eddie, very relieved, is on terra firma again.

By the nature of his job as a comedian, Eddie Cantor is quite individual; a comedian cannot be otherwise. Yet so strong is the social spirit in America to-day that he can find ample material for humour in the social scene: in the discussion which is pervading America about finance, work, schemes and other matters of national importance, as well as the international situation, and even in the foibles and mannerisms of President Roosevelt himself, all guyed in the utmost friendliness and good humour.

XXXVII

THE main trends in the American cinema are overwhelmingly in the direction of sound, healthy, objective reality in alliance with social purpose. The American film has prospered because, for one reason, it paid no heed to the laments of the coterie. Rather, it has catered for people who live in the closest touch with reality.

If a balance were struck between winners and non-winners ever since the film industry began, it would be found that those films that were financially successful and which made the widest appeal, were those that met the healthy, instinctive needs of the people. On the losing side would be found those films that describe the inversions or perversions of certain types, the emphasis upon one instinct only, and all the concomitants of what we have described as subjectivism: greed, selfishness, suicide and sadism. In other words, all the predilections that are concerned with the unhealthy stress upon the ego.

It happens occasionally, of course, that a film in this second category makes money, but this will be more through luck than judgment. The success may be due to some unusual angle on sex, or the private life of a king perhaps may have given it a special novelty or topical value, or it may be colour and spectacle.

In the main, it is quite safe to say that films that suffer from subjectivism are the Jonahs of the film industry. There are degrees of subjectivism in otherwise quite worthy films. *The Good Earth*, a socially estimable film, contains one pernicious element, the Fuehrer principle in a father who exercises his supreme authority and selfishness by beating his grown-up son. A little more of this kind of thing in a given production, and you may be certain it will be left at the post in the Box-Office stakes.

There are elements of subjectivism, regrettably, in Walt Disney's *Snow White and the Seven Dwarfs*. Where, oh, where is the objectivity, the freshness, the spontaneity of *The Three Little Pigs*? *Snow White* made a lot of money, not because of the pre-Nazi Germanic horror of the forest or of the witch, but because of its novelty as the first full-length cartoon colour film, in much the same way as *The Jazz Singer* made a fantastic sum of money because it was the first talkie film. But when producers began copying *The Jazz Singer* slavishly, they were soon pulled up with a jerk.

Much of the décor and the appearance of the Queen in *Snow White* resembles the style adopted by Fritz Lang in *The Nibelungs*, and there is the Caligari element in the personification of evil for its own sake in the witch. The forest full of eyes and menacing talons, the knife poised for what seemed minutes on end above the head of Snow White, the preposterously evil-looking hands and arms of the witch, all this is evil exaggerated and personified, the essence of evil emphasized. Such conceptions in the dynamic film medium are socially destructive, profoundly pernicious, frightening and inhibiting. There is nothing funny or elevating about them. They are simply exercises of the designers craft, like the German films with their art for art's sake.

This evaluation may be easily substantiated. Small models of the delightful seven dwarfs and Snow White are being sold everywhere, but nobody wants a model of the witch.

The contribution that Disney has made to the well-being of the world in giving us the joy and sanity that came with Mickey Mouse and the best of his Silly Symphonies is almost as incalculable in our own time as Chaplin's during the years of war. The real world has always been Disney's field of observation and expression —why not stick to it?

The fantasy element of Disney's work in the past has been greatly beneficial to the world, but we know where the Germanic fantasy to which Disney has resorted in *Snow White* has landed the country of its origin.

The Western has always been a good influence. You sometimes get a lot of shooting and rough and tumble fighting, but in all the conflict the good men and the bad men are nearly equally matched, and the bad man comes to a bad end, and justice triumphs, which is as it should be.

But during the revival of the first-feature Western, a couple of years ago, there came a film like *Texas Rangers* that provided a lamentable exception to this rule. In this film were introduced all the abysmally backward ideas of the earliest European settlers, who thought that one white man was equal to twenty skulking Red Indians.

To balance this, however, we got the fine sensitivity of the colour film *Ramona*, which gave the Red Indian point of view, and was the native's first real break in the history of the film.

There has been a remarkable and welcome resurgence of films of the vigorous early pioneering days, all conveying the spirit of the birth and growth of a new nation. In an otherwise excellent film of this type, we get the spectacle of a father beating his son with an old-fashioned strap designed for the purpose, and later a horrible stand-up fight between father and son. The film is called *Of Human Hearts*, made by M.-G.-M.

This is the twentieth century and the film is a twentieth-century medium. To employ this medium for the portrayal of such outworn, barbaric, fascist notions simply will not do.

A group of pictures quite unusual in the American

scene have made their disquieting appearance recently, all at about the same. These deserve our special attention because they are each subjectivist almost from beginning to end. We describe them as subjectivist, but the public have already expressed the same conviction in much more concrete terms, by staying away from them.

In this group there are three films. These are *Jezebel* made by First National, *Frou-Frou* and *Three Comrades* both by M.-G.-M., all unfortunately sunk in the morass at varying degrees of depth.

About the worst of the three is *Jezebel*. Mr. William Wyler is both producer and director, and Miss Bette Davis as the aristocratic girl of the South, Miss Julie, monopolizes the screen for almost the entire length of the picture.

The film starts with an irrational situation, when Miss Julie, from unbounded egotism and personal pique, defies the convention of 1852 which demands that an unmarried girl at a Ball shall appear in a white dress.

Instead, she insists on being dressed in red, which the inhabitants of New Orleans associate with the women of the Red Lamp district. Miss Julie knows the implications of her obtuseness, she knows the strength of Southern conventions, she knows she will be frowned upon and ostracized if she appears in red at the Ball, she knows that her conduct will shame her family and may put her escort, her fiancé, in the very difficult situation of having to fight a duel to the death for her sake if she is insulted.

She knows all these things, and yet she insists on carrying her egotistic folly to the uttermost limit. Thus the film starts with the same kind of psychological falsity and impossible cussedness as films of the type of *The Divorce of Lady X*, sponsored by Mr. Korda.

A psychologically false premise starts an avalanche of false situations and creates a number of personal tragedies

JEZEBEL. Camera and Microphone busy recording the fuss about the red dress amid the white dresses *(First National)*

FROU-FROU. As in JEZEBEL, the repellent notion of women fighting duels *(M.-G.-M.)*

and two duels, in one of which a man loses his life. And it all arises out of the initial stupidity of wearing the dress of a prostitute at a place where all are expected to wear white. The inevitable accompaniment to a story with such an egotistical starting-point is irrational complication all along the line, and the inevitable advocacy and practice of all the ingredients of Nazism: rigidity, stupidity, race, blood, soil, sadism, senseless frustration, beating, duelling and shooting.

The conduct of Miss Julie is presented in a thoroughly unfavourable light and she never gains the sympathy of the audience nor that of her friends. The film is full of negative ideas of no interest to an average healthy audience. The proper place for such manifestations is a mental home where the patient will be under observation by kindly specialists.

The atmosphere of the picture from beginning to end is febrile and pathological. Bette Davis acts the part of Miss Julie with that queer sadist smile to be seen in films of the *Dr. Caligari* type. The kind of smile that sends a tremor down the spinal column. The exertion of power, supremacy of the ego, is exercised no matter who suffers, no matter who is humiliated. Julie's ego must triumph, and only at the end, the end of a path strewn with tragedy, is there some form of atonement on her part, but it is submerged in the general social catastrophe of a plague of yellow fever that descends upon the district.

The background of this picture is strongly reminiscent of the dark films of Germany made in the period of social depression immediately after the war. *The Student of Prague* is recalled by the overhanging dark foliage, the shadows, the top-hatted caped figures, the twisted symbols, the strong contrasts between light and darkness.

We have seen in our examination of so many German and English films that the manifestations of subjectivism, egotism and irrationality are always accompanied by hints and threats of beating, of sadism, exhibitionism and other aberrations.

Like conditions—like effects. In *Jezebel*, you see advocated in three distinct instances the subjugation of women by men by the use of physical force. The senior male tells the junior male what he would have done had he been Julie's fiancé. He would have, 'cut me a hickory, and beat the living daylight out of her.' A woman friend of Julie says portentously: 'Spare the rod and spoil the child,' and the fiancé acting upon senior advice, takes a silver-headed cane with him to interview Julie in her bedroom, and when he leaves after a violent quarrel, says he regrets he has not used it upon her!

Later, Julie herself treats the Yankee woman from the North, now the wife of Julie's ex-fiancé, with the most cruel sadism, taunting, provoking and threatening, going to the length of saying she wishes women could meet their enemies openly and fight duels, and kill and be killed.

A story of this character can offer no solution, because everything and everybody is rigid and unbending. Only a major catastrophe can resolve it, and Yellow Jack does the job, bringing with it the dead carts, flights, the cordon sanitaire to cut off the infection, whilst the middle class drowns its sorrows in whisky. The atmosphere of this backward Southern state in the city of New Orleans of 1852 is well conveyed. We have presented for our delectation the workings of the slave-owning mentality which carries with it (necessarily for its own preservation) formal rigidity in customs and conventions down to the apparently most trivial things, such as the colour of a frock or the correct mode of address in conversation.

The projection of such an environment from the dark ages to the twentieth century tends only to retard the social process and to confuse the issues in the minds of men. Especially when a worthy character like a doctor—

a doctor, not a gangster—is made to say: 'I'd cut me a hickory, and beat the living daylight out of her.' General Goering in his worst paroxysms could hardly have bettered this.

The reception accorded to *Jezebel* in this country and in America was extremely poor. That is quite understandable. To sit in the sixpennies at a cinema in a working-class district is to sense how impatient the people are with the irrational antics of a woman who is self-centred to the point of lunacy.

It would hardly seem possible that *Jezebel* and *The Life of Emile Zola* could emerge from the same country. But they did, and what is more they were made by two producing companies working in the closest association—Warner Brothers and First National.

Frou-Frou, directed by Richard Thorpe, with Luise Rainer in the name part, is almost identical in spirit and background with the story of *Jezebel*. It too is located in the New Orleans district in the semi-barbarous times of slavery before the Civil War. The same sort of utter unthinking selfishness is reproduced here, not quite the egotism of the vicious little minx, Julie, but the egotism of a flighty, light-headed plaything of a girl, an incredible creature.

Melvyn Douglas as a prosecuting attorney at a trial fires upon an accused man as he tries to escape out of the courtroom window, and kills him. Going to dinner with Frou-Frou and her father he says: 'A little killing like that always gives me an appetite.' Frou-Frou, who has witnessed the killing, looks at him coquettishly, as they take their seats at table, and says: 'What an honour, to sit beside one who has just killed a man.'

Frou-Frou like Miss Julie takes the centre of the picture for the duration. Married, she runs off with a lover. The convention of the South demands that there be a duel between the lover, when he returns, and the wronged husband. The duel is fought, and the lover dies. She herself finally dies a long drawn out death, full of coughing consumption, morbid self-pity and nostalgias for all the things that might have been. As the family gather round her death-bed she utters one final request; she wishes to be buried in 'the white dress with the pink rose-buds, that father brought me from Paris.'

Even in death, she is still incurably full of herself.

The obsession about the uniform of Jannings' doorman, and that of the Russian General, the red dress of Miss Julie, Frou-Frou's white dress with pink rose-buds, and General Goering's uniform with the knobs on, all derive from the same pathological source, an incredibly unhealthy preoccupation with the ego, subjectivism of the worst kind.

Three Comrades is from the book by Erich Maria Remarque. The overhanging cloud of defeatism and despair that hovers over this picture is ghastly in its effect. Three comrades returning from the war enter civilian life. Most of the film is taken up with the usual German intellectual exercise of hair-splitting and word-spinning. No firmness. No resolution. Everything is vague and misty. One of the friends falls in love with a girl. Of all the millions of German girls he might have fallen in love with, he has to fall in love with the mistress of a wealthy man. Another recommendation is that she suffers from consumption, a legacy of the war years. The other two friends have been told about the consumption, but the boy she marries is kept in the dark about it until after they are married, when on her honeymoon she collapses.

Then she tells him. She will have to go to an expensive sanitorium to get cured, but the new husband is prepared to sell up his garage to save her. There is a lot of moaning and morbidity at the bedside. The doctor has warned her not to move from the bed after the operation. If she obeys, she will live and be healthy. If she moves she will die. If

THE CONFESSIONS OF A NAZI SPY (*First National*)
With Edward G. Robinson, directed by Anatole Litvak

she obeys, however, it will cost the young man his garage, so she gets up from the bed, stretches out her arms to her husband at the window, and drops down dead. Property before life.

A nice story to make an American picture with.

There is an incident in this picture that reproduces the morbid, senseless cruelty of *The Blue Angel* almost exactly. One of the comrades is invited to a swell party, and he is obliged to borrow a rather ill-fitting dress suit. At the party he makes an unfortunate turn, and his coat splits at the seam and his white collar unfastens.

All the others sitting at his table burst out in outrageous laughter, enjoying the discomfiture of the young man with immense glee. Now Emil Jannings as the humiliated young man would have made a real fine job of it, just as he did in *The Last Laugh* and *The Blue Angel*; but Robert Taylor who played it, thank heaven, is a sane American, and so he did not get the idea that Remarque was driving at. Taylor simply looks down coldly at these fools with utter contempt.

Fetish-worship, property worship and humiliations, vague political conflicts in the streets that are settled by murder on a personal plane. A perfect picture of pre-Nazi intellectual confusion.

Thus we get, in *Jezebel*, pestilence and death; in *Frou-Frou*, duelling and death; in *Three Comrades*, despair, suicide and death. A well-matched trio.

The emphasis of the American Constitution is upon human values. The emphasis in these three films is upon property values. They have no message for America or for any other part of the world, and it is unlikely that the film industry will fall into the same errors once the reasons for the failure of these films are fully appreciated.

There are the most encouraging signs that the American producers will, as always, be the first to snap into it, and will give the peoples of the world that which they are awaiting. The same First National who slipped up on *Jezebel* have more than corrected the balance and tipped the scale heavily on the side of social sanity as well as good Box-Office by giving us *The Confessions of a Nazi Spy*. No longer the elevation of the ego and its corollary of pestilence and despair as in *Jezebel*, but the elevation of the will of the people, and the determination that the people shall prevail. First National have demonstrated how quickly the defensive instincts of America react to the menaces within their midst.

The spy trials, the abrogation of a treaty with the Japanese aggressors, the smashing blows that the American people are delivering against the blight of the Fuehrer principle contrast vividly with the paralysis which seems to have gripped so many of the film producers in Europe. As powerful and as impressive as the American sky-scrapers of concrete and steel is the call of President Roosevelt resounding throughout the world:

Men are not the prisoners of fate, they are only prisoners of their own minds.

This is the background against which *The Confessions of a Nazi Spy* rises like a landmark, a beacon as full of light and power for the future as were the most outstanding milestones in the past history of the American cinema. With this beacon as a guide, the path that Europe must follow is clear.

There are many who regard the cinema with open or subconscious hostility. Writers appear who beat their breasts and cover their heads with ashes, because they think the profession of writing is being superseded by the cinema and radio. They bring out into the open, and sometimes at book length, what must have been rankling in the bosom ever since the moving picture began.

Those who think that way are in much the same position as were the holy professional scriveners or writers upon parchment in the Middle Ages, when they saw the menace of the printing press confronting them. Then as now, loud lamentations and gnashing of teeth. Then as now, with as little cause for consternation. In an attempt to stem the progress of the printing press, they called it the work of the devil, and invoked bell, book and candle, happily to no effect.

At this distance in time we can see how unjustified their objections were, because we know that the Press has enabled an infinitely greater number of writers to reach, not the minute handful of the Middle Ages, but tens upon tens of thousands of readers.

The film to-day is having a widespread cultural effect upon the world's peoples, and if only we can make up our minds to advance and assist this process, the public for all other means of expression will be increased to incalculable proportions, and the world will be a better place to live in.

INDEX

334